Nelson
A Medical Casebook

NELSON

A MEDICAL CASEBOOK

by

Dr Ann-Mary E. Hills

Foreword by Colin White

SPELLMOUNT

British Library Cataloguing in Publication Data:
A catalogue record for this book is available
from the British Library

Copyright © A-M. E. Hills 2006

ISBN 1-86227-321-9

Published in the UK in 2006
by
Spellmount Limited
The Mill, Brimscombe Port
Stroud, Gloucestershire, GL5 2QG

Tel: 01453 883300
Fax: 01453 883233
E-mail: enquiries@spellmount.com
Website: www.spellmount.com

1 3 5 7 9 8 6 4 2

Printed in Great Britain by
Oaklands Book Services
Stonehouse, Gloucestershire GL10 3RQ

Contents

Dedication

For my family: my husband Peter and Andrew and Rossana,
Catherine and Jim, Robert, Myrran, Oliver, and Freya.

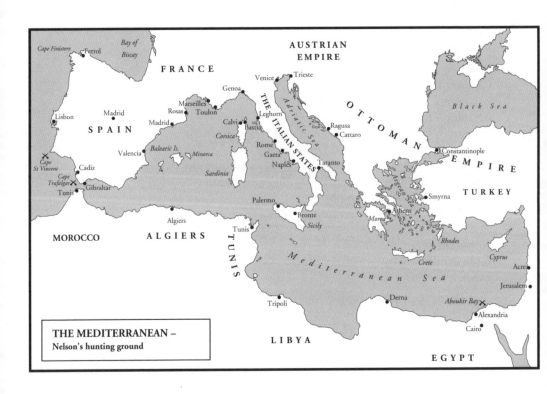

THE MEDITERRANEAN –
Nelson's hunting ground

Foreword
by Colin White

My London taxi driver was absolutely certain. 'Of course Nelson wore a ruddy eye patch,' he told me. 'You look at his statue next time you're in Trafalgar Square, you'll see!'

We were discussing a news item that had appeared that morning in most of the national newspapers – even in the tabloid that was lying on the seat next to him. An historian had discovered a hitherto unpublished letter that, it was claimed, established once and for all that Nelson never wore the famous black eye patch – and my driver was irate at such rampant revisionism.

What he didn't know (and I quickly decided not to tell him!) was that I was the historian who had made the discovery public. During the course of my researches into Nelson's correspondence, I had indeed come across a letter that showed that in 1797, when Nelson went before a medical board who had to decide if he was entitled to a pension, the board members could not tell, simply by looking at him, whether he was blind in one eye. In other words, there was no external disfigurement – and thus no need for a patch to cover it up.

This was scarcely hot news in the field of Nelson studies – it was established long ago that the black patch was a myth. But, when the news broke in the national press, it caused a mini media frenzy and I spent the best part of two days in and out of TV and radio studios, and constantly on the mobile phone, discussing the 'find' with excited journalists from all over Britain – and even overseas as well. It was an indicator of just how much the media's interest in Nelson was beginning to hot up as the Trafalgar bicentenary approached.

In fact, the most important revelation contained in the letter had nothing to do with Nelson's appearance. It was a throw-away phrase that he used when talking about the occasion when his eye was wounded. He wrote, 'I was carried to my tent from the Battery.' That reference to Nelson being *carried* was important. No previous description of the wounding had mentioned this before: all the accounts and illustrations, based on his own rather casual remarks about the incident in his letters home, depicted him reeling slightly as he was hit in the face by a shower of sand and pebbles. Now, for the first time, we had primary evidence that he was knocked flat by the blow – indeed possibly even knocked out, since he was clearly unable to walk.

The emergence of new material such as this has been one of the most exciting aspects of the Trafalgar bicentenary. It has enabled historians to refresh and revitalise the familiar story, often in quite striking ways. Among the areas in which new insights have emerged is Nelson's health and, in this field, Dr. Ann-Mary Hills has been one of the leading lights. In a succession of conference papers, lectures, articles and TV programmes, she has challenged long-accepted views, and thrown fascinating light on hitherto unexplored areas. She also has a gift for making the subject accessible to non-medical audiences. No one who has seen her demonstration, with a human skull and a blancmange, of the effects on Nelson's brain of the sharp blow to the head that he received at the Battle of the Nile can put the disturbing image of the quivering blancmange out of their mind!

Now, for the first time, she has brought the results of all her work together in a single volume. The last study of Nelson's complete medical history was Surgeon Commander P. D. Gordon Pugh's influential and much-quoted, book *Nelson and his Surgeons*. However, that volume was slim, running to only sixty-six pages, and it was published almost forty years ago, in 1968. Both medical science, and Nelson scholarship, have moved a long way since then and so a new and updated study of Nelson's health and wounds is long overdue. Dr. Hills has put all of us in her debt by providing one.

Just as two doctors will often interpret a living patient's symptoms in dramatically differing ways, so medical historians often diverge when diagnosing the illnesses of historical characters. Not everyone, therefore, will agree with all of Dr Hills' conclusions. But none of the other experts working in this field have made so complete and detailed a study of Nelson's entire medical history as she and, as a result, this book is uniquely comprehensive. Here, within one cover, you will find detailed examinations of all of Nelson's wounds – including some you probably did not know he had. His many illnesses are also dealt with in full and some interesting diagnoses are suggested. His death is dealt with in graphic, and often very moving, detail and we are made aware of just how terrible a way of dying it was – and how heroically Nelson bore his suffering. And, because modern medical practice is as interested in the mind and spirit as in the body, there is a full examination of Nelson's 'gene-pool', and his personal psychology, with interesting diversions into his royal ancestry and his ability as a wordsmith.

Writing to Lord Sydney in June 1785, the young, relatively unknown, Captain Horatio Nelson referred (as he often did) to his weak constitution, adding '…my health is a loss I must be content to suffer, my only consolation is that I lost it in the service of my country.' Twenty years later, just weeks before Trafalgar, and by then a famous admiral and peer of the realm, he wrote to a close friend, 'God knows I want rest, but self is entirely out of the question.' This admirable book enables us to appreciate fully just how high a personal price Nelson paid for his devoted service.

And, just in case you were wondering: the statue on the top of Nelson's column in Trafalgar Square, does *not* have an eye patch. But don't tell my taxi-driver!

Colin White
Portsmouth

Acknowledgements

The research and writing of this book has been spread over many years; and in this period of time friends, family and colleagues have been consistently supportive. Every author needs exhorters and encouragers. I have been very lucky with mine. Hilary Green was an excellent sounding board for my first drafts. Valerie Austin looked very critically at my prose. Jill Jackson, Patricia Payne, Margaret Scuffham and Penny Morrish were all delightfully positive. Beverley Matthews, Librarian of Tonbridge School, obtained for me, on loan over the years, an eclectic selection of rare books and documents together with photocopies of articles needed for my research and, bless her, she consistently turned a blind eye to return-by-dates. Francis Cazalet was a great help with the genealogy, and on Nelson's religion. Anthony Hoskins was extremely generous in giving me his research on Nelson's antecedents.

Medical colleagues forbore to comment on my ignorance and gave willingly of their time. Professors Michael Green, John Hampton and Leslie Le Quesne offered me their extremely erudite opinions. Indeed Professor Green altered my life: he assured me that Spirits of Wine had the same degree of alcohol content as French Vermouth, so that I now think of the inadequate preservation of Nelson's body whenever I drink my favourite alcoholic beverage. Surgeons John Bell and Mick Crumplin were so very helpful when I was considering the medical aspects of Nelson's eye problems and of his death respectively. My meetings with them were comprehensive, and very constructive. Dear friend and physician Sylvia Watkins still does not entirely agree with me over Nelson's tropical illnesses, but went ahead looking long and hard at every one of his medical problems for me. Needless to say medical mistakes in this book are mine alone.

'Nelsonics', colleagues from the Nelson Society especially Victor Sharman, Nick Slope, Sue Morris and Elizabeth Baker all were supportive from the very first, as was Peter Warwick from the 1805 Club. Small parts of the text first saw the light of day in the respective journals of these two societies. Throughout the whole gestation period Colin White, Nelson Expert Extraordinary, has ever been available instantly to answer wide-ranging queries; and always been prepared to argue the merits of Nelson's right eyebrow, facial scarring, the correct placement of foreign awards on Nelson's coat, and much, much more, with delightful friendliness and good humour. Such knowledgeable support has been invaluable.

Without the basic secretarial and computer skills of Hazel Faux and Liz Jones, together with their consistent practical help this book would not have been completed; I owe them both an immense and affectionate debt.

Workers at Spellmount, led by Jamie Wilson, have been helpful, considerate and kindly to one who was a complete publishing novice.

Last but not least, my family have been marvellous through thick and thin. I am sure their attitude, when the last word is finally written, will be one of 'loving relief'.

> ... we came off victorious, and they have behaved well to us, for they wanted to take Lord Nelson from us, but we told Captain as we brought him out so we would bring him home, so it was so, and he was put into a cask of spirits.[6]

This 'mutiny' was confirmed in the *Naval Chronicle* published at the end of 1805, by an anonymous correspondent:

> It was certainly the intention of Lord Collingwood to have sent the body of Lord Nelson home in the *Euryalus*, until a very strong reluctance was manifested by the crew of the *Victory* to part with so precious a relic, to which they felt almost an exclusive claim: they remonstrated through one of their boatswain's mates against the removal upon a ground that could not be resisted; he said, the Noble Admiral had fought with them, and fell on their own deck; that if, by being put on board a frigate, his body should fall into the hands of the enemy, it would make their loss doubly grievous to them; and, therefore, that they were one and all resolved to carry it safely to England.[7]

A hero who inspired such affection and respect, a lifelong sufferer from ill health and severe trauma, who had an extraordinary recorded effect upon all who met him, and even some who never did; such a man deserves to have his illnesses and wounds examined and his character and genius explored in relation to those misfortunes.

In 1984 the then Director of Post-graduate Medical Education at Oxford, in an article in the *British Medical Journal,* suggested:

> The retrospective diagnosis of the medical circumstances of famous persons is a pastime which fascinates doctors ... Such speculations can be extremely entertaining, particularly to lay persons. But are they serious contributions to medicine, or to the knowledge of History?[8]

Obviously, in this author's opinion, they are both. So much is known about Nelson's health because he was, as his last chaplain wrote: 'Such a fascinating little fellow,'[9] and so good at describing his own symptoms. The clues in the primary sources are still available, and all have been consulted for this book.

Notes:

1. Nicolas, Sir N. H. *Dispatches and Letters of Vice Admiral Lord Viscount Nelson* vol I p.476 (hereafter Nicolas)
2. ibid vol VII p.214
3. *The Times* 2nd December 1805 p.2
4. 'Nastyface, J.' *Nautical Economy* 1836
5. Quoted in Moorhouse. E. *Letters of English Seamen* 1910 p.302
6. Quoted in Pocock, T. *Horatio Nelson* 1987 p.333 (hereafter Pocock)
7. *Naval Chronicle* vol XIV 1805 p.505–507
8. Potter, J. 'Personal View' *British Medical Journal* 1984 vol 289 p.47
9. Morrison, M. S. *The Hamilton & Nelson papers* 1893–1894 vol 2 p.274 letter 860 (hereafter Morrison)

Nelson's Casebook and Naval Career in Brief

If modern doctors had been able to clerk and examine Lord Viscount Nelson, early on the morning of the Battle of Trafalgar, they would have recorded that the patient looked somewhat older than his 47 years, was of height about 5 ft. 6ins. but extremely thin, appeared clearly in a state of suppressed excitement, very animated and, given the fact that he was about to go into battle, remarkably cheerful.

Doctors would have noted that his Lordship had lost his right arm, had at least three eye problems, showed considerable scarring of his forehead above his right eye (some of it keloid) and that the outer half of his right eyebrow was replaced with scar tissue.

His Lordship would probably have stated that he was currently fit and well, subject only to occasional 'spasms' (due to intestinal problems, his current medical practitioner had told him) but also suffered from occasional right-sided abdominal swelling due to a traumatic hernia which enlarged when he coughed.

However, full clerking of any patient includes their past medical history (PMH) and His Lordship's PMH was extraordinary. This is what he would have provided in chronological order:

- 1775 Malaria: Invalided home from Indian waters, life despaired of. Depression (aged 17)

- 1780 On Nicaraguan expedition: Poisoned by Manchineel tree.
- Gravely ill with malaria, probable scurvy and a tropical illness (aged 21)
- Limb problems of power and sensation (aged 21–22)
- Severe weight loss
- Gum papilloma: syphilitic? (aged 23)

- 1782 Unwell while on *Albemarle:* Unknown cause (aged 23)
- Full-blown scurvy (aged 23–24)

- 1787 Very unwell: Unknown cause (aged 29)
- 1787–1793 Eye strain: Intermittent (aged 29 to 35)

- 1794 Cut on the back (aged 30)
- Concussive injury to right eye at Calvi, resulting in loss of sight in that eye. Marked scarring over right eye – lost outer half of right eyebrow. Also recurrence of malaria

- 1795 'Flux and fever' (aged 37)

- 1797 Blunt concussive wound to right side of abdomen giving rise to severe symptoms and later, a post-traumatic hernia, and recurrent post- traumatic abdominal pains and swelling
- Compound fracture by a musket ball: Right arm amputated: post operative infection (aged 38)

- 1798 Severe head injury due to concussive injury by langridge shot – probable skull fracture. Physical symptoms persisted at least fourteen months. Mental symptoms persisted for longer (aged 39)

His Lordship would also have stated that all his adult life he had been subject to bouts of depression directly relating to stress in his life and that when stressed he slept poorly and also lost his appetite and so lost weight.

He would have mentioned that ever since his right eye injury at Calvi, he had been troubled intermittently with recurrent episodes of pain in his injured eye. Additionally he had suffered from at least one episode of infection in his 'good' left eye and he had noted that the vision in that eye was now deteriorating.

As a further aide-memoire to the following chapters, here is a summary of Nelson's family history:

Aged 9	Mother died
12	Left home, to join Royal Navy
28	Married Frances Nisbet (nee Woolward)
29-34	Unemployed on half pay
35	Met Sir William & Lady Hamilton for first time
40	Met Sir William & Lady Hamilton for the second time
42	First daughter born. Parted from wife
43	Father died
44	Sir William Hamilton died
45	Second daughter born and died
46	Exchanged rings with Lady Hamilton in quasi marriage ceremony after attending Holy Communion.

Nelson's naval career in summary:

1771 March	joins *Raisonnable* at Greenwich under Captain Maurice Suckling
August	sails to West Indies on merchantman
1772 July	returns to England
1773 June–September	expedition to Arctic
November	sails on *Seahorse* for East Indies as Midshipman
1775	invalided home suffering from malaria
1777 April	passes exam for Lieutenant and joins *Lowestoffe* as 2nd Lieutenant
July	returns to West Indies
1778 September	made 1st Lieutenant of *Bristol*
December	appointed Commander of *Badger* brig
1779 June	Post Captain of *Hinchinbroke*
1780 January–April	Nicaraguan Expedition captures Fort San Juan
April	appointed to command *Janus*: too ill to take up appointment
August	invalided home on *Lion*
1781 January–August	on half pay mainly at Bath
August	Captain of *Albemarle* in North Sea
1782 April	sails for Quebec and West Indies
1783 July	returns home
November	visits France
1784 March	appointed Captain of *Boreas* in West Indies
July	meets Mary Moutray
1784–1787	employed in implementing Navigation Acts
1787 July	back in England
December	Trial of James Carse
1787–1792	'On the Beach' with half pay
1793 January	appointed Captain of *Agammemnon;* sails to Mediterranean
1793 July–1796 March	active in Mediterranean
1794 April–May	Siege of Bastia, sustained cut on back July right eye wound at Calvi
1796 March	promoted to Commodore
June	transferred to *Captain*
1797 February	Battle of Cape St. Vincent; receives abdominal wound
February	promoted to Rear-Admiral of the Blue
May	transfers to *Theseus*
July	loses right arm at Tenerife
September	returns home in *Seahorse* and convalesces in Bath portrait painted by Lemuel Abbott

1798 March	hoists flag in *Vanguard* joining fleet at Cadiz
April–July	searches for French fleet across Mediterranean
August	Battle of the Nile, receives head wound
September	reaches Naples and stays with Hamiltons
December	rescues Neapolitan royal family and transfers them to Palermo
1799 January	appointed Rear Admiral of the Red; reclaims Naples from French
1800 July–November	travels home with Hamiltons overland
1801 January	promoted Vice-Admiral of the Blue
March	transfers to *San Josef* and sails with Hyde Parker to Baltic; transfers to *Elephant*
April	Battle of Copenhagen
July	returns to England, appointed to command anti-invasion forces in Channel
August	two attacks on *Boulogne* fail
October	Britain and France sign armistice
1802 March	Treaty of Amiens
1803 April	Napoleonic War begins
May	appointed Commander-in-Chief Mediterranean; transfers to *Victory*
July	joins English Fleet blockading at Toulon
1804	blockades Toulon
1805 May to July	chases combined fleet under Villeneuve to West Indies and back
August	arrives in Merton for 27-day leave (see Appendix III)
September	rejoins *Victory* and takes command at Cadiz
21st October	Battle of Trafalgar; mortally wounded

CHAPTER I
Ancestry and upbringing

Nelson had forbears of distinction. Through his mother, Catherine Nelson (nee Suckling), his gene pool was fascinating. Not only can branches of Catherine's family tree be traced back a thousand years but many noble figures, some of royal blood, are found there. It is possible to link Nelson to William the Conqueror and to Alfred the Great.

Nelson himself was proud of his Suckling blood, although he never seems to have traced his origins with any enthusiasm. It is extraordinary that Catherine Suckling and Edmund Nelson produced Nelson at all, if we consider their other male offspring: there was Maurice – worthy, dull, who never married the woman he lived with; William – pompous, acquisitive, mean – an archetypal anal-retentive character; Edmund – a failed shop-keeper, gambler and lowly curate; and Suckling – a complete nonentity.

By some kaleidoscopic quirk of fate and a unique rearrangement of DNA, Edmund and Catherine Nelson conceived in Horatio, their sixth child, an individual of great intelligence and with a most extraordinary personality.

Every individual inherits a unique pattern of DNA sequences from their parents. Cellular DNA contains all of the genetic information required for the development of cells into tissues, organs and the complete organism that is a unique human being. By a complex treble-coiling process, DNA is incorporated with chromosomes, and virtually every human cell contains 46 chromosomes as 23 pairs, with one of each pair derived from each parent. Each parent inherits half his or her genes from each of their parents and so backwards up the family tree.[1]

Each human conception is unique, but characteristics can appear repeatedly through the generations or alternatively a characteristic can be dormant for generations, and then reappear in a later member of a family (for example red hair appears in some families time and again.) A deformity of the little toe-nail appears in the author's family but can skip one or two generations.

Almost half a century after Nelson was killed, the book *The Royal Descent of Nelson and Wellington* pointed out that: 'The Royal descent of Lord Nelson, by several lines, has altogether escaped the notice of his

1

biographers.'[2] This is almost as true today as it was in 1853, the year the book was published.

Nelson's father's family came originally from Lancashire, and bore arms. What is known of the Nelson ancestors is given in 'Descent VI' at the end of this chapter.[3]

Far more interesting is Nelson's ancestry on his mother's side. The author G R French was aiming in his book to link Nelson and Wellington in their joint ancestry. He went back only to King Edward I. Successive biographers have ignored French's genealogical information. For example, Oman only mentioned the families who married into the maternal side of Nelson's family.[4] No-one has looked properly and fully at the incredible number of royal ancestors Nelson possessed.

In March 1997 the *Journal of the Society of Genealogists* published as its first article a piece entitled 'Mary Boleyn's Carey Children – Offspring of King Henry VIII?'[5] The author, Anthony Hoskins, sought to prove, on balance of probabilities, that the two children of Lady Mary Boleyn were not sired by her husband, Sir William Carey, but were the children of Sir William's master, King Henry VIII. Part of Hoskins' conclusion was:

> Finally, if as is probable, the Careys were Henry VIII's children, certain interesting observations can be made. Rather than his issue becoming extinct with the death of Elizabeth 1st in 1603, King Henry VIII has instead a numerous posterity in both England and America.

One of the numerous footnotes in this extremely well researched and very convincing article listed 'Admiral the Viscount Nelson' amongst other English descendants of either William Carey or Henry VIII by Mary Boleyn. In actual fact the exact paternity of Mary Boleyn's two children is not relevant. Nelson is directly descended from Henry Carey, Lord Hunsden, her only son, and *both* the possible fathers are descended from King Edward III (father of John of Gaunt) and therefore from William the Conqueror (see Descents I and II.). Nelson was descended through his mother from William the Conqueror through two of the illegitimate children of John of Gaunt and his mistress Catherine Swynford. (John of Gaunt was the fifth son of King Edward III and his wife Queen Philippa.) He had four children by Catherine and Nelson is descended from the oldest, John, and the youngest, Joan. John of Gaunt married Catherine, his third wife, in 1396. One year later their children were legitimised and ennobled as the Beauforts. This was the first example of legitimisation in English legal history. With regard to his own beloved (illegitimate) daughter Horatia, this legal precedent would have fascinated Nelson had he known of it.

If William Carey was the father of Henry Carey, Lord Hunsdon, then Nelson was directly descended from:

Saint Margaret of Scotland
Eight kings of England: William the Conqueror, Henrys I, II & III,
John, and Edwards I, II & III
Philip IV, King of France
Eleanor of Aquitaine, Queen of France and England.
Matilda, Queen of England
Malcolm III, King of Scotland
Ferdinand III, King of Castile
Warwick the Kingmaker

If King Henry VIII was the father of Henry Carey Nelson was descended from a total of eleven rulers of England: the nine given above, plus Henry VII and Henry VIII.

Henry VIII and his father Henry VII are considered to be the founders of the Royal Navy. Nelson would have been very pleased to acknowledge descent from these two highly intelligent, but utterly ruthless men. It is fortunate that psychopathy (a severe personality disorder which Henry VIII almost certainly possessed) is not a hereditary mental condition.

Finally, Nelson is descended from Alfred the Great because Alfred's six times great grand-daughter Matilda, daughter of St. Margaret of Scotland and her husband King Malcolm IV of Scotland married King Henry II of England[6] (see Descent IV).

The author believes that characteristics both physical and mental are inherited from forebears, not just immediate family. In the Nelson and Suckling genes were ancestors who had been formidable leaders, and men and women of high intelligence. The Nelson ancestors had been men of influence in their own local spheres. Suckling royal ancestors included the cleverest and most powerful rulers of Anglo-Saxon and Norman, Plantagenet and Tudor England. Extraordinarily all those genes for intelligence, character, leadership and personality seem to have come together in one man: Horatio Nelson.

Nelson's father, Edmund Nelson (1723–1802) had been educated at home and then at Caius College, Cambridge. Ordained there, he met his future wife, Catherine Suckling, after he was appointed to his first curacy, in Beccles, Suffolk. By marrying Catherine he did well for himself, since her family was undoubtedly higher up the social scale than his. It was thanks to Catherine's great uncle, Lord Walpole, that Edmund Nelson was given the living of Burnham Thorpe in 1755 and it was there, three years later, that his sixth child, Horatio, was born.

Edmund is a slightly less shadowy figure than his wife. 'It has fallen to my lot to take upon me the care and affection of a double parent'[7] he wrote after his wife died, and true to her memory, he never remarried. He seems to have been a strict parent. However, in one very important way Edmund was a model for his famous son. When speaking and worshipping in his church a clergyman acts as intermediary between a congregation and their Maker. Nelson would have seen that although his father was somewhat diffident, whimsical and unworldly, he still had a defining part to play in the lives of his parishioners by christening, marrying, burying and exhorting them. A sea captain's role runs parallel to that of a clergyman, with the 'bonus' that a sea captain, in the 18th century, also had the power of life and death over his men.

Edmund wrote letters to his other children about 'Yr Bro,' and they all knew it was Horatio he was talking about. When Nelson was unemployed for five years 'on the Beach,' it was Edmund who gave Nelson and his wife a home, and he remained very useful to Nelson while he was serving abroad, because it was with her father-in-law that Fanny Nelson spent so much of her time when Nelson was at sea. Edmund continued to succour and support Fanny when Nelson's affair with Lady Hamilton led to the break-up of his marriage. On hearing of the news of the Battle of Copenhagen the letter he wrote to his illustrious son shows Edmund's personality clearly. A clergyman first and foremost, he was not afraid to rebuke Nelson for his behaviour.

Bath April 1801

MY GOOD, GREAT AND AFFECTIONATE SON, – He who created all things, He to whom all creatures bow, He by whom the very hairs of our heads are numbered, has covered your head in the day of battle. He has bestowed upon you great abilities and has granted you His grace to use them to His glory, the good of your fellow creatures and the salvation of your own soul ...

Yesterday I received your joyous news, but all things have their alloy, Lady (Fanny Nelson) was heavily affected with her personal feelings at not receiving a line from your own hand. In all things may you have a right understanding.[8]

Edmund died in April 1802. Both Nelson and Fanny were warned that he was failing in health. Nelson declared (rather frequently) that he was too unwell to attend his father's deathbed or his funeral. (Almost certainly he was embarrassed at the possibility of meeting Fanny there, and so avoided going.) Fanny did attend. Some measure of the regard with which Edmund Nelson was held in Burnham Thorpe, was noted by his son-in-law, Thomas Bolton, husband of Edmund's daughter Susannah. Bolton wrote of the service, when Edmund Nelson was buried there 'the church was crowded, everyone lamenting the loss of a friend ...'[9]

Nelson's mother – Catherine (nee Suckling) – was born in 1725, the daughter of the Reverend Maurice Suckling and his wife, Mary (nee Turner). Mary Turner was related on her mother's side to the Walpoles and so Catherine was the great niece of Sir Robert Walpole, first prime minister of Great Britain. It was his maternal grandfather, Maurice Suckling, who gave Nelson his Royal Ancestors.

Little is known of Catherine and what is known is almost all second-hand, but his mother's personality and influence continued with Nelson from the day she died to the day he was killed. She hated the French, *he* hated the French. In a letter to a friend, Hugh Elliott, he spelled it out: 'My mother hated the French.'[10] This letter, dated 8th October 1803, was written 36 years after Catherine's death.

All his life, reinforced by his mother's opinion, Nelson pursued his career in fighting the French. Although he hardly ever underestimated them, in his heart of hearts he believed he could always beat them: it seems that he despised them slightly. His stay in France as a young man before the French Revolution repeatedly reinforced in his mind the superiority of England with its better roads, better inns, better use of resources and presence of influential 'middling sort' (i.e. the middle classes) of people, of which he and his family and friends were a classic example. To him, they were the backbone of England. He had quickly spotted there were no middling sort of people in France and he probably believed there was no proper 'backbone' to France.

In a large family, parental hugging and loving can be in short supply and only months before he was killed, Nelson wrote a letter to an old Norfolk acquaintance paraphrasing a passage from Shakespeare's *Henry V*: 'the thought of former days brings all my mother to my heart which shows itself in my eyes.'[11] Sent on 14th May 1804 from *Victory*, the correct quotation from Shakespeare's Henry V is 'And all my Mother came into my eyes and gave me up to tears.' The picture of one of the most influential men in the western world, so sad if not actually crying at the thought of his mother, some 35 years after her death, is incredibly moving. Perhaps in this we have a pointer to some of the powerful effect the 'motherly' Lady Hamilton had upon Nelson. Although the original use of the word 'mother' here by Shakespeare refers to the feminine, gentler side of the speaker's nature (it is Exeter witnessing the death of York on the battlefield) we feel that Nelson's paraphrase really does show him thinking back to his mother.

A formal, somewhat primitive portrait of Catherine exists, showing a large-bosomed figure. Her face is arresting as she looks full at the painter with a confident gaze. The nose and lips were inherited by her famous son. Her eldest daughter, Susanna, wrote, 'But somehow the Navy must always be interesting to me. I may say I suck'd it with my mother's milk, for she was quite a heroine for the sailors.'[12] Susanna also commented (rather daringly) after her mother had died that she had 'bred herself to death.'[13] Catherine was, alas, typical of her age, since one last piece of primary evidence can be shown. She married Edmund Nelson in May 1747 and her obstetric history was as follows:

1. Edmund	1750.	Died aged 2
2. Horatio	1751.	Died same year
3. Maurice	1753	
4. Susannah	1755	
5. William	1757	
6. Horatio	1758	
7. Anne	1760	
8. Edmund	1762	
9. Suckling	1764	
10. George	1765.	Died aged 1
11. Catherine	1767	

Catherine died in December 1767 aged 42, when her youngest child was nine months old having had eleven children in eighteen and a half years; almost certainly from what has been called the 'attrition of childbirth'[14] suffered by vast numbers of women before the advent of birth control.

It is known that Nelson attended two schools – the first being the Royal Grammar School at Norwich, where he was sent as a boarder at an early age shortly after his mother died when he was nine. Later Horatio was removed from Norwich and sent to Sir William Paston's School nearer home at North Walsham. It has been said 'the education there had a more liberal curriculum,'[15] by comparison with most other boys' schools. Unusually for the time, the school had a French language teacher, although Nelson was never, ever, a linguist.

Nelson's two uncles on his mother's side – Maurice and William Suckling – were very important to him throughout his early life. Maurice was a lieutenant in the Royal Navy by the age of 19, serving under Admiral Byng in the Mediterranean. Appointed captain at the age of 30, he was sent to the West Indies where his ship *Dreadnaught* was one of three British ships to fight a successful action with a superior French squadron on 21st October 1757 (a day ever afterwards celebrated annually in the Nelson family). In 1761 he served in the Channel under Lord Hawke. After some years on half pay during a Peace, he was appointed to *Raisonnable* in 1770 when war with Spain over the Falkland Islands appeared to be a possibility and it was then that he took the young Horatio Nelson to sea with him for the first time.

At the age of 50 Maurice was made Comptroller of the Navy, the senior officer of the Navy Board. The Navy Board was responsible for all the technical and financial aspects of the Navy, so his post was a very responsible one, especially in time of war. He died three years later when still in office. Childless himself, his legacies greatly assisted all the children of his sister, Catherine.[16]

William Suckling, Nelson's other maternal uncle, lived in a large house in Kentish Town where Nelson stayed from time to time. He was an official in the Customs and Navy Office and in contrast to Nelson's somewhat unworldly and impoverished father, was a wealthy man. Nelson was extremely fond of his uncle who was twenty-nine years his senior, and once referred to him as 'my best friend.'[17] He wrote to his uncle frequently, regarding him as not only a man of the world, but also a source of good advice. He was also a relative who could be 'touched' for money should the need arise! Nelson discussed in his letters to William things he did not mention to anyone else in the world, for example, his urinary problems following his abdominal wound. He wrote more than once, asking for money, when he had at various times fallen in love with young ladies whilst abroad; the last such occasion was when he met his future wife. Here is part of a letter he wrote in just those amorous circumstances:

'Life is not worth preserving without happiness; and I care not where I may linger out a miserable existence ... I shall ever be a well-wisher to you and your family and pray they and you may never know the pangs which at this instant tear my heart.'[18]

He asked for legal advice with regard to his somewhat over-zealous implementation in the West Indies of the Navigation Acts, which threatened to ruin him.[19] He also seems to have 'off-loaded' onto his uncle in more than one letter: for example, on 7th February 1795 he wrote to Fanny a somewhat bland letter about his time in Corsica. On the same day he wrote to his uncle a letter which was almost twice as long as the one to Fanny, full of financial details and mentioning a 'cut across my back,' a wound he received at Bastia, and containing many heartfelt moans about lack of recognition (always a very important factor in Nelson's life.)

I have got upon a subject near my heart, which is full when I think of the treatment I have received: every man who had any considerable share in the reduction, (of Corsica) has got one place or other – I, only I, am without reward.[20]

When William Suckling died in 1798 Nelson found he had been left £100 and was one of his uncle's executors. Fortunately there seem to have been others, as Nelson was 'inactive in a foreign court.' (Naples) at the time and would not have been much help in clearing up his uncle's financial affairs. However, he did put his feelings about his uncle in writing 'I loved my uncle for his own worth.'[21]

The 'Nature versus Nurture' debate within developmental psychology over the relative importance of biological predisposition (Nature) and environmental influences (Nurture) as determinants of individual human development continues. Current thinking by developmental psychologists seems to be that what should always be considered is the *interaction* of Nature and Nurture to bring about a finished person, with belief that all complex human attributes, such as intelligence, temperament and personality are the end products of a long and involved interplay between biological predispositions and environmental forces.[22]

What were Nelson's biological predispositions? His Nature components were firstly, genes for longevity. In both his parents' families, but especially on the Nelson side, there were a significant number of people who lived for longer than three score years and ten, and to judge from the post-mortem report, Nelson, too, would have lived to a great age had he not been killed. Two of his siblings lived into their mid-seventies, and, in an age when life was still nasty, brutish and short, longevity was a rare gift.

Nelson's next biological predisposition was intelligence of genius level. It is his intelligence which singles Nelson out from his siblings, and his contemporaries. He seems never to have forgotten anything he read or heard; his letters from an early age contain quotations from a wide range of sources. He was able to marshal complex facts with apparent ease, and throughout his life always maintained a grasp of the main thrust of his work and duty, while at the same time not losing sight of any important minutiae. It requires a powerful IQ to be able to do this for month after month, and year after year, and this Nelson had, and did.

However, intelligence is not the same as character and personality. Nelson developed a character and a personality which were the epitome of Thomas Edison's dictum that Genius is 10% inspiration and 90% perspiration. Throughout his life, he was always prepared to work hard; and the stories of his youth – almost certainly from his brother William – indicate in Nelson a mature character at an early age. It is also obvious that Nelson possessed an extraordinary personality. For example: 'He had just returned from Tenerife, after losing his arm,' wrote Lavinia Spencer (wife of the First Lord of the Admiralty) 'He looked so sickly it was painful to see him and his general appearance was that of an idiot; so much so, that when he spoke and his wonderful mind broke forth, it was a sort of surprise that riveted my whole attention.'[23] Nelson seems to have had, throughout his life, the same effect on almost all his acquaintances and friends that he had on Lady Spencer in the spring of 1798. He was genuinely charismatic and this aspect of his personality is explored in Chapter XII.

Nelson was born with a wiry fitness. Although thought by the family to be small and feeble, Nelson was basically extremely tough physically. He clearly survived childhood illnesses and, later, withstood and survived illnesses which killed many of his contemporaries. His physical toughness also enabled him to recover from four severe wounds sustained over a period of only four years.

What were the characteristics Nelson acquired? His most important 'nurture' components were, firstly, parents who were upright citizens and typical of the 'middling sort of people'. They were genuinely religious,

8

law abiding, hard working, careful with money and caring of others less fortunate; and they passed on all these attributes to Nelson. Next, but extremely important, he was born into the middle of a large and united family, with an excellent additional 'support' system of relatives, so that although time for one-to-one loving and physical contact between Nelson and his parents must have been short, the *quality* of what he was given must have been good, since throughout his life Nelson, although requiring support himself, was always able to give help to others. The family in Burnham Thorpe Parsonage were none of them spoilt. There existed a relatively harsh physical home environment. There was no spare money, no indulgence of the children. All were expected to make their own way in the world, but also to help one another to do so. Thus, throughout his life, Nelson knew he could expect support from his father, his uncles and his siblings. He also knew that it was his role in the family to help them if they needed it. The inherent stability of such a family system was incredibly important to all its members, not least to Nelson.

The next two environmental forces that tempered Nelson were the two parts of his early education. He was subjected to an old-fashioned, very hard-working environment at the schools he attended. He then was subjected to a relatively harsh environment on board ships in his teens. This environment was tempered with *graded* training, which meant that Nelson as a young officer was taught how to lead others at a relatively early age. Such training ensured he was able to accept responsibility for the lives and well-being of subordinates throughout the whole of his naval career.

As the son of a Church of England clergyman, born into the middle of the 18th century, Nelson received from his earliest years a very genuine religious faith, of a fatalistic order, which lasted all his life and was always a support to him.

All the above—the family, the good teaching, the structured education, the religious faith, gave Nelson a form of innate self-confidence that enabled him to make friends with older men and women. They, in turn, enjoyed his company, became his mentors when he was young, and continued as his life-long friends. His principal guides were:

His uncles: Maurice & William Suckling
Captain Skeffington Lutwidge of the *Carcass*
Captain William Locker of the *Lowestoffe*
Cuthbert Collingwood
Admiral Sir Peter and Lady Parker
Earl St. Vincent
Alexander Davison

It was this innate self-confidence which enabled Nelson to take unpopular stands – for example when he was trying to implement the Navigation

Acts in 1774, in the West Indies, or when he supported in court the traitor Edward Despard, in February, 1803, without being fearful of the consequences to himself.[24]

Nelson served with Despard on the San Juan Expedition of 1780. Twenty-three years later Despard was accused of high treason, having plotted with others to kill King George III. Despard asked Nelson to appear as a witness for the defence, which Nelson did. So strongly did Nelson try to support Despard that although the latter was found guilty, the jury recommended him to mercy 'on account of the high testimonials to his former good character and eminent services.' Although this recommendation failed to save him, the original sentence of 'hanging, drawing and quartering' was changed to 'hanging and beheading after death.'

DESCENT I: WILLIAM THE CONQUERER[25]

WILLIAM THE CONQUERER King of England b. 1027 d. 1087	m.	MATILDA (daughter of Count of Flanders)

‖

HENRY King of England b. 1068 d. 1135	m.	MATILDA (daughter of Malcolm III, King of Scotland)

‖

MATILDA b. 1103 d. 1167 proclaimed Queen of England	m.	GEOFFREY PLANTAGENET, Count of Anjou

‖

HENRY II King of England b. 1133 d. 1189 France)	m.	ELEANOR OF AQUITAINE (formerly Queen of

‖

JOHN King of England b. 1167 d. 1216	m.	ISABELLA

———————————————||

||

HENRY III   m.   ELEANOR OF PROVENCE
King of England b. 1207 d. 1272

———————————————||

||

EDWARD I   m.   ELEANOR OF CASTILE
King of England b. 1238 d. 1307   (daughter of Ferdinand III,
                                         King of Castile)

———————————————||

||

EDWARD II   m.   ISABEL (daughter of
King of England b. 1284 d. 1327   Philip IV, King of France)

———————————————||

||

EDWARD III   m.   PHILIPPA OF HAINAULT
King of England b. 1312 d. 1377

———————————————||

||

JOHN OF GAUNT   m. (3rd wife) CATHERINE SWYNFORD
Duke of Lancaster b. 1340 d. 1399   (nee Roelt)
(First of three direct lines of descent)

———————————————||

||

JOHN BEAUFORT   m.   MARGARET (daughter of
Earl of Somerset b. 1371 d. 1410   Thomas Holland, Earl of Kent)

———————————————||

||

EDMUND BEAUFORT   m.   ELEANOR (daughter of
Duke of Somerset b. 1406 d. 1455   Warwick the Kingmaker)

—————————————————| |

| |

ELEANOR BEAUFORT   m.   SIR ROBERT SPENCER

—————————————————| |

| |

MARGARET SPENCER   m.   THOMAS CAREY

—————————————————| |

| |

WILLIAM CAREY   m.   Lady MARY BOLEYN

—————————————————| |

| |

HENRY CAREY, lst Lord Hunsdon

DESCENT II: JOHN OF GAUNT

Alternative 1[26]

JOHN OF GAUNT   m. (3rd wife)   CATHERINE SWYNFORD
Duke of Lancaster   (nee Roelt)
b.1340 d. 1399

v----------------------------------^

JOHN BEAUFORT   m.   MARGARET HOLLAND
Earl of Somerset b. 1371 d.1410   (daughter of Earl of Kent)

v----------------------------------^

JOHN BEAUFORT   m.   MARGARET
Duke of Somerset b. 1404 d. 1444   (daughter of John Beauchamp
                                                            of Bletso)

v----------------------------------^

MARGARET BEAUFORT   m.   EDMUND TUDOR
b. 1443 d.1509   Earl of Richmond

```
                      v--------------------------------^
```

HENRY VII   m.   ELIZABETH OF YORK
King of England   (daughter of Edward IV,
b. 1457 d. 1509   King of England)

```
                    v--------------------------------^
```

HENRY VIII   Refer back
King of England b. 1491 d. 1546

Alternative 2

JOHN OF GAUNT   m. (3rd wife)   CATHERINE SWYNFORD
Duke of Lancaster   (nee Roelt)

```
                    v--------------------------------^
```

JOAN BEAUFORT   m.   RALPH NEVILLE
b. 1380 d. 1445   Earl of Westmorland

```
                    v--------------------------------^
```

CICELY NEVILLE   m.   RICHARD
b. 1415 d. 1495   Duke of York (Protector
                                          of England)

```
                    v--------------------------------^
```

EDWARD IV   m.   ELIZABETH WOODVILLE
King of England   (nee Rivers)
b. 1442 d. 1483

```
                    v--------------------------------^
```

ELIZABETH OF YORK   m.   HENRY VII
d. 1503   King of England

```
                    v--------------------------------^
```

HENRY VIII   Refer back
King of England b. 1457 d. 1546

DESCENT III: HENRY VIII[27]

HENRY VIII
King of England
b. 1491 d. 1546

Lady MARY BOLEYN
doubly adulterous
union

—————————————||

||

Probable issue:
HENRY CAREY   m.   ANNE MORGAN
1st Lord Hunsdon b. 1525 d. 1596

—————————————||

||

JOHN CAREY   m.   MARY HYDE
3rd Lord Hunsdon b. 1556 d. 1617

—————————————||

||

HON. BLANCHE CAREY   m.   SIR THOMAS WODEHOUSE
d. 1651   2nd Bart

—————————————||

||

ANNE WODEHOUSE   m.   ROBERT SUCKLING
b. 1617 d. 1653

—————————————||

||

ROBERT SUCKLING   m.   SARAH SHELTON
b. 1643 d. 1708

—————————————||

||

Rev. MAURICE SUCKLING, DD.   m.   ANNE TURNER

d. 1730

CATHERINE SUCKLING m.   Rev. EDMUND NELSON, MA
b. 1725 d. 1767

————————————————————||

||
HORATIO NELSON
1st Viscount Nelson b. 1758 d. 1805

DESCENT IV: ALFRED THE GREAT[28]

ALFRED THE GREAT   m.   EALSWITHA
King of England d. 901

————————————————————||

||
EDWARD THE ELDER   m.   EADGIVA
King of England d. 925

————————————————————||

||
EDMUND THE ELDER   m.   ELGIFA
King of England d. 946

————————————————————||

||
EDGAR THE PEACEABLE   m.   ELFRIDA
King of England d. 959

————————————————————||

||
ETHELRED   m.   ELGIFA
King of England d. 1016

————————————————————||

||
EDMUND IRONSIDE   m.   ALGITHA
King of England d. 1017

15

EDWARD THE OUTLAW   m.   AGATHA
Prince Royal d. 1057

——————————————| |

| |
MARGARET (Saint Margaret)   m.   MALCOLM III
Queen of Scotland d. 1093   King of Scotland

——————————————| |

| |
MATILDA   m.   HENRY I
Queen-Consort of England d. 1118

——————————————| |

| |
MATILDA   m.   GEOFFREY PLANTAGENET
proclaimed Queen of England   Count of Anjou
  b. 1103 d. 1167

——————————————| |

| |
HENRY II
King of England   Refer back to William the Conqueror, Descent I
b. 1133 d. 1189

DESCENT V: THE NELSONS

RICHARD NELSON   m.   ?
of Maudsley, Lancs. Alive in 1508

——————————————| |

| |
THOMAS NELSON   m.   CECILY MAXEY
of Wrightington, Lancs

WILLIAM NELSON   m.   JUDITH CLINTON
of London d. 1618

———————————————————| |

    | |
THOMAS NELSON   m.   ELIZABETH
Mayor of Lynn. b. 1580 d. 1654

———————————————————| |

    | |
EDMUND NELSON   m.   ALICE
of Wendling, Norfolk. b. 1629 d. 1645

———————————————————| |

    | |
WILLIAM NELSON   m.   MARY SHENE
of Scanning & Durham.
b. ?1654 d. 1711

———————————————————| |

    | |
EDMUND NELSON   m.   MARY BLAND
Rector of East Bradenham.
b. 1693 d. 1747

———————————————————| |

    | |
EDMUND NELSON   m.   CATHERINE SUCKLING
Rector of Burnham Thorpe.   b.1725 d. 1767
 b. 1722 d. 1802

———————————————————| |

    | |
HORATIO NELSON
1st Viscount Nelson b. 1758 d. 1805

Notes

1. Davidson *Textbook of Medicine* Haslett, C. et al (eds) 2004
2. French, G. R. *The Royal Descent of Nelson and Wellington* 1853 p.45 (hereafter French)
3. Leigh: *Chronical Scrip Book* part IV July 1879 p.365–89
4. Oman, *Nelson* 1947 p.7 (hereafter Oman)
5. Hoskins, A. *Mary Boleyn's Carey Children: Offspring of Henry VIII?* Genealogists Magazine 25(9) March 1997 p.345–52
6. French p.195
7. Quoted in Pocock, 1987 p.1
8. Naish, G. P. B. *Nelson's Letters to his Wife* 1958 p.586 (hereafter Naish)
9. Quoted in Pocock p.272
10. Nicolas vol V p.238
11. ibid vol VI p.18 & Shakespeare's *Henry V* Act 4 Scene 6
12. Morrison vol II letter 936 p.308
13. ibid vol II letter 700 p.206
14. Hudson, R. (ed) *The Grand Quarrel* 2000 p.xvii
15. White, C. *Nelson Encyclopaedia* 2002 p.220
16. ibid p.227
17. Nicolas vol I p.187
18. ibid vol II p.479–80
19. Examples: ibid vol I p.146 & 161
20. ibid vol II p.6
21. ibid vol III p.323
22. Shaffer, D. R. *Development Psychology* 1996 p.43
23. Edgcumbe, R. (ed) *The Diary of Frances, Lady Shelley* 1912 p.77–8
24. Nicolas vol V p.42
25. French p.196
26. Louda and Maclagan *Lines of Succession* table 5 p.20
27. Hoskins: Personal communication to the Author
28. French p.195

CHAPTER II

Illnesses and Doctors

Nelson's formal education ended when he was 12 years and 5 months old. He joined his uncle, Maurice Suckling's ship *Raisonnable* in March 1771 but then transferred with him to *Triumph* five months later. *Triumph* was a stationary guard ship on the Medway, so, to gain sea-going experience, Suckling arranged for Nelson to join a merchant ship going to the West Indies. He was away for thirteen months. Taken back on *Triumph* in September 1772 he spent the next nine months learning to handle the ship's boats between the mouth of the Thames and the Pool of London. Nelson recorded:

> Thus by degrees I became a good pilot for vessels of that description from Chatham to the Tower of London, down the Swin, and the North Foreland and confident of myself amongst rocks and sands.[1]

Nelson then joined an 'Expedition towards the North Pole.' He served on a bomb-ketch, *Carcass*, whose captain, Skeffington Lutwidge, became a life-long friend. The expedition lasted three months and included young Nelson's close encounter with a polar bear.

After *Carcass* was paid off Nelson was appointed Midshipman on a frigate, *Seahorse*, and sent to the East Indies. For two years *Seahorse* journeyed to Madeira, Basra, Madras, Bengal, Trincomalee, Calcutta and the remote islands of Amsterdam and St. Paul (40 degrees south). Eventually Nelson became ill and was invalided home on *Dolphin*. He recovered sufficiently on the six-month journey home to be at once employed, on his return to England, as acting Lieutenant on *Worcester*, on convoy duties between England and Gibraltar. Promoted Lieutenant in April 1777 he sailed again for the West Indies on *Lowestoffe*. Within 18 months he was appointed First Lieutenant of a 50-gun ship –*Bristol* – and then commander of a sloop – *Badger* – at just 20 years old. Three months short of his 21st birthday, he was made Post Captain of *Hinchinbroke*.

Most of Nelson's illnesses occurred when he was a young man. Due to his service abroad, they included tropical disease and poisoning, but, typically for a serving naval man of the late 18th century, he also suffered from

19

deficiency diseases and seems to have been exposed to possible sexual disease as well. In the tropics he suffered from sunstroke.

Throughout his life Nelson suffered from reactive anxiety and depression. He also experienced severe and prolonged post-traumatic depression after the Nile head wound. His last surgeon, Beatty, recorded that he experienced severe 'chest' spasms. Beatty thought they were gastro-intestinal in origin. In addition to these illnesses, Nelson suffered from seasickness, and while it may not be regarded as an illness in the true sense of the word, it is also examined here in this chapter.

Having been eighteen months on the East Indies station, Nelson, aged 17, arrived back in Bombay in December 1775, with a severe fever. The exact diagnosis is not known, but it was very probably malaria. Nelson was seen by the surgeon of *Salisbury* (the flagship of Sir Edward Hughes, his Admiral in the East Indies) and ordered home on *Dolphin*, a 20-gun ship whose Captain was James Pigot.

Nelson seems to have kept to his sickbed for almost the whole voyage and, as was the normal procedure at the time, a barrel was on board in which to take his body back to England should he have died whilst on the voyage home. Towards the end of the voyage he went through the so-called 'Radiant Orb' experience.

He later opined that Captain Pigot had saved his life – having been transferred to *Dolphin* 'more dead than alive'. *Dolphin* reached England via Simonstown, South Africa, in September 1776. Nelson does not seem to have landed there but the fresh vegetables supplied to *Dolphin* while she stayed in the harbour for about four weeks, on the way home, would have helped all on board considerably.

Recovered from the severe illness which had necessitated his return to England, Nelson served on the *Worcester*. Having passed his Lieutenant examination, in April 1777 he was appointed to the frigate *Lowestoffe*, whose captain was William Locker.

Captain Locker (1731–1800) entered the Royal Navy aged 15, and served in the West Indies, the Mediterranean, India and China. He was present at the French defeat of Quiberon Bay. During service, again in the West Indies, with Nelson as one of his lieutenants, Locker exerted an enormous influence over the younger man who, (more than 20 years later) wrote 'I have been your scholar; it is you who have taught me to board a Frenchman … it is you who always told me 'Lay a Frenchman close and you will beat him' and my only merit in my profession is being a good scholar.'[2]

In 1779 Locker returned to England because of ill health. He was appointed Commander-in-Chief at the Nore in 1792 and Lieutenant-Governor of Greenwich Hospital a year later. He died in 1800. (It was Locker who urged Nelson to sit for the painters John Francis Rigaud and Lemuel Abbott.)

Despite the fact that his uncle Captain Maurice Suckling had dismissed the child Nelson in a famous quotation 'Poor Horace ... who is so weak'[3] Nelson seems by 1780 to have been a physically tough and robust young man. By the time he was appointed Captain of *Hinchinbroke*, in June 1779, just before his 21st birthday, Nelson had crossed the Atlantic at least four times, travelled extensively in the Middle East, in the Far East, and across the Southern Indian Ocean. He had also been within 10 degrees of the North Pole on the Spitzbergen expedition. He was already one of the most travelled men of his age. But between 1780 and 1782 Nelson suffered from a succession of life-threatening illnesses.

The expedition to San Juan, Nicaragua, consisted of seven troop transports escorted by *Hinchinbroke*. The whole expedition sailed from Jamaica on 3rd February 1780 and made its way slowly southwards calling at islands off the coast of Honduras and Nicaragua, the Costa de Mosquitoes, and even stopping off for 3 weeks at Cape Grace a Dios, where a shore camp was set up in a location particularly bad for mosquitoes, even for that area. Nelson seems to have gone on shore only once in the seven weeks. Having arrived at the mouth of the San Juan river there was no need for Nelson to leave his ship and to join the land expedition. Once he had delivered the soldiers in the transports to their destination he could have anchored his ship off the land and waited until the land forces re-emerged from the jungle, requiring transport home. The object of the expedition was to 'force a passage to the Pacific' across the isthmus joining North to South America and 'bring about a communication between sea and sea.'[4] Nelson insisted on leading the rowing boats that carried the troops up the San Juan river and he also assisted the military with their cannon fire against Fort San Juan, held by Spanish troops. Fortunately for Nelson he then received orders to return to Port Royal, Jamaica, to take command of a larger ship, *Janus*.

On land, the first apparent pathological problem for Nelson on the San Juan expedition was poisoning by the highly toxic sap of a local tree. Clarke and M'Arthur wrote:

> During this arduous service, Captain Nelson and some of his men narrowly escaped being poisoned. They had inadvertently endeavoured to quench their excessive thirst by drinking at a spring into which some branches of the manchineel apple had been thrown: a subtle poison that is used by the Indians for their arrows. Nelson suffered severely from its effects and it is the opinion of His Royal Highness, the Duke of Clarence, from whom this anecdote was received, that the delicate health of his friend thus experienced a severe and lasting injury.[5]

Actually this does not seem medically very likely. The dilution of the sap in the pool of water seems to have prevented extreme toxicity and next day, Nelson was back on active service, laying his 'battery of one gun' as a colleague put it, with success against the castle of San Juan.

Hippomane Manchinella or the manchineel tree grows to a height of some thirty feet and is a native of central America and the West Indies, where it grows in the coastal areas but not inland. The most toxic part is the sticky white sap that oozes from any broken part and is very soluble in water. But the sawdust inhaled when the tree is cut down can cause coughs and sore eyes, nose, larynx and chest, and any part of the tree, from the apple-like fruits to its leaves and bark, can produce toxic symptoms. The severity of these is related both to length of exposure time and amount of toxic material with which the victim comes into contact. It is thought that more than one toxic substance is produced by the tree but the exact poisons are still not yet fully known. Direct contact with sap causes severe skin blisters. Eating the green/yellow crab apple-type fruit causes vomiting, abdominal pain, bloody and profuse diarrhoea, shock and death, with post mortem showing an intense inflammation of the entire lining of the digestive tract. A consultant radiologist published an article in the British Medical Journal in 2000 giving a horribly clear modern account of the oral and pharangeal symptoms consequent upon eating just one bite from a manchineel 'apple.' While on holiday he ate a piece of 'apple' and on recounting the experience to the locals, 'elicited frank horror and incredulity, such was the fruit's poisonous reputation.'[6]

Nelson is thought to have drunk water contaminated by the sap and suffered an attack of stomach pain and dysentery, fortunately not prolonged. He did not bother to mention the episode in his memoir of his services, and seemed to recover fully from it. However, he was almost certainly 'incubating' four much more serious illnesses.

Most of Nelson's biographers seem to believe the main illness he suffered from on the Nicaraguan campaign was yellow fever, and that this was why he nearly died on the expedition. But the medical information available from contemporary sources, including Nelson's letters, Dr. Benjamin Moseley's book, *Treatise on Tropical Diseases,* and *Hinchinbroke's* log, do not confirm the diagnosis. Although this description of yellow fever comes from a naval doctor's account of a mid-nineteenth century outbreak, the symptoms of yellow fever must have been very well known to the naval doctors of Nelson's day. 'Intense fever coming on suddenly and the symptoms gradually becoming worse, violent delirium, yellow skin, black vomit, collapse and death. The vomit was constant, copious and black or brownish.'[7] Nothing like that was described by those associated with the *Hinchinbroke* or the San Juan Expedition. Moreover, when Captain Cuthbert Collingwood took over the *Hinchinbroke,* the illness of the sailors on board was said to show symptoms of 'Fevers, Fluxes and Scorbictic Ulcers.'[8] Flux is an old-fashioned word for diarrhoea and scorbictic ulcers are the type associated with scurvy.

If, in an illness, the medical symptoms (what the patient complains of) and signs (what the doctor looks for and notes) can be seen to fit into a diagnosis of one illness, no doctor should make two diagnoses. However, it is the author's opinion that the only way to explain all the medical problems Nelson suffered from at this time is to show, from primary sources, that he had no fewer than four illnesses in the period from April 1780 to August 1781. Whilst one of these was malaria which will be discussed in detail later, the other three – incipient scurvy, tropical sprue and peripheral neuropathy – were part of a continuum, which formed a ghastly, life-threatening process during this period.

From the medical point of view, the following is what probably happened. The *Hinchinbroke* took seven weeks to travel from Jamaica to the mouth of the San Juan river, during which time everyone was eating ship's food. Nelson seems to have gone ashore only once. British sailors were extremely conservative about their food and by the time the ship arrived, it is highly likely they were all in a pre-scurvy state, lacking in vitamin C. Scurvy sufferers have not only a lack of bodily vitamin C, but also suffer from folic acid deficiency and lack of other B vitamins. Folic acid is one of the B group of vitamins, and is an essential substance found in liver, kidneys, vegetables, fruit, nuts and yeast – none of which foods would have been readily available to Nelson or his men. Folic acid and B vitamins are easily destroyed by cooking. Absorbed in the small intestine, a lack of them produces a form of anaemia and, rarely, psychiatric upsets. Lack of folic acid can also cause a condition called peripheral neuropathy: the symptoms of which are weakness, pain and altered sensation in the limbs. The human body does not have large reserves of folic acid and B vitamins, and cannot synthesise them. They need therefore to be eaten, and absorbed, regularly.

First medical reports in English of a condition subsequently called tropical sprue were made by a British doctor in the West Indies in 1759.[9] Many further reports followed and on one occasion it was described as 'Cachectic Diarrhoea.' The exact organism which causes it is not known. The illness is interesting because it has an incubation period covered by that which Nelson gave to Dr. Moseley: 'The fever which destroyed the army and navy attached to that Expedition was invariably from 20–30 days before it attacked the newcomers.'[10] This incubation period is much longer than that of other acute tropical gastro-intestinal infections, or illnesses. Sprue is usually a chronic illness but it can have an acute onset and it also causes folic acid deficiency. What is more, in people with an already low folic acid level, (e.g. due to developing scurvy) sprue is rapidly progressive. Acute sprue symptoms are diarrhoea, fever, malaise, weakness, and weight loss which can lead to cachexia and death (note below). It is the author's belief that Nelson and his men were in a pre-scurvy state and therefore low in folic acid and then succumbed to an acute attack of tropical sprue with its attendant problems. Recalled away from the Nicaraguan expedition on 28th April 1780, to go back to Jamaica to take command of a new ship, *Janus*, Nelson was so extremely weak when he arrived back at Port Royal in the sloop *Victor*, that 'he had to be taken on shore in his cot.' Clarke and M'Arthur say this was due to being 'so completely debilitated by the dysentery and worn by fatigue.'[11] (Even in modern times sprue can be a dangerous illness. The grandfather of a friend of the author died of sprue in the 1920s. The husband of an acquaintance was diagnosed, in India in the 1970s, with terminal cancer, and sent home to England ostensibly, to die. This was a case of mis-diagnosis, and fortunately modern treatment for tropical sprue effected a complete cure.)

Severe prolonged dysentery also causes loss of essential body fluid components such as sodium, potassium, and iron, and is prostrating. Anaemia due to poor absorption of iron also causes fatigue. No wonder Nelson was so weak. His life was immediately saved by not going to Green Bay Hospital (the naval hospital in Jamaica, which had an appalling reputation for failing to cure its patients) but by being taken at once to stay with Cuba Cornwallis – a freed slave who had once belonged to Nelson's fellow captain, the Honorable William Cornwallis, and being given, by her, herbal remedies which probably contained large amounts of vitamin C, folic acid and B vitamins. Nelson was clearly rushed to her care when he got back to Jamaica. She was described as 'a well born and respectable negress, who saved the lives of many naval officers.'[12]

Any modern researcher into Nelson's health must, across two centuries, warm to Admiral Sir Peter Parker and his wife Margaret. Parker was naval Commander-in-Chief of the Jamaica station. About a month after he got back to Jamaica Nelson left what Clark & M'Arthur called 'The Lodging House of his faithful Negress' and 'was removed' to the Parkers' house near Port Royal, Jamaica, where both Lady Parker and her housekeeper, Mrs. Yates, sat up with him by turns, and even the Admiral himself 'constantly watched' by Nelson's bedside. Clarke and M'Arthur's account continues: 'his aversion from taking medicine was great, and the only method which these friends could devise was to send it by the Admiral's youngest daughter, then a child; who afterwards was often recognised by Nelson as his little nurse.'[13]

It is not known exactly how long Nelson stayed in the Parker residence, but, like many a conscientious patient before and since, he tried to return to work 'as soon as his health was in the smallest degree re-established' and rapidly relapsed. He was forced to write officially to Sir Peter at the end of August 1780:

> Having been in a very bad state of health for these several months past, so bad as to be unable to attend my duty on board the *Janus*, and the faculty having informed me that I cannot recover in this climate,

I am therefore to request that you will be pleased to permit me to go to England for the re-establishment of my health.[14]

Two days later, in a kindly letter, Sir Peter replied:

The report of the Surgeons who have examined into your complaints, confirms my opinion of the absolute necessity for your immediate return to Europe, and you have therefore my leave to go to England by the first opportunity, with my very sincere wishes for your speedy recovery; being with true esteem,
    Sir, your most obedient humble servant,

P. PARKER[15]

The report of the surgeons makes ghastly reading. On 1st September 1780 the three naval doctors, Wood, Bruce and Melling who had examined Nelson at the behest of Sir Peter Parker, wrote:

We have Strictly and Carefully inquired into the Nature of the Complaints of Captain Horatio Nelson, of his Majesty's Ship the *Janus*, and find from repeated attacks of Tertian and Quartan Agues, and those now degenerated into Quotidian, attended with bilious Vomitings, Nervous Headaches, Visceral Obstructions and many other bodily Infirmities, and being reduced quite to a Skeleton, we are of the opinion his remaining here will be attended with fatal Consequences. Would therefore recommend an Immediate Change of Climate as the only Chance he has for recovery.[16]

Clearly the three doctors recognised that Nelson was suffering from agues, (malaria) but were at a loss to diagnose his other illnesses. Sir Peter's official report home read in part 'Captain Nelson is so emaciated and in so bad state of health that I doubt whether he will live to get home.'[17] Nelson was not yet 22 years old.

He sailed back to England with his friend Captain the Hon. William Cornwallis, on the latter's ship, *Lion*, and said later of Cornwallis, his 'care and attention again saved my life.'[18] but the voyage, back across the Atlantic, took almost three months and one must presume Nelson's bowels, affected by the sprue, were poor at absorbing what shipboard nutrition they were given. In any event, by the time Nelson arrived in England he was suffering from what seems to have been a recurrence of peripheral neuropathy. He stayed for a short time at the Parkers' London house, but then travelled to Bath to recuperate.

Peripheral neuropathy has many causes: it can be a symptom of infections such as influenza and diphtheria; metabolic illnesses such as diabetes, and it can be associated with some neoplasms, for example, cancer of the lung. Nelson's symptoms, as given in his letters, were severe pain, altered sensation, and weakness of his limbs so severe that he could not walk or properly use his arms. He suffered these symptoms for months.

Common sense dictates that across such a distance in time the diagnosis of some of Nelson's illnesses 1780–1782 must be speculative. But deficiency of certain of the B group of vitamins – most especially B_1, B_6 and Nicotine acid can cause sensory and motor polyneuropathy[19] – the symptoms Nelson described. These B vitamins are water soluble. Legumes, pork, liver, nuts and yeast provide B_1, in the diet and an almost identical list of foodstuffs supply B_6. Nicotine acid is found mainly in meat, fish and wholemeal cereals. Even if present in *Hinchinbroke's* shipboard fare – which it is known was of a poor standard – absorption would have been severely reduced once diarrhoea took hold. In the final analysis the author is of the opinion the illness affecting Nelson originally caused a complex interaction of poor availability and reduced absorption of several vitamins. This left him with sensory and motor symptoms which waxed and waned over many months.

Bath is a spa town famous for its medicinal waters which contain a high concentration of iron, as the sulphide, making them taste so vile. (Many sulphides have an offensive taste and smell – it is hydrogen sulphide which gives bad eggs their unpleasant odour.) But of course iron, if it can be absorbed, helps to cure anaemia. The effects of the chronic diarrhoea, in lowering Nelson's body folic acid and vitamin B complex, which in turn caused the peripheral neuropathy, left him with a much longer intermittent illness, the symptoms of which, typically, he reported faithfully to his old friend Captain Locker, in a series of letters written from Bath. They reveal much about the writer's physical and mental state. The first was written on 23rd January 1781:

I have been so ill since I have been here, that I was obliged to be carried to and from bed, with the most excruciating tortures, but, thank God, I am upon the mending hand. I (am) physicked three times a day, drink the waters three times, and bathe every other night.[20]

Five days later he wrote:

> Although I have not quite recovered the use of my limbs, yet my inside is a new man, and I have no doubt, but in two or three weeks, I shall be perfectly well.[21]

This letter suggests that the chronic diarrhoea Nelson suffered from was improving. On 15th February, he wrote:

> My health, thank God, is very near perfectly restored, and I have the perfect use of all my limbs, except my left arm, which I can hardly tell what is the matter with it. From the shoulder to my fingers' ends are

as if half dead, but the Surgeon and Doctors give me hopes it will all go off. I most sincerely wish to be employed, and hope it will not be long.[22] [Then six days later] As to my picture, it will not be the least like that I am now, that is certain, but you may tell Mr. Rigaud to add beauty to it, and it will be much mended.[23]

In this letter Nelson was referring to a portrait of himself, which John Francis Rigaud R.A. had started to paint, at the behest of William Locker, when he was a young lieutenant. Because of his overseas duties Nelson had not been able to complete the sittings required by the artist. X-rays of this picture suggest that the original portrait gave Nelson a much more rounded face. The alterations Rigaud made on Nelson's return to England three years later included altering his face to make it longer and thinner, changing the uniform to that of a captain and painting in a representation of Fort San Juan in the background.

Rising optimism, shown in the letters of February, probably caused Nelson to leave Bath in mid March, but symptoms recurred in May when he wrote to Locker: 'I have relapsed very much.'[24] Another good description of his symptoms was given in this letter to his brother William:

I have entirely lost the use of my left arm, and very near of my left leg and thigh, and am at present under the care of a Mr. Adair, an eminent Surgeon in London, but he gives me hopes a few weeks will remove my disorder.[25]

It is highly likely recurrences of diarrhoea, which he does not mention, but which can happen with sprue, most probably reduced folic acid and multi-vitamin B absorption again and tipped Nelson back into peripheral neuropathy. It was not until August 1781 that he was able to hoist his pennant on his next ship, *Albemarle*. Even then he was not fully recovered since he wrote to Locker in late October 1781, that he had been 'so ill, as hardly to be kept out of bed' but he gave no further details of his symptoms.[26]

When Captain Cuthbert Collingwood had taken over the *Hinchinbroke* from Nelson in April 1780, the ship and the crew were in a terrible state. Collingwood had only the most primitive resources. The ship was washed all over with vinegar, twice. As it was leaking very badly, fires were lit in iron pots and placed in the lower deck to try and dry out the living quarters. Men had to be drafted from other ships to help to sail *Hinchinbroke*, so ill were her crew members. It is medically significant that the drafted men did *not* go down with the same illnesses. The food too, must have been abysmal. When *Hinchinbroke* got back to Port Royal, in September 1780, large amounts of stores of beef and pork in barrels were got out of the hold, surveyed, condemned, and thrown overboard. *Hinchinbroke's* log tells, in a flat, factual way, of the continuing tragedy. In May 1780 alone at least 16 named shipmates died. On two separate days 70 seamen had fevers and then 90 seamen were sick. In mid-May Collingwood tried to help the most severely ill by putting them ashore to live in tents. On 17th May 1780 the log reported 'eighty-six men exceedingly ill with fevers, fluxes and scorbictic ulcers and the number daily increasing.'[27]

The complete medical picture is a very complex one. It is postulated that *Hinchinbroke's* original crew continually ate ship's food, and at some time drank contaminated water. They then died of a double illness, a mixture of scurvy and tropical sprue. Nelson, shipped away to take command of another ship, the *Janus*, back at Port Royal, Jamaica, escaped. The exact sequence of events was the same for all. Poor food induced a low folic acid and vitamin B complex state so that when they drank contaminated water and they were infected with tropical sprue it was in the acute form. After the prolonged incubation period they were prostrated by fevers and the fluxes, and the sick absorbed even less of all nutrients including folic acid, multi-vitamin B and vitamin C. In Nelson, prostration occurred with a combination of peripheral neuropathy with weak limbs, loss of sensation and severe limb pains, as well as chronic severe diarrhoea. In his men, superimposed scurvy was, it seems certain, the last straw and they died – and died – and died.

There is one last confirmatory clue to Nelson's deficiency illness. Severe lack of folic acid, in about 20% of cases, causes psychiatric problems, and abnormal thought processes. Nelson did not experience such problems but Dr. Benjamin Moseley, the senior doctor to the Nicaraguan Expedition (who was conspicuous by his absence, having prudently stayed in Jamaica, leaving the medical care of the expedition to a deputy, Dr. Thomas Dancer) looked after some of the survivors later. He commented on 'intellects impaired and senses at times disordered in some who had been long ill on the Spanish Main.'[28] One last important medical fact; as has been mentioned neither Collingwood nor Moseley went down with this illness nor did the seamen drafted on to *Hinchinbroke* from other ships: this means the illness was not infective – it could not, for example be attributed to typhoid fever or to lice infestation and subsequent typhus. The members of the San Juan expedition drank contaminated water on the way to their destination and that was their fatal undoing.

Any theory deserves to be challenged. In 2002 the author suggested that tropical sprue was one of the many illnesses from which Nelson suffered in the years 1780–1782. This was disputed by John Sugden in 2004. His challenge, although backed by two tropical medicine experts, does not – in the author's opinion of course! – stand up. Firstly, contrary to what is postulated by John Sugden, sprue *can* be found in acute epidemic form.[29] Next, his experts suggested that (a) malaria combined with typhoid fever was 'a reasonable possibility' or (b) malaria and bacillary (bacterial) dysentery. But (and it is a very important but) typhoid fever has a characteristic rash never reported in *Hinchinbroke's* log, and both typhoid fever and bacillary dysentery are highly infectious and transmissible, whereas the sailors transferred to *Hinchinbroke* from other ships did not catch the illnesses which were killing *Hinchinbroke's* own crew. One of the experts considered the original numbers of *Hinchinbroke's* crew were likely to have been suffering from 'vitamin deficiencies and under nutrition' which concurs with the author's original article.

Modern text books describe backache, headache and back pain as being symptoms of Yellow Fever and the illness is said to have a short incubation period of three to six days. This does not agree with the 20–30 days given very clearly by Nelson in his account of the Expedition.

Similarly, dengue fever has been suggested as the cause. But this illness too has a short incubation period, (two to seven days) and the marked pains in the joints and bones that have given dengue the alternative title of 'break bone fever' were not described in accounts of the appalling illness which affected the Nicaragua expedition. In addition, dengue fever has an obvious rash which shows itself three to five days after the onset of symptoms and can be accompanied by desquamation, or shedding of a superficial layer of the skin. This symptom was not described either.

The report of the three doctors, Wood, Bruce and Melling, shows that at the same time as he suffered from the sprue and the peripheral neuropathy, Nelson was suffering from malaria.

Malaria is the pre-eminent tropical disease. For example, figures quoted in July 2004 stated that 'malaria sickened 300 million people last year and killed 3 million'[30] – probably both sets of figures are a gross underestimate. The mortality of the disease is the three million deaths; but the morbidity (what the three hundred million living sufferers experience) exerts a terrible toll. All these people experience very high fevers, lassitude, anaemia, depression, and chronic severe ill health.

The full complexities of the life cycle of the malaria parasite are not a part of this book, but some brief information is necessary which relates to Nelson the malaria sufferer, as will become clear later. Worldwide only four types of mosquito can infect humans with malaria parasites and there are four types of malaria parasite. Two types cause so-called tertian fever: a very high fever (40° C) every alternate day. One parasite causes quartan fever, a fever every third day and one parasite causes the lethal cerebral malaria of the brain with organ failure (which Nelson never suffered from). Malarial type fever occurring every single day is called quotidian fever. The causative microscopic organism for malaria is called a plasmodium and it is present in the saliva of infected, and infecting, mosquitoes. When the mosquito bites a human, hundreds of plasmodia are injected, via the insect's saliva, into the fluid of the blood of the human. Nelson frequently complained in his letters about being bitten by mosquitoes. As he wrote from *Boreas*, in August 1786: 'I have been kept here most woefully pinched by mosquitoes, for my sins perhaps.'[31] But he did not realise the significance of the bites. In 1572, a British merchant navy captain had drawn attention to the association between mosquito bites and malaria[32] but typically this accurate observation was ignored by the medical profession for some 250 years.[33]

Once injected into a human's bloodstream the parasite goes through several stages of its very complex life cycle loose in the fluid of the blood and then each parasite enters a red blood cell and does two pathological things. It multiplies within the cell so as to make more parasites to attack more red blood cells, and it feeds on the oxygen- carrying pigment, haemoglobin, within the red blood cell. Eventually the red cell envelope ruptures, releasing not only the six to eight new parasites but also toxic products of digested haemoglobin, which cause the typical acute malaria attack. Each attack has three stages. In the first, although the patient feels very cold and shivery, a so called rigor, the temperature may go as high as 40°C, often with vomiting and headache. Next comes a hot stage, with the patient feeling burning and possibly becoming delirious. Lastly comes the sweating stage with profuse perspiration. The temperature then drops and the patient, exhausted, feels more comfortable and sleeps. The next day they feel weakened but better.

The cycle is now in place and will persist. It takes between 48 and 72 hours for the cycle to repeat itself depending on which of the cyclical types of plasmodia the patient has been infected with.

The report from naval doctors Wood, Bruce and Melling made it perfectly clear that Nelson had been infected with one forty-eight hour type

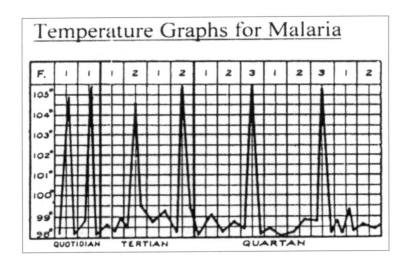

30

of malaria and also the seventy-two hour type since the report stated he had quotidian malaria: fevers of up to 40°C *every day*. The report should make the reader wonder how often similar reports were written for members of the British armed forces serving abroad in those far off days when Britain was reeling from the fight she was waging against the American Colonists, and was losing her First Empire. At the same time she was trying to carve out a Second Empire in the more medically hostile continents of Africa, Asia and South America, where malaria was rife.

Nelson had recurrences of malaria from time to time which he mentioned in his letters. In March 1784 he clearly had tertian fevers, as in a letter to Captain Locker he wrote:

> On last Friday I was commissioned for the *Boreas* ... the same day gave me an ague and fever, which has returned every other day since, and pulled me down astonishingly.[34]

Just over 10 years later, he was writing to his then commanding officer, Admiral Hood, 'This is my ague day ... It has shaken me a good deal; but I have been used to them, and so don't mind them so much.'[35]

In this extraordinary two-year period, the last illness Nelson suffered from was full blown scurvy. In August 1781 Nelson was appointed captain of the *Albemarle*. On 21st October 1781 whilst getting *Albemarle's* ship's company 'in order for service,' Nelson was ill again, but gave no other information about this new bout of ill health or its cause. In *Albemarle* he sailed to Denmark, helping to escort a large Baltic convoy back to England, and was then, in April 1782, sent to St. Johns, Newfoundland, escorting an Atlantic convoy. After this voyage was completed *Albemarle* spent the next two months cruising between Cape Cod and Boston Bay.

Like folic acid, the member of the B group of vitamins mentioned earlier, humans cannot synthesize vitamin C. They have very limited storage capabilities (two-and-a-half to three months) and need to eat vitamin C regularly in foods which contain it: citrus fruits and fresh vegetables especially. Preserved meats such as salt beef and pork, cereals and pulses do not contain vitamin C.

Ascorbic acid (Vitamin C) is essential in the conversion (hydroxylation) of proline to hydroxyproline, an amino acid that only occurs in collagen. Collagen is a fundamental building material in the walls of the blood vessels and in the organic matrix of bone. Lack of Vitamin C eventually results in fragile capillaries and weakened bone tissue. All the symptoms of the illness arise from these facts.[36] So lack of vitamin C eventually leads to fully-developed scurvy, causing many very severe symptoms – abnormal reduced blood clotting, severe haemorrhages into the skin, joints, bowels, nails, and eyes, nose-bleeds, skin ulcers, anaemia, listlessness, lack of bodily strength, breakdown of old scar tissue and old healed bone fractures, and loosening of the teeth. In its full blown form scurvy is a fearful, killing illness. Nelson wrote to Captain Locker, from the St. Lawrence river, on 19th October 1782:

> We arrived here on 1st July and I sailed upon a cruise the 4th and returned to Quebec on the 17th September knocked up with the scurvy having for 8 weeks myself and all the officers lived upon salt beef. Nor had the Ship's company had a fresh meal since the 7th April.[37]

He never neglected a ship's company or fleet of his in like manner again. In a typical act of kindness on Nelson's part, on 17th August 1782 he restored a captured ship to its American captain – Nathaniel Carver – in return for the latter's piloting skills, in helping *Albemarle* when the ship needed to enter shoals. Having got his ship back, Carver, who must have noticed the symptoms and signs of scurvy in the British crew, sailed away but returned to *Albemarle* as soon as possible with fresh provisions. This probably helped to reduce the morbidity. (Working from the information given in Nelson's letter to Locker the *Albemarle's* crew had been without fresh food for 132 days.) Even so, despite the fresh food, when Nelson got back to the harbour at Quebec, some 22 of his crew had to be hospitalised, although not Nelson himself.[38]

An extremely popular medical book in 18th Century England was George Cheyne's *An Essay of Health and Long Life*. First published in 1724 it ran through many editions and was still in print in 1827. Nelson may well have read it since he certainly at times followed some of Cheyne's dietary precepts – a vegetable and milk diet for example. Cheyne had some sensible views on scurvy. He knew that the illness could be reversed and wrote:

> A vegetable diet for a few weeks or months together with drinking water of unfermented liquors (such as tea, coffee, teas made of oranges or other seed or plants) will fasten the teeth when dropping out, cure any cutaneous foulness or eruptions and even any spreading ulcer.[39]

According to William Beatty, Nelson believed (quite wrongly) that salt was the cause of scurvy and Beatty wrote 'early in life when he first went to sea he left off the use of salt and never took it with his food.'[40] Since a low salt diet is known to be associated with good health, low blood pressure and longevity, this may partly explain Beatty's findings when he did Nelson's post-mortem. It is fascinating to read in Nelson's later letters of his efforts to keep the fleets under his command healthy. For example Nelson wrote to William Marsden at the Admiralty from *Victory* at sea 7th August 1804. He told Marsden that the then Physician to the Fleet – Dr John Snipe – had contracted with John Broadbent, a merchant at Messina, for supplying thirty thousand gallons of lemon juice. Typically Nelson praised Dr Snipe for obtaining this vast quantity by his own local effort[41].

Dr. John Snipe has been called one of naval medicine's unsung heroes. He died as a result of an illness he caught at Messina. Nelson, typically, then wrote to the Admiralty to try to get Snipe's widow a pension.[42]

The illnesses of the San Juan expedition could easily have killed Nelson, like so many of his *Hinchinbroke* shipmates. So could the attack of scurvy a year later. Surviving them proves, essentially, that Nelson was extremely resilient.

Medical facts in these excerpts from the Ship's Log of the *Hinchinbroke* from the time Captain Cuthbert Collingwood took command on 1st May 1780 show the high death rate of the crew (numbers in the second column) and the puny resources available to combat the appalling situation:

1st May		Ship very leaky and 70 men with fevers.
		John Stockbridge departed this life (DTL)
2nd May		James Higgins, Surgeon's mate DTL
3rd May		Peter Bird, Seaman died
		Leak in ship considerably increasing
4th May	2	The number of sick increasing daily
5th May	1	
6th May		Sent a party ashore to erect tents on the beach for the sick
7th May		Employed making and thatching the tents
8th May	1	Sent 40 sick to the tent
10th May	2	
11th May		Washed the ship with vinegar and kept fires in iron pots continuously burning on the lower deck
12th May		Employed stopping the leaks
13th May		Employed stopping the leaks
14th May		Employed stopping the leaks
15th May		Stopped the most considerable leaks
16th May	3	
17th May	1	86 men exceedingly ill with fevers, fluxes, [diarrhoea] and Scorbictic ulcers, and the number daily increasing
18th May	1	
19th May		Brought all the sick on board from the tents
20th May	1	Washed the ship with vinegar
21st May		Weighed and stood to sea in company the *Resource* and *Cartel* appointed to carry the Spanish garrison of Fort San Juan to some port in the Spanish Dominion agreeable to their capitution
22nd May		All the old leaks sprung out afresh and the Ship makes 12 and 15 inches water an hour

25th May		The Ship very leaky, the number of sick increasing
26th May	1	
27th May	1	
23rd June		Smoked the lower deck and washed it with vinegar
24th June	1	The Ship's company very sickly
25th June	1	
26th June		Smoked the ship with brimstone
29th June	1	
lst July		The Victor's men [Victor was an accompanying vessel] employed in watering us, having of this Ship's Company scarce enough to bury the dead and remove the sick
4th July	4	
6th July	2	H.M. sloop Victor sailed hence and a sloop with sick troops under her convoy
7th July	1	Made the signal for Masters of merchant ships to determine what number of seamen were in port fit for service. Found that in all the transports there were only 20 men, the rest sick and dead
8th–17th July	17	
18th July	5	The ship very leaky, the whole Ship's Company sick
19th–24th July	13	
25th July	1	The leaks in the ship considerably increasing [43]

And so it went on. In the first nine days of August no fewer than 20 sailors and 3 marines died. On 3rd August the Log states:

> The whole Ship's Company sick and men from 2 other ships Diamond and Pelican were drafted to complete the wood and water and fitting the ship for sea.

On the day after, 30 men were lent from the Pelican and ten from the Diamond to work the ship to Jamaica. When the Hinchinbroke reached Jamaica she had access to fresh food and was situated in a far healthier climate. Nevertheless she at once sent 23 men to the hospital. Men on board continued to die but in far fewer numbers since by now almost all Hinchinbroke's original crew must have been dead or in hospital, and had been replaced with healthier seamen from the other ships.

One last indication of the ghastly voyage was noted in the Log. On 20th September the Ship's Company were employed 'getting up the bad provisions to be surveyed.' On 21st they were 'loading the long boat with provisions condemned by survey and sending them all on shore.' On 28th September, after a period of intense activity by port carpenters caulking the ship, poor *Hinchinbroke* received '105lb. fresh [sic] beef, which was condemned and hove overboard' and the next day not only were provisions supplied found to be short weight but '3 barrels of pork and some tierces of beef' (casks holding 42 gallons capacity) were hove overboard after being 'condemned by survey'.

The work of two naval surgeons, James Lind and Gilbert Blane, was of vital importance as it radically improved the health of the Navy in Nelson's time, although Lind's research was done before Nelson was born. It was that major part of Nelson's genius that was basic hard work, mentioned earlier, that ensured the implementation of their life-saving ideas. As commander of fleets, Nelson frequently wrote at his desk for up to eight hours a day, constantly working to maintain and improve the health and well-being of the men under his command. The stress upon him was very considerable but he always accepted that his was the ultimate responsibility and he never shirked this grinding duty. Much of his time was spent in ensuring that the men on board the ships in the fleets he commanded were fed as well as possible, for month after month, and year after year. A significant factor in Nelson's popularity with the men of his ships and fleets lay in the fact that he was continually working to maintain and improve the health of the sailors under his command, and they knew this was so.

The first detailed description in English of scurvy was by Sir Richard Hawkins in 1593.[44] Hawkins wrote that the best cure for the illness was sour oranges and lemons. No attention seems to have been paid to his accurate medical observation. The mortality rate for scurvy in Royal Navy ships due to lack of citrus fruits during the next 150 years was as disgraceful as it was tragic.

James Lind (1716–1795) took his M.D. in Edinburgh in 1748. He was appointed physician to the Royal Naval Hospital at Haslar in 1758. Lind had read Hawkins' account and in testing his comments became a medical pioneer. Lind performed one of the first ever controlled medical trials on board *Salisbury* in 1753. He took twelve seamen, all suffering from scurvy, and divided them into six pairs. All twelve lived in the same conditions and were given the same basic food. In addition, each pair were given daily one of the different alleged remedies for scurvy which were current at the time:

Quart of cider
Oil of vitriol
Vinegar
Sea water

Mixture of garlic, myrrh, radish & Peru balsam
Oranges and lemons

The pair given oranges and lemons every day were considered by Lind to be restored to health and fit for duty by the sixth day of the trial. They were put to nurse the other ten men, *all* of whom remained in varying degrees of ill health with continued symptoms of scurvy. Lind published his findings in his book, *A Treatise on the Scurvy,* in 1753.[45]

The year before Nelson was born Lind had published another book on *The most Effectual Means of Preserving the Health of Seamen.*[46] Lind's researches and published writings make it all the more awful that, for example, Nelson himself and all his crew on board *Albemarle* in 1782 became seriously ill with scurvy, especially as Nelson seems to have known it was lack of fresh food that was the cause. It was only in 1795 that lemon juice began to be issued generally to the Royal Navy and scurvy gradually disappeared from the British Fleets. And this was very largely due to the efforts of Doctor (later Sir) Gilbert Blane implementing Lind's findings in a practical manner.

Sir Gilbert Blane (1749–1834) trained in Medicine at Edinburgh, and following distinguished naval service became Physician to the Fleet under Admiral Rodney in the West Indies. Blane was an important medical link in the chain of events in preventative medicine, which led from James Lind's published account of his medical trial against the scurvy to the issuing in 1795 (42 years later!) of regulations for the universal use of lemon juice in the Navy.

The innovations he instituted were of vital importance. It was Blane who presented two 'memorials' to the Admiralty. The first, dated 13th October 1781, showed that one in seven seamen died from disease on the West Indies Station, and advocated supplying wine, fresh fruit and other provisions to prevent scurvy. He also arranged for stricter enforcement of sensible sanitary arrangements on board every ship in the fleet, thus reducing morbidity and mortality due to fevers, infections and unhealthy, damp shipboard conditions.

By the time of the second 'memorial' to the Admiralty (16th July 1782) Blane was able to prove that by the implementation of the changes advocated in the first memorial, the mortality rate on board ships on the West Indies station had fallen to one in twenty. Rodney himself noted that there had not been a single death amongst the 900 men on his own ship *Formidable* over a period of six months.

In 1793, although he had left the Navy ten years before, Blane recommended to one of the Lords of the Admiralty – Admiral Sir Alan Gardner – that lemon juice should be given to fit men to *prevent* illness as well as to men showing scurvy symptoms so as to cure them. The suggestion was put into effect with such good results that two years later, regulations were issued for the universal use of lemon juice throughout the Royal Navy. It was Blane's force of character and good connections with the Admiralty that ensured the practical implementation of Lind's findings.

In 1785 Blane wrote *Observations on the diseases of seamen*. This book went through three editions (the last in 1803 incorporated 'a pharmacopaeia for the naval service') and was most influential. He retired from actual naval service in 1783, and took up a position on the staff of St. Thomas' Hospital, London. Thereafter his rise to medical influence on land was very rapid. He was appointed Physician to the Prince of Wales, one of the Commissioners for sick and wounded seamen (virtually the medical board for the Navy) and gave advice, with other eminent physicians, to prevent the importation of plague (with the British army returning from Egypt) by drawing up the rules which formed the basis of the Quarantine Act of 1799. He also was asked for his medical opinion on keeping contagious fevers out of prisons and convict ships and improving the medical service in India. When the Walcheren military expedition of 1807 experienced the most appalling loss of life due to illness (and not to war) it was Blane who was sent out to report on the medical situation, despite the fact that he was a naval doctor, not an army one. When the expedition was recalled, largely on medical grounds, it was Blane who organised the return of the sick and wounded. For these acts, and his report, Blane was given a baronetcy in December 1812. Blane wrote widely on medical matters and became an international figure consulted by foreign rulers on matters medico-political. The *Dictionary of National Biography* quotes no fewer than 14 dissertations written by him and this is almost certainly an understatement. But his greatest work was undoubtedly his recognition that bad conditions on board ships of the British Fleets were capable of remedy, especially by implementing Lind's previous findings. Admiral Rodney wrote:

> To his [Dr. Blane's] knowledge and attention it was owing that the English fleet was, notwithstanding their excessive fatigue and constant service, in a condition always to attack and defeat the public enemy.[47]

Nelson seems never to have met Blane, but he certainly implemented Blane's recommendations in his own fleets.

Nelson was involved when the Navigation Acts were introduced in July 1783. The Acts stated that all trade by Britain and her colonies should be done by vessels that were British-built and manned by mostly British sailors. After the American War of Independence, American-built and manned vessels no longer had, or were allowed, the same rights under the Navigation Acts as they had previously enjoyed, since they were now foreign nationals.

The West Indies islanders were keen for the trade in sugar, rum and molasses to be resumed after the war ended and for the status quo from before the War of Independence to return: in other words, for the Americans to enjoy the privileges of British colonials. Nelson's Commander-in-Chief, Rear Admiral Sir Richard Hughes, was prepared to waive the Navigation Acts for American vessels in West Indian waters. Nelson, second-in-command to Hughes, was not.

Nelson had turned back every American ship he sighted and it was at this time that Nelson seized Nathanial Carver's ship but let him go for his navigational co-operation. Nelson had to show considerable moral courage in flouting Hughes' illegal orders. On his arrival in *Boreas* at Barbados Bay in June, he had found 'that the Bay was full of Americans, who were lading and unlading [sic] without molestation.' Two other captains, Sotherby and Boston, showed him the orders from Hughes 'which had not a syllable in them indicating a wish to see the Navigation Act was attended to.'[48] Nelson went on:

Captain Collingwood told me he was very much afraid that the Navigation Act was not in the least attended to by the Admiral ... The Captains Collingwood [Cuthbert – later Nelson's great friend and second-in-command at Trafalgar, and his brother Wilfred, who died out in the West Indies] were the only officers, with myself, who were even attempting to hinder the illicit trade with America.[49]

In October 1799, in his *Sketch of My Life*, Nelson wrote:

This Station [Leeward Islands] opened a new scene to the Officers of the British navy. The Americans, when colonists, possessed almost all the trade from America to our West India Islands; and on the return of Peace, they forgot, on this occasion, that they became Foreigners, and of course had no right to trade in the British Colonies. Our Governors and Custom-house officers pretended, that by the Navigation Act they had a right to trade; and all the West Indians wished what was so much for their interest.

Having given Governors, Custom-house Officers, and Americans, notice of what I would do, I seized many of their vessels, which brought all parties upon me; and I was persecuted from one Island to another, so that I could not leave my Ship ... I was supported, when the business came to be understood, from home: and I proved, [and an Act of Parliament has since established it] that a Captain of a Man of War is bound to support all the Maritime Laws, by his Admiralty commission alone.[50]

Nelson wrote to his Uncle William for legal advice regarding the Navigation Acts, asking him to get his solicitor to answer a string of questions, and ending the letter '... get me some legal advice upon all this matter.'[51] Almost certainly William did give advice, although the letter he wrote back does not survive. In any event Nelson proceeded to uphold a very unpopular law, to his own detriment, in the short, medium and long term. Although in the right, the unpopularity Nelson acquired whilst implementing the Navigation Acts followed him back to England when his term of service in the West Indies was finished and was instrumental in keeping him without occupation and 'on the Beach' for five years after 1787.

Venereal disease was common in the 18th-century Navy, and a sufferer, prior to 1795, had to pay a fine of 15 shillings to the surgeon who treated him, (when at that time the monthly wage for an Ordinary Seaman was just under £1). So, naturally, many cases went un-reported and untreated. Nelson seems never to have suffered from venereal disease, but at one stage in his life, when only twenty-three, he clearly believed he did have a venereal condition.

A Treatise on the Teeth was a book published in 1797, written in English by a dentist, Chevalier Ruspini. In the book Ruspini extolled the virtues of a tincture of his own invention by giving examples where its use had proved efficacious. One such was that of Captain Nelson who was case III in Ruspini's book. He wrote:

> Some years since Captain Nelson of the Royal Navy, whom I accidentally met with at Portsmouth, showed me a fleshy excrescence, which whenever he shaved, gave him uncommon pain. He applied to one of the surgeons at the hospital, who assured him the case was venereal, and had prepared him to go through a mercurial course. I gave my opinion of the complaint and the surgeon, upon a consultation, having no objection to its being extirpated, I removed it with a bistory and the cure was completed in a few days, without any other application than the tincture. I saw this gentleman two years afterwards, when his perfect state of health confirmed my prognostic, and convinced the hospital surgeon of his mistake.[52]

It has been calculated that the most likely time for Ruspini and Nelson to have first met was February 1782, when Nelson was 23 years old. There was only one Captain Nelson in the Royal Navy at this time.

From what Ruspini wrote, Nelson seems to have been prepared to believe he had venereal disease until Ruspini reassured him and removed the benign papilloma from inside his mouth with the bistory – a form of scalpel. A 'mercurial course' (pills containing the heavy metal mercury) was the specific treatment for syphilis in those days, which Nelson must have known, and he accepted this as well. Clearly the cause was not venereal, and benign fleshy gum growths are quite common. However, Nelson's subsequent childless marriage must have left lingering doubts in his mind – especially as Fanny had been so rapidly fertile with her first husband. Making Lady Hamilton pregnant would subconsciously have been not only a great joy but something of a relief to a man of 41, with a past history of exposure to venereal infection.

In a letter to his fiancée, 'My Dearest Fanny,' written from Carlisle Bay, Barbados on 25th March 1786, Nelson wrote of his next illness: '… going about … so much in the sun has given me violent headache, but a little rest will I trust remove it again.'[53] This was clearly an episode of heat exhaustion.

In July 1787, Nelson arrived back in England on board *Boreas*. He had been so ill on the voyage across the Atlantic it was not expected he would live to reach England although the symptoms of his illness are not known, so that a diagnosis cannot be made. His early recovery was not helped by being separated from his new wife, (whom he had married in March 1787, and who had sailed to England with her uncle and her son on a comfortable West Indiaman) because *Boreas* was not paid off until 30th November 1787.

Two months later Nelson was asked to speak for the Defence on behalf of a man, James Carse, who had been the cooper on *Boreas* for nearly four years[54] and who was being tried for the murder of a prostitute, whose throat he was said to have cut. Carse's lawyer entered a plea of insanity on his behalf. Nelson, in the course of his evidence to the Court, made two extremely interesting medical comments. Firstly he said of Carse, 'At the island of Antigua … he was struck with the sun, after which time he appeared melancholy.' Nelson went on 'I myself have been affected with it, I have been out of my senses; it hurts the brain.' Nelson also compared the cooper's personality with his own, acknowledging that while the accused was 'So quiet a man, and never committed a fault during the time I knew him,' he himself was 'hasty' and he used this adjective about himself twice in giving evidence. He added, 'I myself have been struck in the brain, so that I was out of my senses.'[55] Carse was found guilty but insane, and spared execution. The cooper of *Boreas*, like Nelson, probably suffered from heat exhaustion.

Heat exhaustion is caused by over-exposure to heat (usually, but not always, the sun) accompanied by loss of salt and water through sweating, and inadequate replacement of one or both of these. The symptoms Nelson mentioned were headache and collapse, but sufferers can also show nausea, tachycardia (rapid heart rate), hyperventilation (excessive breathing), weakness, thirst, and muscle pain. They are, on examination, dehydrated, with low blood pressure. Modern treatment consists of fluids by mouth and skin surface cooling (fans, and wet cloths on the body, head and limbs).

Untreated, heat exhaustion can progress to heatstroke, a life-threatening medical emergency associated with the loss of normal temperature control mechanisms. This does not seem to have happened to Nelson.

Throughout his life Nelson almost always described his episodes of illness clearly in his letters; only very occasionally did he suffer bouts of ill health that he did not describe well. In September 1786 he wrote to William Locker that he had 'been since June so very ill (till lately) that I have only a faint recollection of anything which I did. My complaint was in my breast ... The Doctor thought I was in a consumption.'[56] Fascinatingly, he had written to his Uncle William earlier in July 'I wish I could tell you I was well but I am far from it. My activity of mind is too much for my puny constitution. I am worn to a skeleton.'[57] Of course it was over all this time that Nelson was having to contend with the problems of his attempts to implement the Navigation Act in the West Indies, which caused him so much stress. His letters during this time were otherwise completely lucid. Anxiety, depression and stress were almost certainly responsible for his physical complaints and symptoms.

Judging by comments in his letters, it appears that Nelson was one of those people who, when under stress, stop eating. It is known for example, that he failed to eat properly in the days before the Battle of Copenhagen. He wrote to Alexander Davison in April 1805, 'Captain Conn will call upon you. He will tell you of my present anxiety. I can neither eat, drink or sleep.'[58] Later he was to write that he had lost so much weight with anxiety he could scarcely keep his rings on his fingers.[59]

So what were Nelson's heart and lung problems? In Nelson's day, without access to investigative instruments now taken for granted – X-rays, scanners, electrocardiograms, stethoscopes – any patient losing weight and complaining of chest pain would have been automatically suspected by his doctor of having consumption (tuberculosis of the lung). Working backwards, it is known from Beatty's post mortem that Nelson's heart and lungs were not only free of any evidence of TB but exceptional, '... so perfectly healthy ... they resembled those of a youth rather than a man who had attained his forty-seventh year.' It is also known that Beatty suspected Nelson's chest spasms were caused by indigestion and a condition called globus hystericus. The first mention of globus hystericus in medical literature was in 1787, and it is a condition basically due to atypical contraction and spasm in the oesophagus. Patients with lower oesophageal problems can get heart pain because the same nerves supply both organs (which is why people who have had a heart attack frequently think they have got indigestion; and vice versa). Beatty wrote:

> His Lordship's health was uniformly good with the exception of some slight attacks of indisposition which never continued above 2 or 3 days nor confined him in any degree with respect to exercise or regimen.[60]

Beatty said Nelson had three attacks in twelve months and was alarmed by them. Beatty diagnosed:

> These complaints were the consequence of indigestion, brought on by writing for several hours together. His Lordship had one of these

attacks from this cause a few days before the battle but on resuming his accustomed exercise he got rid of it. This attack alarmed him as he attributed it to sudden and violent spasm but it was merely an unpleasant symptom (globus hystericus) attending indigestion.[61]

This is not at all typical of heart pain, which is worsened by effort and eased by sitting.

In 1968, Surgeon Commander Pugh wrote in his book *Nelson and his Surgeons* that Nelson's symptoms 'should be more properly attributed to Effort Syndrome or Soldier's Heart ... at this distance of time it is, of course, impossible to speak with any certainty upon these matters.'[62] Later biographers have omitted the caveat, and some modern biographies have stated that Nelson had a condition variously called 'Da Costa's Syndrome', 'Soldier's Heart' or 'Effort Syndrome.' This is not true.

Da Costa, an American Union Army doctor, wrote an original paper in 1871, ten years after the patients (soldiers of the Union Army in the American Civil War) were actually seen by him.[63] He was the first person to recognise that in time of war, i.e. under extreme personal fear and stress, the hearts of combatants could, and did, beat faster, uncontrollably, and that this condition could persist after the precipitator, the stress or the danger, had ceased. Da Costa in his original paper said the stress of war also produced palpitations, diarrhoea, pain over the heart, shortness of breath, exhaustion and dizziness. Nelson, or Beatty, would have mentioned such symptoms if they had occurred, but they never did.

In 1941 a British cardiologist, Paul White, coined the term 'Da Costa's Syndrome' to collect together a group of illnesses hitherto individually described.[64] These included 'Soldier's Heart' and 'Effort Syndrome,' conditions caused by a disturbance of part of the nervous control of the heart resulting from intense repetitive emotional stimuli, when fear and anxiety about the person's safety, or their present or future security, are the dominant emotion. The same symptoms: breathlessness, palpitations, pain over the heart, exhaustion and dizziness are the physical complaints of sufferers from 'Soldier's Heart' or 'Effort Syndrome.' These are not the complaints of Nelson, a man accustomed to 'generally walking on deck six or seven hours in the day', as Beatty reported, and on occasion 'not quitting the deck during the whole night.'[65] Da Costa was writing about ordinary men caught as combatants in a major civil war. White was writing in the middle of World War II, and with a degree of hindsight, knowing that 65,000 British soldiers with the symptoms outlined had in the First World War been declared unfit to fight and had been labelled, for want of proper diagnoses, malingerers or 'shell-shocked'. The author's opinion is that Nelson experienced oesophageal spasm, as Beatty believed. He did not suffer from Da Costa's Syndrome. Any anxiety he experienced was usually associated with situations where he was in command of British

Fleets pursuing enemy fleets and unable to locate the latter because of lack of information. (For example, the pre-Nile chase, or the pursuit of the French Fleet across the Atlantic in the summer before Trafalgar.) 'You know,' he wrote to Lady Hamilton in July 1803, from *Victory* en route to Toulon, 'I hate being kept in suspence [sic].'[66] Nelson never suffered from medical symptoms relating to fear of, or in, battle.

On one occasion only, a particular heart symptom Nelson wrote about was extremely complex. On 30th May 1804 he wrote to Dr. Baird:

> The health of this Fleet cannot be exceeded; and I really believe that my shattered carcass is in the worst plight of the whole Fleet. I have had a sort of rheumatic fever, they tell me; but I have felt the blood gushing up the left side of my head, and the moment it covers the brain I am fast asleep: I am now better of that; and with violent pain in my side and night sweats, with heat in the evening, and quite flushed. The pain in my head, nor spasms I have not had for some time. Mr. McGrath, who I admire for his great abilities every day I live, gives me excellent remedies.[67]

Whatever Nelson was suffering from in spring 1804 it was not rheumatic fever – the symptoms he gave in his letters are not those of that illness. Professor John Hampton, in a personal communication to the author, is of the opinion that this cardiac problem could have been simple extra-systoles (erratic extra heart beats probably originating from the upper chambers, or atria, of the heart, a benign medical condition). In his experience patients have complained of 'blood rushing to my head' when E.C.G. tests showed extrasystoles to be the cardiac abnormality. 'Violent pain in my side' suggests symptoms relating to his traumatic abdominal hernia (see Chapter IV) while the sweats, heat and flushed face could all have been indicative of pyrexia (high temperature)of a non-specific cause. Certainly, from Beatty's post mortem findings, Nelson was basically a very fit man.

In his later years, Nelson seems to have been prone to sore throats, severe coughs and aching teeth: 'my cold is now got into my head and I have such dreadful pain in my teeth that I cannot hold up my head'[68] which suggests sinus infection associated with the cold. He described his frequent upper respiratory tract infections in letters to Lady Hamilton and of course, by repeated coughing and so increasing the pressure in his abdomen, he exacerbated the problems associated with his abdominal hernia. He clearly believed his lungs were weak. For example he wrote to Alexander Ball in June 1801: 'My dear Invaluable Friend, I have been even at Death's door, apparently in a consumption.'[69] However, had he been able to read his own post-mortem report it is likely he would have been very surprised at how normal were the findings.

The last aspect of Nelson's illnesses to consider is his mental health, as Nelson seems to have suffered throughout his life from bouts of depression, often accompanied by anxiety. Depression can be divided into two types: 'endogenous' and 'reactive'.

'Endogenous' depression can again be divided into two forms: (A) Manic-depression when the patient, often very rapidly, can swing from a manic mood with over-talkativeness, over-activity, over-spending and surreal mental beliefs into the other extreme of the illness showing a deep depression with slow but often suicidal thoughts, total lack of energy, weight loss and total inability to feel pleasure in anything at all (anhedonia). Manic-depression is not a common condition, and it has a strong genetic component. (B) Endogenous depression where the patient never enters into a manic phase, but alternates periods of normal thought and behaviour with bouts of depression, is fairly common. Endogenous depression also tends to run in families. There have been suggestions in biographies of Nelson that he was a manic depressive. This diagnosis can be dismissed once and for all. First there was no family history, and there were in Nelson himself no recorded instances of over-spending, over-talkativeness, or pathological over-activity; nor were there any abnormal mental beliefs – although he was capable of marked jealousy where Lady Hamilton was concerned. There are no bouts of *unexplained* depression in Nelson's life.

'Reactive' depression is when a low mood occurs as a result of perceived depressing external circumstances or as a result of specific illnesses, or being non-specifically 'run down.' In other words, if the patient's doctor probes deeply enough he can almost always find a *cause* for the patient being depressed. This type of depression is often accompanied by anxiety and worry about current circumstances.

Episodes of 'reactive' depression, sometimes accompanied by anxiety, can be traced throughout Nelson's life from the age of 18. Nelson, the patient, had insight into his condition. Shortly before he was killed, he was asked if he would have changed anything in his life, and it is said he replied that he would have worried less.

Many illnesses, among them influenza, malaria, concussion from head wounds and recurrent pain from old wounds can of course make a patient reactively depressed, as can guilt feelings, prolonged absence from loved ones, clashes with employers, over-work and stress in employment, and worry regarding employment prospects or about money. All these worries affected Nelson during his life, and he reacted to all of them with bouts of depression and anxiety.

The first depressive episode recorded in Nelson's life was perhaps the most famous, the so-called 'Radiant Orb experience.' Aged 18, having been separated from all his friends on board *Seahorse*, Nelson was sent home from India in a state of severe ill health, (almost certainly suffering from malaria) and fully expected to die on the journey. As the ship he was sent home in, *Dolphin*, neared England, Nelson had a remarkable 'inner' experience, and he remembered this experience, almost two decades later, in some seven sentences. The first few sentences were depressive in content:

> I felt impressed to an idea that I should never rise in my profession. My mind was staggered with a view of the difficulties I had to surmount, and the little interest I possessed. I could discover no means of reaching the object of my ambition. After a long and gloomy reverie, in which I almost wished myself overboard ...[70]

Clarke and M'Arthur wrote: 'The spirits of young Nelson, which were lowered by this severe illness, were frequently much depressed.'[71] As was to happen with other bouts of depression in the future – for example, his reaction to the pre-Copenhagen delays of Sir Hyde Parker, or when Nelson was separated from his mistress at a time when Lady Hamilton was expecting their first child, or later, after the death of his third daughter – Nelson had the extraordinary ability to 'kick-start' himself out of the depressed episode by his use of self-initiated (and totally positive) thoughts and actions, and he had the 'radiant orb' experience:

> ...a sudden glow of patriotism was kindled within me, and presented my King and Country as my patron. My mind exulted in the idea. 'Well then,' I exclaimed, 'I will be a hero, and confiding in Providence, I will brave every danger.' The spirit of Nelson revived; and from that hour, in his mind's eye, as he then declared to Captain Hardy, a radiant orb was suspended which urged him onward to renown.[72]

The 'sudden glow of patriotism', like the extraordinary physical activity before the Battle of Copenhagen began, are examples of this gift. Hoisting King and Country into 'prime spot', as it were, was very sensible. They were the fount of all earthly honour in the eighteenth century, and this enabled Nelson in all his life thereafter, when, as he saw it, petty local considerations clashed with the greater good of his country and her laws (for example in the row over the Navigation Acts) to act so far as he could for the laws and overall good of his country, even if it made him extremely unpopular. 'To serve my King and destroy the French, I consider as the great order of all, from which little ones spring'[73] This would explain why Nelson felt very threatened when his behaviour towards his wife and his living with his mistress caused King George and the Court to show him their disapproval.

After the severe Nile head wound and concussion which shaded so quickly into besotted love for another man's wife, in the knowledge that it would destroy his marriage and bring a sea of troubles down upon his head, Nelson was seemingly unable to shake himself free of profound depression, which seems to have lasted some two years. This is clearly shown in his letters of the time, and the Guzzardi portrait, painted at least five months after the Nile wound, shows a depressive *facies* [facial expression and demeanour – usually applied in description of patients with psychiatric problems]. This was an example of post-concussive depression (see Chapter VI).

The actual 'Radiant Orb' expression may well be a subliminal quotation from the third verse of Joseph Addison's hymn *The Spacious Firmament on High*:

> What though nor real voice nor sound,
> Amid their radiant orbs be found.

It is known Nelson quoted from Addison at other times; but there is another possible explanation. The largest golden orb in England is the one on the top of St. Paul's Cathedral, in the City of London. Weighing twenty-two tons, and surmounted by an enormous gold cross, it would have been a dominant part of the sky-line to the young Nelson, learning to navigate from Chatham to the Tower of London in 1772. At that time Sir Christopher Wren's Cathedral was just beginning to be used as the burial place of the heroes of the First British Empire. It may be that, by extension, the golden orb, with its cross, atop the Cathedral, became a symbol of religion's domination over the world for Nelson – the 'radiant orb,' urging him onward to renown as a warrior. 'I will be a hero, and confiding in Providence...' The word 'Providence' is spelt by Nelson with a capital letter, and in the author's opinion can only mean God.

It is possible to find in Nelson's letters, expressions of the anxiety, depression and exhaustion he felt during times of extreme stress. For example, when outside Toulon, having been on board *Victory* for 22 months without setting foot on shore:

> I have suffered very much from anxiety[74] ... My health does not improve, but because I am not confined to my bed, people will not believe my state of health.[75]

About the chase after the French Fleet to the West Indies in 1805 Nelson wrote, 'What a race I have run after these Fellows; but God is just, and I may be repaid for all my moments of anxiety.'[76] Then, after wrong information was given to him, which meant he did not come up with the French Fleet in West Indian waters: 'It has made me very sorrowful.'[77] Lastly, chasing back across the Atlantic after the French Fleet, Nelson wrote in his private journal:

Midnight, nearly calm, saw three planks, which I think came from the French Fleet. Very miserable, which is very foolish.[78]

Whilst suffering from all his known bouts of reactive depression with anxiety Nelson nevertheless remained fully capable of functioning as a naval officer at whatever rank he held. Perhaps the most important example is that the depression and anxiety associated with 'the Long Chase' after the French across the Atlantic and back again, did not affect Nelson's leadership as Commander-in-Chief of the British Fleet. What his depression did do was to cause him to experience poor sleep, and loss of appetite, with consequent weight loss. His letters and actions, even when he was fraught with anxiety and very 'low,' at no time show loss of control, inertia, or a failure to complete the day's work each day. He does seem, by writing what he felt, to have used his private journal and his letters to close friends and relatives, as a means of relieving his depressive and anxiety symptoms. On 19th April 1805, when he had failed to find the French Fleet in West Indian waters, Nelson wrote to an old and trusted friend, Sir Alexander Ball, ' I believe this ill-luck will go near to kill me; but as these are times for exertions, I must not be cast down, whatever I feel.'[79]

In the past much has been written about Nelson's ill-health and he has been labelled a hypochrondiac, a malingerer[80] and 'possessed of congenital self pity.'[81] These labels can be strongly refuted.

Nelson's father possessed a tendency to look at life from a slightly pessimistic point of view but Nelson, although he expressed thoughts of unhappiness, anxiety and distress in personal letters, especially to Lady Hamilton, did not stay in an introspective or self-pitying frame of mind for long, except after the severe head wound of 1st August 1798 (see Chapter VI). The refutation of Nelson as a malingerer is on pages 75 and 76.

In addition, there is a general belief that Nelson was always seasick when afloat – and one can see why the idea is so appealing – but it's not quite true. There is no evidence that he suffered from seasickness as a young man. He never mentioned or confirmed it in any letters to his wife, or any other relatives or friends. In 1793 after his five years 'on the Beach', Nelson returned to sea as captain of *Agamemnon* and took with him his stepson, Josiah Nisbet. In three letters to Fanny he made no mention of suffering from seasickness himself but wrote, 'Your son was a little seasick for a day or two but soon got over it … Now Josiah has got the better of seasickness I think he gets stout.'[82]

However, six years later, in his letters to Lady Hamilton, he did begin to record episodes of his own seasickness. For example, he first mentions in a letter to Lady Hamilton in 12th May 1799, 'I am seasick.'[83] Then in August 1801 he wrote to her 'I am so dreadfully seasick I cannot hold up my head!'[84] From *Amazon*, off the Kent coast, on 8th October 1801 he wrote

'It came on [bad weather] in one hour, from the weather like a mill-head, to such a sea as to make me very unwell.'[85]

There was also a very revealing comment in a letter to Lady Hamilton from *Victory* in the Mediterranean, off Toulon on 18th October 1803 'You know, my dear Emma, that I am never well when it blows hard.'[86] He wrote again on 14th April 1804, from *Victory* off Toulon: 'I am so seasick that I cannot write another line.'[87] So, towards the end of his life he did suffer, in rough seas.

He also told Earl St. Vincent and Alexander Davison. For example, to his old Commander on 5th October 1803 from *Victory* off Toulon: 'I am – don't laugh – dreadfully sea-sick this day …'[88] and to Davison (also off Toulon) 'Such a place for storms of wind I never met with, and I am unfortunately, in bad weather, always sea-sick.'[89] A fascinating example of Nelson's motion sickness on land occurred when, disgracefully, he abandoned his wife the first Christmas (1800) after his return to England following the Battle of the Nile. He spent the festive holiday at the incredible estate of William Beckford, an extremely wealthy relative of Sir William Hamilton, with the Hamiltons themselves. Beckford took Nelson for a drive in his phaeton. The phaeton is a very well sprung four-wheeled vehicle, pulled by two horses, and it does tend to 'rock.' Driven at speed, Nelson began to feel unwell very quickly and asked Beckford to stop. Nelson jumped out of the vehicle and walked home.[90]

Motion sickness is not a true sickness. It can be caused when patterns of motion differ from those previously experienced – the rocking of Beckford's phaeton would seem to be a specific example. Nelson had very probably never travelled so fast on land in his life. On sea and on land, it is caused when three pieces of information (from the eye, the vestibular part of the ear, and the proprioceptors of the body) are sent to the brain and do not present a coherent picture to that organ of actual body motion. The results are nausea, vomiting, pallor, yawning, anxiety, panic, hyperventilation, fatigue and weakness. Triggers include an apparently moving horizon – almost certainly present as Nelson sat in the phaeton, and always present in a ship at sea – and other illnesses: and it is known Nelson was not well on the occasions when he wrote the letters to Lady Hamilton. Why Nelson's motion sickness should apparently have such a late life onset it is not possible to say.

Nelson had strong views on doctors! In a letter to the Duke of Clarence in August 1794, he wrote: 'One plan I pursue – Never to employ a Doctor – Nature does all for me and Providence protects me.'[91] Nevertheless at least 48 doctors and a dentist are known to have treated Nelson when he was ill or assessed him after wounds or illnesses:

1. Surgeon Dalzell (*Seahorse*) – Invalided home in 1776
2. Surgeon J. Davis (*Dolphin*) – During 6 months voyage

3. Thomas Dance – Nicaragua
4. Robert Wood
5. Archibald Bruce – Report 'Reduced to a skeleton'
6. James Melling
7. Dr. Jameson – Surgeon on *Janus*
8. Surgeon, Portsmouth – Advice regarding gum papilloma
9. Chevalier Ruspini – Dentist regarding gum papilloma
10. Robert Adair – Consulted regarding neuropathy
11. Dr. Woodward – Consulted regarding neuropathy
12. Mr. Nichols – Dresses arm at Bath, paid £12
13. Michael Jefferson – Calvi eye wound certificate 1794 Post-op arm treatment 1797 Nile head wound 1798
14. John Harness – Regarding Eye Certificate 12.8.1794
15. William Chambers – Regarding second Eye Certificate
16. A. Cruickshaw – Regarding third Eye Certificate }
17. H. Leigh Thoring
18. Thomas Eshelby – Amputation right arm
19. Louis Remonier – Assists amputation
20. Eye Doctor, Palermo – Electric treatment to blind eye
21. William Falconer – Post-op arm treatment, Bath
22. Mr. Cruikshanks – Post-op arm treatment, London }
23. Mr. Thomas   Nephew assisting in consultation
24. James Earle – Consultation over slow healing of arm
25. John Rush – Consultation over arm
26. H. Carrickshawk – Saw Nelson in September 1797 }
27. H. Leigh Thoring   and issued 3rd eye certificate;
28. Thomas Keate   Keate consulted 19.10.1797
29. Mr. Bayly – Advice on phantom limb problems
30. Dr. Weir – Physician to Earl St. Vincent's Fleet
31. Surgeon of *Captain* – Consulted re abdominal wound }
32. John Gunning
33. Isaac Minors
34. William Lucas
35. Joseph Warner
36. Charles Hawkins – See Nelson at Private Court of }
37. George Chandler   Examiners re. his eye on 12.10.1797
38. Samuel Howard   and his arm on 1.3.1798, or both
39. William Cooper
40. William Long
41. Thomas Trotter – Acute conjunctivitis
42. Andrew Baird – Late aspects of abdomen wound
43. Benjamin Moseley – Consulted regarding worsening vision, left eye
44. Dr. Magrath – 'Gives me excellent remedies' 1804
45. Lambton Este – Gives details; eyes & abdominal wound

46. Dr Snipe – '… says I am a bad patient'
47 Sir William – Blizard saw Nelson several times, possibly regarding his pensions. Was in Nelson's funeral procession
48. William Beatty – Last surgeon, does post-mortem

(In all probability this list is not complete!)

Nelson's attitude to the medical profession in 1793 was perhaps a reasonable one. A popular contemporary couplet ran:

God and the patient both agree,
God cures the patient, and the doctor takes the fee.

But in his lifetime lemon juice was ordered for the Navy both to cure and then to prevent scurvy, and vaccination became much more widely available to prevent smallpox. Thousands of lives were saved by these two measures alone. Nelson himself implemented preventative medicine on the advice of Dr John Snipe, ordering ship's watering parties to be given Peruvian Bark, which contained quinine, before they were sent on shore to marshy areas where mosquitoes, and therefore malaria, were thought to be present.[92]

Some of the doctors who came into contact with Nelson were very eminent men in their day, as was the dentist Chevalier Ruspini, who went on to become Dental Surgeon to the Prince of Wales. Adair was Surgeon General to the Army, as was Keate, who was also Surgeon to the Prince of Wales. Trotter and Baird were both Physicians to the Fleet, as were Gillespie and Snipe. Moseley's famous book *A Treatise on Tropical Diseases on Military Operations*, as mentioned earlier, was in its fourth edition by 1803. Cruikshanks was an anatomist who had been William Hunter's partner for nine years, and was the author of the first English work on the lymphatics. Earle was knighted when he was appointed Surgeon-extraordinary to King George III. Rush was Inspector General of Hospitals, and later one of the three members of the Army Medical Board. And when Nelson appeared before the private Court of Examiners of the Surgeons' Company on 12th October 1797, Gunning was Master of the Company that year, Earle would be Master the next year, and Hawkins, Minors, Howard, Lucas and Warner were all Past Masters. (see Chapter V) And, of course, William Beatty became one of the most famous medical men of his day, on the strength of being the last doctor to look after Nelson, and writing a book about his death.

Nelson suffered most of his severe named illnesses before he was 25. Throughout his life he was prone to colds and coughs which he does not seem to have talked about freely until he began to write to Lady Hamilton. (Perhaps he felt she was a more sympathetic ear than his wife; more likely it was a part of the extraordinary way in which his letters to Lady Hamilton appear to have flowed in a 'stream of consciousness' manner, so that he put down, for her, and only for her, every idea, thought, and physical symptom that was registering in his brain at the time of writing.) He never seems to have mentioned his seasickness to Fanny, possibly for the same reason, so that it is not possible to say whether he suffered from the condition as a young man.

In an extraordinary letter to the Duke of Clarence, in which he quoted *Cymbeline*, the relatively obscure Shakespearean play, Nelson put forward his own totally un-medical reason for his survival in the face of disease and trauma. He wrote 'I am here the reed among the oaks: all the prevailing disorders have attacked me, but I have not the strength for them to fasten upon. I bow before the storm, whilst the sturdy oak is laid low.'[93] The correct reason was almost certainly his wiry, tough constitution.

It is the author's opinion that Nelson was basically very fit and this trait enabled him to survive severe illnesses which would have killed less robust individuals. His tropical illnesses he was lucky to survive. His experience of scurvy taught him a lesson he never forgot, so that when he himself rose to a position of great naval authority, he made it one of his most basic and important aims to ensure the good health and physical well-being of the men in the ships under his command. This in turn completely altered the balance of power between the British ships under Nelson and those of the enemy. It enabled Dr Gillespie, for example, to quote figures for the health in Nelson's Fleet in the two years before Trafalgar which would have astounded Villeneuve and Gravina, commanders of the French and Spanish Fleets respectively. Throughout all ages of warfare up to the Second World War, illness has always taken a greater toll of the combatants then actual battles. Indeed, even in the Second World War, malaria decimated British troops in the Far East until the proper implementation, by the newly arrived General Slim, of anti-malarial prophylaxis.[94] The health of Nelson's fleets was extraordinarily good. His own suffering, most especially as a young man, taught him that prevention was better than cure, so that hard work by Nelson and his officers resulted in unconquerable British fleets at sea, manned by fit, active and optimistic crews. The lessons learned by Nelson as a result of his own personal experience of severe illness undoubtedly contributed later in his life to the victories of the fleets under his command.

Notes

1. Nicolas vol I p.4
2. Nicolas vol III p.260
3. Quoted in Oman p.10
4. Clarke and M'Arthur *The Life of Admiral Lord Nelson, K.B.* vol I p.36 (hereafter Clarke and M'Arthur)
5. ibid
6. Strictland, N. H. J. *British Medical Journal* 2000 vol 321 p.428 (hereafter B.M.J.)
7. Herrick, C. E. J., personal communication to the author
8. Public Record Office ADM 51/442 p.20 May 17th 1780 (hereafter P.R.O.)
9. Captain William Hillary Quoted in *Oxford Textbook of Medicine* 3rd Edition 1996 vol 2 p.1931. (Hereafter Oxford Textbook)
10. Clarke and M'Arthur vol l p.38
11. ibid p.40
12. ibid p.40
13. ibid p.41
14. P.R.O. ADM 1/242 p.533
15. Nicolas vol I p.35
16. P.R.O. ADM 1/242
17. P.R.O. ADM 1/242 p.525
18. Nicolas vol I p.10
19. *Cecil: Textbook of Medicine* 2004 p.357
20. Nicolas vol I p.36
21. ibid p.37
22. ibid p.38
23. ibid p.39
24. ibid p.41
25. ibid p.42
26. ibid p.48
27. P.R.O. ADM 51/442 p.20 May 17th 1780
28. Clarke and M'Arthur vol I p.38
29. *Oxford Text Book* 1996 p.33, and Kuvan and Clark *Clinical Medicine* 5th edition 2002 p.294
30. *Time Magazine* 26th July 2004 vol 164 No.3 p.58
31. Nicolas vol I p.188
32. Keevil, J. J. *Medicine & the Navy* 1959 vol I p.123
33. Hutchinson and Hunter *Clinical Methods* 12th edition 1949 p.30
34. Nicolas vol I p.100
35. ibid p.462
36. Maat, G. J. R. and Elshout, A. M. L. *Organorama* 1982 p.23
37. Nicolas vol I p.66
38. Clarke and M'Arthur vol I p.51
39. Cheyne, G. *An Essay on Health & Long Life* 8th edition 1734 p.184

40. Beatty p.78
41. Nicolas vol VI p.142
42. White, C. *Nelson: The New Letters* 2005 p.119
43. P.R.O. ADM/51/442 p.30 21st, 28th, 29th September 1780
44. Lloyd, C. *The British Seaman* 1968 p.46
45. James Lind, *Dictionary of National Biography* 2004
46. Lind, J. *An Essay on the most effectual means of preserving the Health of Seamen in the Royal Navy* 1757
47. Sir Gilbert Blane *Dictionary of National Biography* 2004
48. Nicolas vol I p.171
49. ibid p.179
50. ibid p.11
51. ibid p.147
52. Britton, C. J. *New Chronicles of the Life of Lord Nelson* 1946 quotes Ruspini's account. Reference supplied to the author by Professor L. Le Quesne C.B.E.
53. Naish p.26
54. Quoted in Sugden, J. *Nelson: a Dream of Glory* 2004 p.374 (hereafter Sugden)
55. ibid p.375–6
56. Nicolas vol I p.199
57. Ibid p.186
58. Ibid vol VI p.400
59. Quoted in Hibbert, C. *Nelson a Personal History* 1994 vol 6 p.114–9 (hereafter Hibbert)
60. Beatty p.78
61. ibid
62. Pugh p.5
63. Da Costa, J. M. 'On irritable heart, a clinical study of a form of functional cardiac disorder and its consequences' *American Journal of Medical Sciences* 1871 vol 761 p.17
64. White, P. 'Da Costa's Syndrome or Effort Syndrome' B.M.J. 1941 vol I p.767
65. Beatty p.80
66. *Nelson's Letters to Lady Hamilton* 1814 vol I p.117
67. Nicolas vol VI p.41
68. *Nelson's letters to Lady Hamilton* vol I p.74
69. Nicolas vol IV p.401
70. Clarke and M'Arthur vol 1 p.14
71. ibid p.13
72. ibid p.14
73. Quoted in Dixon, N. *On The Psychology of Military Incompetence* 1976 p.331 (hereafter Dixon)
74. Nicolas vol VI p.357
75. ibid p.392
76. ibid p.460
77. ibid p.461

78. ibid p.464
79. ibid p.410
80. Keynes, M. *Horatio Nelson Never was Blind* Medical Biography 1998 vol 6 p.114–9
81. Walker, R. *The Nelson Portraits* 1998 p.6 (hereafter Walker)
82. Naish p.77, 79, 82
83. *Nelson's Letters to Lady Hamilton* vol I p.9
84. ibid p.64
85. ibid p.160
86. ibid vol II p.20
87. Quoted in Pocock p.221
88. Nicolas vol V p.223
89. ibid p.261
90. Beckford *Memoirs* 1859 vol II p.127 Quoted in Mahan A. T. *The Life of Nelson, the Embodiment of the Sea Power of Great Britain* 1897 p.449 (hereafter Mahan)
91. Nicolas vol I p.476
92. Ibid vol VII p.318
93. Ibid vol I p.476
94. Dixon p.341–2

CHAPTER III

'His Eye in Corsica' – and a First Look at the Portraits

After his five years of unemployment Nelson was given the 64-gun ship *Agamemnon*, when England went to war with Revolutionary France in February 1793. *Agamemnon* sailed to the Mediterranean in June 1793 and came under the command of Lord Hood. Nelson was young (35), fit, and *Agamemnon* was extremely active under his command. She took part in the capture of Toulon and also visited Naples – where Nelson met with Sir William and Lady Hamilton for the first time.

After the French recaptured Toulon in December 1793, other bases for the British Mediterranean Fleet had to be found. As Corsica was in revolt against the French and trying to establish its own independence, the two fortress towns of Bastia and Calvi in northern Corsica, occupied by the French, were attacked in a preliminary move toward capturing the whole island. Bastia fell in mid-May 1794 after a combined naval and military operation, which involved Nelson and his sailors manhandling naval guns inland over awkward and rocky land. During the course of the siege of Bastia, Nelson received a 'cut on the back'[1] but how, from what, and to what degree of severity no one knows. He mentioned it briefly, twice only, and some weeks after it happened. It seems not to have impeded his service in any way.

The naval guns having successfully assisted in the capture of Bastia, a month later the British combined forces attacked Calvi on the West coast. Heroic efforts by the men from *Agamemnon* again shifted heavy naval guns two-and-a-half miles over extremely difficult terrain. (So difficult that, rather like the British High Command at Singapore in 1942 who believed the jungle could not be penetrated by Japanese forces, the defenders at Calvi did not believe troops could attack them from the area of the island to which Nelson and his men manhandled their guns.) Then batteries were constructed. On the 4th July so near to the town were the British batteries that they were within range of the guns of fortress Calvi. After at least one narrow escape, when an enemy shot destroyed a British battery magazine near to where Nelson was standing, but left him unhurt, on 12th July 1794 he was wounded in the right eye, right eyebrow and face.

Apart from his letters, the first intimation that Nelson had any form of eye trouble comes from his early posthumous biographers, Clarke and M'Arthur who wrote about his time 'on the Beach' between 1787 and 1792: 'He sometimes also employed his time, when his eyes would admit of it, in reading.'[2] This suggests Nelson easily suffered from eye strain.

There is no record of further eye trouble until Calvi. On 12th July 1794 Nelson noted in his journal: '… at seven o'clock I was much bruised in the face and eyes by sand from the works [breastworks] struck by shot.'[3] On the same day he wrote to Admiral Lord Hood: '… I got a little hurt this morning; not much as you may judge by my writing.'[4]

Hood replied on the same day: 'I am truly sorry to hear you have received a hurt, and hope you tell truth in saying it is not much.'[5] Hood also wrote on 15th July to Sir Gilbert Elliot, then Viceroy of Corsica, 'Captain Nelson has received a hurt in the face by the contents of a sandbag which had large pebbles in it: he speaks lightly of it, but I wish he may not lose the sight of an eye.'[6] This letter suggests Hood obtained details of Nelson's injury from another witness and not only from Nelson himself.

Nelson's next letter to Hood may have provoked Hood's two letters as it was less sanguine. 'My eye is better and I hope not entirely to lose the sight.'[7] On 14th July he wrote to one Thomas Pollard at Leghorn about 'being half blinded by these fellows, who have given me a sharp slap in the face.'[8] On the same day he wrote a brief letter to his wife making no mention of his eye wound at all. But on 16th July he wrote to his uncle, William Suckling, (to whom he confided later such details as his urinary problems after the abdominal wound at the Battle of St. Vincent that he mentioned to no one else) giving much more detail:

> My right eye is entirely cut down; but the surgeons flatter me I shall not entirely lose my sight of that eye. At present I can distinguish light from dark but no object … I feel the want of it; but such is the chance of War, it was within a hair's breadth of taking off my head.[9]

Nelson wrote to Sir Gilbert Elliot on 17th July, confirming the details:

> Our loss has been trifling, not twenty killed and wounded: amongst the latter, in a slight manner, is myself, my head being a good deal wounded, and my right eye cut down; but the surgeons flatter [me] I shall not entirely lose the sight, which I believe, for I can already distinguish light from dark.[10]

This suggests Nelson was initially totally blind in the injured eye but then that a change in his symptoms occurred. Five days later he wrote to Hood and was frankly pessimistic. 'My eye is troublesome, and I don't think I shall ever have the perfect sight of it again.'[11] On top of all his other problems Nelson appears to have had a recurrence of malaria, writing on 31st July to Hood: 'This is my ague day … it has shaken me a good deal; but I have been used to them, and now don't mind them so much.'[12]

Finally he wrote to Fanny on 1st August 1794 'Except a very slight scratch towards my right eye … I have received no hurt whatsoever.'[13] Even this was untrue since he had received the 'sharp cut to the back' weeks before, which he did not bother to tell his wife about until 18th August. Well aware that Fanny worried a lot ('I well know your anxiety of mind'[14] he had written just before the Calvi injury) he must have presumed the letter of 1st August had prepared her a little, because in the letter of 18th August he gave a lot more clinical detail: 'As it is all past, I may tell you, that on 10th July [actually 12th July] a shot having hit our battery, the splinters and stones from it struck me with great violence in the face and breast. Although the blow was so severe as to occasion a great flow of blood from my head, yet I most fortunately escaped having only my right eye nearly deprived of its sight: it was cut down but is so far recovered, as for me to be able to distinguish light from darkness. As to all the purposes of use, it is gone; however the blemish is nothing, not to be perceived unless told.'[15]

The official dispatches of General Stuart and Admiral Lord Hood did not mention Nelson's eye wound, a fact which is not really surprising since it is clear from the above quotations that he played down the severity of the wound and its effects. But it is equally clear he had to all intents and purposes lost the sight of his right eye so he was justified in writing to Hood almost three months after the injury date:

> Not any notice having been taken in the Public List of Wounded at the Siege of Calvi, of my eye being damaged, I feel it but justice to transmit to your Lordship two certificates … and I have to request that your Lordship will take such measures as you may judge proper that my Sovereign may be informed of my loss of an eye in His Service.[16]

As Nicolas notes 'Lord Hood did not fail to recommend his case in the strongest manner to the First Lord of the Admiralty.' The two certificates both wrongly give the date of the injury as 10th July. This is not surprising, as no doctor appears to have seen Nelson at the time of the eye injury, and he himself had given the wrong date to his wife. In all probability, he gave the wrong date to the two medical men as well. The first certificate was signed by John Harness, Physician to the Fleet. Harness was an excellent doctor and had in the past recommended that ascorbic acid could be used by the British Fleet to prevent scurvy.

Harness was in Bath during the second week of December 1794, where he met Fanny. 'Dr. Harness I am very much pleased with, he spoke so handsomely of you and did tell me many little things which to bystanders might be thought trifling, but to me highly gratifying.'[17] Harness, clearly, had met Nelson personally, and it was he, with Jefferson, who noted the dilation of the pupil of Nelson's right eye.

Michael Jefferson also signed the first certificate calling himself 'Surgeon attending on shore.' Nelson had thought him 'a very good sort of man' when he sailed with him on *Agamemnon* from Sheerness in April 1793, calling him 'Surgeon landed for the care of the Seamen,' in his letter to Lord Hood of 2nd October 1794. In addition, he was the Surgeon to whom Nelson paid £24. 3s. 0d. for attending him in London in respect of his arm injury in the winter of 1797. One must also say it was Jefferson who totally failed to appreciate how severely Nelson was wounded in the head at the Battle of the Nile. Jefferson may only have been a non-commissioned mate (and not, as he wrote, a surgeon) when he signed the first certificate.

The second certificate was signed by William Chambers incorrectly calling himself 'Surgeon General to the forces in the Mediterranean.' Both certificates made quite clear the severity of the injury and the first describes 'the wound of the iris of the right eye which has occasioned an unnatural dilation of the pupil.' This can be clearly seen, both in the oil sketch painted by Sir William Beechey in 1800 (now in the National Portrait Gallery) and in the portrait by Lemuel Abbott painted in 1798 (now in the National Maritime Museum, Greenwich). If years *after* the injury, two separate and presumably unacquainted painters, at two different times, painted a similar pathological sign, that is, a dilated and irregular right pupil, in the sitter, one can be absolutely sure that the pathological sign was present. The 'several small lacerations about the face' can be seen in a painting called the Leghorn Miniature (1795) as two small scars: one below the outer end of the right eyebrow and one below the outer end of the left lower eyelid. Here are the certificates of Harness and Jefferson, and of Chambers:

CERTIFICATE:

These are to Certify, that Horatio Nelson, Esquire, Commander of his Majesty's Ship *Agamemnon*, did, on the 10th day of July 1794, while Commanding the Seamen before Calvi, receive a wound of the iris of the right eye, which has occasioned an unnatural dilation of the pupil, and a material defect of sight.

Given under our hands, on board his Majesty's ship *Victory*, off Calvi, this 9th day of August 1794

JOHN HARNESS,
Physician to the Fleet.
MICHAEL JEFFERSON
Surgeon attending on Shore.

These are to Certify Captain Horatio Nelson of his Majesty's Ship *Agamemnon*, now serving on Shore at the Siege of Calvi, was on the 10th day of July last, wounded in the face and right eye, much injured by stones or splinters, struck by shot from the Enemy. There were several small lacerations about the face: and his eye so materially injured that in my opinion, he will never recover the perfect use of it again.

W. CHAMBERS

Surgeon to the Forces in the Mediterranean.

Calvi, August 12th 1794[18]

A third medical certificate about Nelson's right eye will be quoted later. At least four portraits clearly show the loss of the lateral part of the right eyebrow and possibly a fifth:

1. The Leghorn Miniature of 1795
2. The Guzzardi painting of 1799
3. The Schmidt miniature of 1800
4. The Bowyer Miniature of 1800 and also
5. The Dresden Life Mask (eyes closed) of 1800.

This is not part of the Nile head wound, as if it were it would not be present in the Leghorn Miniature. It is a permanent scar from Calvi. If the force of the sand and pebbles removed totally and permanently part of the hair-bearing skin of Nelson's eyebrow, then the impact was considerable, and the wound of the face must have been a very deep one. This explains Nelson's description, as above, 'The blow was so severe as to occasion a great flow of blood *from my head*.' (author's italics.)

On 31st January 1795 Nelson wrote again to his wife: 'Lord Hood told me that my loss of one eye should be represented to the King. Lord Chatham carried my papers to the King but now he is out, [of office – he was succeeded by Lord Spencer in December 1794] all hopes will be gone away. My eye is grown worse, and is almost total darkness; and very painful at times; but never mind, I can see very well with the other.'[19] The intermittent severe pain is suggestive of glaucoma or possibly sympathetic ophthalmia. The comment 'never mind, I can see very well with the other.' is typical of Nelson: utterly pragmatic.

However, one must have sympathy for Nelson in his later comments to his uncle:

The taking of Corsica has cost me … £300, an eye and a cut across my back and my money I find cannot be repaid me. Nothing but my anxious endeavour to serve my country makes me bear up against it; but I sometimes am ready to give it all up.[20]

Nelson wrote to Earl Spencer just over one year after his eye injury, on 19th July 1795:

> The doubts which had arisen respecting the damage my eye had sustained ... made it, your Lordship said, impossible to say whether it was such as amounted to the loss of a limb. I have only to tell your Lordship that a total deprivation of sight for every common occasion in life is the consequence of the loss of part of the crystal of my right eye.[21]

Nelson, who was fond of quoting Shakespeare, may have been thinking of a quotation from the poem *Venus and Adonis* comparing the eyes to crystals (though the ocular-crystal metaphor is often found).

Although it is fair to believe an abnormal physical sign is present if two or more artists show it at different times, it must be remembered that artists are not medically trained, nor are they clinical observers. Therefore, one should not be too surprised if mistakes are made – even the gross ones of Andras and Hoppner who, in their effigy and portrait respectively, made Nelson's left eye the abnormal one. The artistic convention for an abnormal eye is to omit the so-called corneal highlight (a small bright white dot near the centre of the eye). This convention is clear in the Schmidt miniature of 1800, but was not used by all artists: the Fuger painting of 1800 has no abnormality of the eyes at all. But artists can and do show gross eye pathology secondary to infection (Picasso's Blue Period painting 'Woman with a Wall Eye', for example). The lack of gross abnormality in his right eye is confirmed by the Life Masks of Nelson, now known to have been created in Dresden in 1800. A life mask with the eyes open has had to be 'worked' – the life mask maker has had to alter the mask to show open eyes. A life mask with the eyes closed has not been interfered with by the maker and so is a more accurate representation. The Nelson closed eye mask does show slight loss of right eye globe size only. The difficulty the authorities faced is understandable, in effect Nelson had two apparently normal eyes though he said he could not see out of the right one; but they could see nothing objectively wrong with the eye. The official examiners appear to have missed the abnormal pupil, and the smaller globe size. Unfortunately no report of their examination has survived. It is because of this lack of objective findings that Nelson need be quoted so extensively. He maintains a consistent account all the way through.

Nelson continued at sea until 1st September 1797. Not even the severe abdominal wound which left him with a very painful abdominal hernia for the rest of his life drove him home. It was only after the loss of his arm at Tenerife that he was invalided back to England. So, of course, the official medical examinations of his eye had to wait over three years.

Less than three weeks after he landed back in England Nelson obtained a third medical certificate. Dated 20th September 1797 and signed by two doctors, it says:

This is to certify that we have examined the right eye of Admiral Sir Horatio Nelson and that we found the sight entirely lost without the smallest hopes of his ever recovering it again.

H. CARRICKSHAWK
H. LEIGH THORING[22]

Like the Court of Examiners at the Company of Surgeons at Lincoln's Inn Fields on 12th October 1797, they could only have used a magnifying glass to examine the eye. They just stated the injury received by Nelson was fully equal to the loss of an eye. So, only one of the certificates (the first) contains any type of description of the eye.

Nelson possibly 'used' his blind right eye during the Battle of Copenhagen. He definitely 'used' it in the post-battle negotiations. William Stewart, commanding the marines on board *St. George* recorded that towards the end of the negotiations when the Danes were baulking at the length of the armistice, Nelson, in a break from the negotiating table, while walking with Stewart up a grand staircase to the Palace dining room, said: 'Though I have only one eye, I see all this will burn very well.'[23] Presumably what he said was overheard: the armistice was signed after the meal, that same evening.

He kept a 'Journal of the Siege of Calvi by Captain Horatio Nelson, who commanded the seamen employed on the expedition' from 10th June 1794, when the *Agamemnon* 'left Lord Hood at sea,' to the 10th August, when the English took possession of the town.

In the journal, for 8th July 1794, Nelson recorded how he had nearly been blown up by a shell which 'burst in the centre of our battery amongst the General, myself and at least 100 of us, but wonderful not a man was hurt, although it blew up our battery magazine.'[24] Four days later his luck ran out. Nelson wrote:

The enemy opened a heavy fire at daylight from the town and San Francisco, which, in an extraordinary manner, seldom missed our battery; and at 7 o'clock, I was much bruised in the face and eyes by sand from the works struck by shot.[25]

This was the only reference he made in the journal to his wound and, having been carried to his tent the day of the injury, on the following day he returned to his post despite his injuries. The entry for the 13th July is a particularly full one and in a manner typical of him, Nelson was at great pains to praise by name a colleague, the Canadian Captain Hallowell: 'I must here acknowledge the indefatigable zeal, activity and ability of Captain Hallowell and of the great readiness he ever shows to give me assistance in the laborious duties entrusted to us.'[26] As the Journal was destined for Lord Hood, Nelson was drawing Hood's attention not to his own problems but the hard work of others. In the Journal entry for 29th July he mentioned some eight junior officers by name 'for their constant assiduity and attention.' Throughout his life, whenever he could, Nelson always gave praise.

To summarise the probable trauma and its lasting effects:

(a) The stones, splinters and sand would have been flung so rapidly into Nelson's face and eyes he would have had no chance to close his eyelids. So the likelihood of corneal abrasions would have been extremely high. But in all probability these healed rapidly without long-lasting effects. No abnormalities due to corneal trauma are visible in any of the Nelson portraits.

(b) The trauma would have caused sub-conjunctival haemorrhages with the white of Nelson's right eye becoming blood-red for several weeks, but with complete resolution, as a bruise does, through yellow to white.

(c) The concussive injury to the eyeball of the right eye would have caused bleeding into the anterior chamber of the eye (so-called 'hyphema') causing vision to be severely reduced to only perceptions of light, or possibly of hand movements. 'It was cut down but is so far recovered as to be able to distinguish light from darkness, but as to all the purpose of use it is gone.'[27]

(d) The concussion injury could cause rupture of the iris sphincter giving rise to an enlarged pupil. 'The pupil is nearly the size of the blue part. I don't know the name' (see reference 28). This would be permanent damage and would not recover. Alternatively the iris itself could have been torn (iridodialysis). This produces a pupil which is no longer round but irregular and D-shaped. And this might explain the appearance of Nelson's right pupil in some portraits, for example Abbott, and the Beechey sketch.

(e) Vitreous haemorrhages are very common with blunt concussive injuries, which send shock waves in all directions through the fluid of the eyeball (see diagram of the eyeball and direction of shock waves). If severe, as Nelson's probably was, the haemorrhage is not re-absorbed and loss of sight is permanent.

(f) Two other possible eye lesions may have occurred, both of which cause vitreous haemorrhages as well and both of which frequently occur after concussive eyeball injuries. One is a retinal detachment, which would have been untreatable in Nelson's day and would have resulted in loss of vision. The other is a tear of the choroid layer of the eye which would also result in loss of vision.

(g) The injury from high velocity debris from the exploding projectile was severe, and resulted in either a non-penetrating injury to the globe, or a penetrating injury. A penetrating injury is the most likely, given the sudden and permanent loss of vision. The iris abnormality, if it was a penetrating injury, would have been due to an iris prolapse through a corneal or limbal laceration. This was probably plugged by the iris.

Once the sub-conjunctival haemorrhages, corneal ulceration, the penetrating injury and the posterior chamber lesions were resolved and healed, Nelson would have been left with a sightless right eye which was slightly smaller than the left and which had an abnormal pupil. In all other respects his right eye would appear normal to the naked eye of an examiner, even with a magnifying glass. The direct ophthalmoscope was not invented until 50 years after his injury. His right eye would move normally with the left. None of the Nelson portraits show any evidence of late onset traumatic cataract, or of lens opacity, and Nelson never reported any eye infection at the time of the eye injury.

However, the Life Masks – both the 'worked' one with eyes open and the 'closed' one with the eyes shut, appear to show that the globe of Nelson's right eye was slightly smaller than the left and so do at least four of his portraits:

The Orme chalk drawing 1797–98
The Guy Head oil 1798–99
The Schmidt pastel 1800
The Beechey study 1800
All were painted or created after the Calvi injury.

This is compatible with a severe blunt injury, almost certainly with penetration of the eye giving rise to slight globe shrinking, subsequent enophthalmos (sinking of the globe of the eye in the eye-socket) and the right eye appearing slightly smaller than the left.

The diagram of the eye shows the effect of a direct blow to the front of the actual eyeball. The horizontal arrow within the eye shows the further direction of force towards an important part of the back of the eyeball, the macular region. The other four arrows show the most likely directions of subsequent pressure forces. Eye areas addressed by the five intra-ocular arrows are those most likely to be torn after such an injury as Nelson sustained.

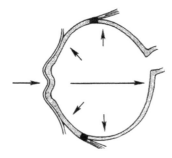

Adapted from Yanuf & Fine, *Ocular Pathology*, 4th edition, 1996 p.142

Nelson also sustained periorbital damage on 12th July 1794. 'The blood was so severe ... it [the right eye] was cut down;' as he described it to his wife, over a month after the injury. The effect of those shards that struck his face and brow was to cause the cuts visible in the Leghorn miniature, a scar beneath the right eyebrow under the supra-orbital ridge and a scar beneath the left eyelid. They also removed permanently the hair-bearing tissue from the outer half of Nelson's right eyebrow. This is shown most clearly in the Beechey sketch and Bowyer's miniature. It is fascinating to see how many of Nelson's portraits avoid showing his right eyebrow either by placing his hair over the outer half, or by painting him facing to the right, showing a left profile.

Several years ago the author had the opportunity to examine medical reports on two patients, each of whom had been struck in an eye by fast missiles. In one the report was written shortly after the event. The examining doctor had noted the following abnormalities in the injured eye: vision was limited to hand movements only; the eye globe contained blood; the cornea (surface of the eye) was superficially grazed; and the pupil was irregularly dilated. In the second report, made some nine months after the injury, the patient had described how she was at first unable to see anything at all with the eye but then began to be able to distinguish light from dark and fingers moving in a bright light situation. She also complained of intermittent pain in the affected eye which was not present every day.

The similarity of the symptoms of these two modern patients with those of Nelson is striking. In neither had the globe of the eye been penetrated during the accident and also in both these cases the two eyes moved normally together, from left to right and up and down.

One last medical observation: at Calvi, Nelson must have been covered in blood at the time of the wound. Head wounds almost always bleed profusely and are difficult to staunch.

Apart from the early eye strain and the trauma of the Calvi wound, Nelson had other eye problems. On 28th January 1801 Nelson wrote to Lady Hamilton from the *San Josef*:

> My eye is very bad. I have had the physician of the fleet to examine it. He has directed me not to write, (and yet I am forced, this day, to write Lord Spencer, St. Vincent, Davison, Troubridge, Mr. Locker etc., but you are the only female I write to) not to eat anything but the most simple food; not to touch wine or porter; to sit in a dark room; to have green shades for my eyes – (will you, my dear friend, make me one or two? Nobody else shall) – and to bathe them in cold water every hour. I fear it is the writing has brought on this complaint. My eye is like blood; and the film so extended, that I only see from the corner farthest from my nose.[28]

Dr. Thomas Trotter M.D., then Physician to the Fleet, described Nelson's eye:

> Violent ophthalmia [inflammation of the eye] in his *only eye* [author's italics] with a membranous substance seemingly spreading fast over the pupil … I prescribed a dark room, and bathing the eye every hour with cold spring water, which in 24 hours had a surprising effect, and in two days more the inflammation was entirely gone.[29]

From Trotter's description and the rapidity with which the problem cleared, it sounds as if Nelson was suffering from a severe bacterial conjunctivitis. It is also possible he had had similar episodes before as there is an isolated reference to 'almost blind … with very great pain.'[30] in a letter to the Minister at Genoa in August 1795, though Nelson had written to his brother William, two months before that he was 'never better in health.'[31]

Thomas Trotter (1760–1832) was a Scotsman. He went to sea as a surgeon's mate aged 20. He wrote an important book about scurvy in 1786 and later had personal influence with Earl Howe, Commander of the Channel Fleets, which meant Howe implemented all Trotter's health suggestions, most especially with regard to the use of lemon juice and fresh vegetables for the ships' crews. Nelson must have been aware of Howe and Trotter's work.

Lastly, it is possible that after the wound to his right eye, Nelson suffered from a condition called Sympathetic Ophthalmitis. This rare condition has been known for over a thousand years in medical literature. Damage to uveal tissue (almost always by a perforating wound involving the iris, ciliary body and / or choroid parts of the eye) produces an immune response, antibodies are made and then these attack the good non-injured eye. Nowadays, topical steroids are used for treatment of the condition, the symptoms of which may either be rapid 'burn out' in the non-injured eye, followed by poor vision and blindness, or photophobia, bruised feelings and discomfort, and intermittent pain associated with various vision impairment symptoms that can go on for years. It is known that Nelson suffered from variable symptoms in his left 'good' eye for the rest of his life after the Calvi wound. The Nelson quotations on pages 60 and 64 were written thirteen months and six and a half years respectively, after his eye injury.

Obviously at this distance in time one cannot make an accurate diagnosis. The fact remains that from the date of his eye injury until he was killed just over 11 years later, at intervals Nelson experienced problems in both eyes which were compatible with a diagnosis of Sympathetic Ophthalmitis in the left eye.

The above were not Nelson's only eye problems. Pinguecula is a degenerative condition of the conjunctiva which is extremely common in adults.

It presents as yellow/white nodules and coloration usually in the nasal side of the iris and pupil of each eye and it is the nasal side of each of Nelson's eyes that it is shown (for example) in the Beechey study portrait in the National Portrait Gallery. The yellow nodules consist of hyaline and yellow elastic tissue and frequently become the site of localised infection.

Pterygium is thought by some authorities to be an extension of pinguecula.[32] It is a fleshy growth of the conjunctiva across the cornea from the nasal side of the eye. Because it frequently occurs in patients exposed to ultraviolet light, sun, wind and dusty and windy environments, it is thought possibly to be an irritative reaction to these elements. Nelson would have been exposed to them day after day, throughout his sea-going life. The degeneration becomes overgrown and vascular and if it impinges on the central part of the eye it can affect the part of the cornea covering the iris and pupil and so affect the field of vision. As noted earlier, Dr Lambton Este perceived this in November 1804: 'A thick opaque membrane had grown over and into a part of the transparent cornea … in the only eye left to him.'[33]

Later in the development of pterygium, scar tissue can form, causing corneal astigmatism. The combination of overgrowth obscuring the vision and scar tissue contracting to alter the eye's ability to focus could, undoubtedly, be responsible for such eye problems as Nelson reported (again to his brother William) in December 1803: 'My eye is every month visibly getting worse and I much fear it will end in total blindness'[34] (actually clinically unlikely). He also wrote to Dr Baird in mid March 1804 'my sight is getting very, very bad.'[35]

Four years previously Nelson had been on shore at Palermo from where, over a period of just over three weeks, he penned six letters to five people in all of which he complained of severe eye problems:

1. H. E. Thomas Jackson, Minister at Turin: 'Pity the sorrows of a blind, and (in constitution) old man.' (1st December 1799)
2. Captain Ball, Chief of the Island of Malta: 'I am almost blind.' (7th December 1799)
3. Evan Nepean at the Admiralty: 'As to myself, I can see, that is all I can say.' (14th December 1799)
4. Commodore Sir Thomas Troubridge: 'I am blind …' (16th December 1799)
5. Earl Spencer: 'I am almost blind – therefore, my dear Lord, excuse my writing more at this moment.' (18th December 1799)

Then most interestingly, he wrote again to:

6. Sir Thomas Troubridge: 'I am undergoing a course of electricity which I begin to think will give sight to my blind eye.' (22nd December 1799)[36]

Fascinatingly, Troubridge replied to this last letter: 'I trust and hope the Electrifying will restore your sight ...'[37] Nelson stayed on at Palermo until 16th January 1800 but this was the last mention, in any letter, of eye problems, or treatment, at that time.

The Leyden Jar is a device for storing quantities of static electricity. It was invented in 1745 by van Musschenbroek of the University of Leyden and independently by von Kleist in Pomerania. In its early form it consisted of a glass phial, partly filled with water, with a narrow neck closed by a cork, pierced by a wire which ran from one end in the water to the other above the cork. It was charged by bringing the end of the wire outside the phial into contact with the prime conductor of an electrical machine. After removing the electrical machine a severe shock could be given to a person who touched the wire of the Leyden Jar.

Because the Leyden Jar could accumulate electricity it was used to give dramatic demonstrations of the passing of a shock from a Jar through large numbers of people holding hands or connected by metal rods they were holding. An operator holding the outside of the Leyden Jar at one end and another operator touching the wire in the cork at the other end, completed the circuit, whereupon all connected in the circle received a shock from the electricity stored in the jar.

A Frenchman, the Abbe Jean-Antoine Nollet, (1700–1770) conducted extensive early investigations into electricity. His most famous (and popular) experiment was to stand two hundred monks in a large circle. Each monk was 'connected' to his neighbours on either side by a piece of wire 25 feet long, held in each hand. When the mile-long 'circle' was completed by connecting the two final ends to a 'charged' Leyden Jar, all the monks involuntarily and simultaneously, jumped into the air, reacting to the electric shock they had received.

Nollet repeated the jumping circle in front of King Louis XV of France, using one hundred and eighty of the King's own guardsmen. Drawing-rooms all over Europe copied these experiments and James Graham would have known all about them. In the author's opinion so too did Nelson and Lady Hamilton.

By 1767 the discovery of a machine, the electrometer, to standardise the shocks from a particular electrical machine and a Leyden Jar meant that the severity of shocks could be controlled. The length of time they could or should be administered, was discussed by such early practitioners using electricity for medical purposes as J. B. Becket in his *An Essay on Electricity*[38] and in 1780 by Thomas Cavallo, in his extremely influential book *An Essay on the theory and practice of Medical Electricity*. (There was a second enlarged edition in 1781). He was able to give precise instructions and recommend measured, gentle methods. Cavallo had been born in Naples but came to England at a young age and wrote in English. His emphasis was on a gentle stream of electricity from a metal point or points which he said felt like a gentle wind on the affected part and he described a stream of very small sparks from a wooden conductor. Cavallo insulated his patient who was then connected to the primary conductor, with the affected part covered with flannel and the end (probably a knob or pointer) of an ordinary conductor passed rapidly over the part to be treated. Most likely the apparatus illustrated in Figure 2 of Cavallo's frontispiece was used for the eye. Cavallo said that inflammation of the eyes required only the most gentle stream of electricity and in his 'General Rules for Practice' wrote:

> It should be attentively observed, to employ the smallest force of electricity, that is sufficient to remove or to alleviate any disorder... The difficulty consists in distinguishing the proper strength of electric power that is required for a given disorder, the sex and constitution of the patient being considered. In regard to this point, it is impossible to give any exact and invariable rules ...
>
> Inflammations of every sort are generally relieved by a very gentle electralisation.
>
> Inflammation of the eyes, the throwing of the electric fluid by means of a wooden point, is constantly attended with great benefit; the pain being quickly abated, and the inflammation being generally dissipated in a few days. In these cases, the eye of the patient must be kept open, and care should be taken not to bring the wooden point very near it, for fear of causing any spark. Sometimes it is sufficient to throw the fluid with a metal point; for in these cases, too great an irritation should be always avoided. It is not necessary to continue this operation for three or four minutes without intermission; but after throwing the fluid for about half a minute, a short time may be allowed to the patient to rest and to wipe his tears, which generally flow very copiously; then the operation may be continued again for another half minute, and so on for four or five times every day.[39]

Carvallo also wrote a vivid account of a patient being given 'electrified' treatment with some success. We must assume that Nelson's treatment was similar:

Authentic physical cases in which Electricity was administered.

The particulars of the following case were communicated to me by Mr. Partington:

Daniel Wiscoyl, aged thirty-six of a strong robust constitution, was sent... to Mr. Partington, in order to be electrified for a violent inflammation in both his eyes. The account he gave of his disorder, was the following: Several dark objects of different shapes and sizes, seemed at first to obstruct his sight. This was succeeded by an inflammation in both his eyes, which increased with such rapidity, that in a week's time he was brought to the degree of blindness that afflicted him till he was electrified. He was immediately recommended to the Westminster Dispensary, where every possible attention was paid to his misfortune by Mr. Ford, the surgeon of that place: but the obstinacy of this poor man, proved useless. Blisters and leeches, besides the other usual means, were applied without any efficacy whatever.

About two months after the commencement of the inflammation, Mr. Ford recommended him to Mr. Partington; who, on examining him, found that the eyelids could not be opened without the help of the fingers, and that when opened, the coats of the eye appeared of an uniform red colour. The sight of the right eye, which was the most affected was so far impaired that when it was turned towards a window, the eyelids being forced open, he could perceive only a red glare of light like a ball of fire; but the rest of the room seemed to be equally dark, so that he could not distinguish any object in it. With the left eye he could distinguish colours, and the shapes of objects that were held to him, but in their sizes he was commonly mistaken. This disorder was accompanied with excruciating pains, shifting from one part to the other, but principally insisting on his temples, and sometimes darting to the back part of his head, or to the center of his eyes.

Mr. Partington began to electrify him, the 21st October 1776; and three days after the inflammation began visibly to abate, and in a fortnight's time it was quite subsided; but the pupil of the eye was so nearly closed, that scarce any of it could be seen. He continued to be electrified every day for five weeks, and the pupil gradually dilated, till he attained a degree of sight sufficient to distinguish objects on the other side of the way. The pains had now entirely left him, so that he omitted the use of electricity, and did not experience any further inconvenience after it.

This remarkable cure was effected by throwing the stream of electric fluid with a metal, and with a wooden point. The first instrument used … consisted in a pointed brass wire, fastened by means of a cork at the smaller end of a conical glass, open at both ends, and passing through the axis of this conical or funnel-like glass, its point came within about half an inch of the larger aperture of the glass. This instrument being designed to throw the electric fluid upon the eye, was to be fixed so that the larger aperture of the glass surrounding the eye, kept its lids open, and the point of the wire was opposite to the pupil, and about half or one inch from it. With this instrument it was observed that a spark often proceeded from the point of the wire, which occasioned an insufferable pain; for which reason Mr.

Partington, who spares no efforts to advance this branch of physic, thought of improving this instrument by fixing a wooden point upon the pointed wire, by which means, the formal inconvenience was entirely removed, and the stream of electric fluid was rendered more efficacious and more easily manageable.

This, as far as I am informed, was the first time that this most excellent method of throwing the electric fluid, vis, with a wooden point, was used.[40]

Two men, one a naval surgeon, the other a portrait painter, are important with reference to Nelson's eyes. The naval surgeon, Thomas Trotter, treated Nelson and recorded what he found at the time of the consultation. The artist, William Beechey has painted what is probably the best portrait of Nelson.

Sir William Beechey was born in Burford, Oxfordshire. He entered the Royal Academy School aged 18. He began by exhibiting small portraits when he was 21 but quickly progressed to life sized ones and he was made an Associate of the Royal Academy just before he was 40, in 1793. He became Painter to Queen Charlotte, wife of King George III, and five years later, having exhibited a large painting of the King and his eldest son reviewing troops, Beechey was knighted and made a Royal Academician. He has been described as a 'very careful craftsman,' which makes the study for a portrait of Nelson of particular interest, showing as it does so many physical abnormalities on Nelson's face and forehead and in his eyes.

The first portrait was painted in 1801 when Nelson had just returned from Naples with Sir William and Lady Hamilton, having travelled overland across Europe via Vienna, Prague, Dresden and Hamburg. The copy in this book was painted posthumously in 1807 for the Drapers' Company. Comparison with the life mask shows how accurate Beechey's painting was. Nelson's large nose and sensuous full lips are faithfully reproduced as are the pronounced supra-orbital ridges. (These give protection to the eyes and are said to be a simian characteristic.) The painting shows the following physical abnormalities:

1. The right pupil is very obviously irregular and enlarged by comparison with the left pupil.
2. The right eyebrow is distorted, puckered and scarred, lacking in colouration compared to the left.
3. The Nile scar is above the right supra-orbital ridge. It is not a straight linear scar but rather stellate (see illustration on front cover).
4. Both eyes have a touch of yellow in their inner aspects (Pinguecula)
5. The right eye appears slightly sunken.

Beechey had already painted Nelson's father in sittings apparently arranged by his wife Fanny, while he was still abroad, as she wrote him a letter to tell him all about it, on 4th March 1800, which was addressed to Palermo. She described how Beechey had broken his own rule, never to go to the house of a sitter, when he heard that he had been asked to paint the father of Lord Nelson.[41] Beechey and Nelson became friends and Nelson stood as honorary Godfather to Beechey's son Charles. It is said that Nelson also gave Beechey the cocked hat he had worn at the Battle of the Nile.

The more painters who tackle a single subject, the more likely it is that variations will appear in the subject's appearance. Richard Walker wrote that only Queen Victoria and the Duke of Wellington (both of whom lived to a great age) were painted more often, by different painters, than Nelson.[42]

Earl St. Vincent wrote to Lady Foster in a famous quotation 'That foolish little fellow has sat to every painter in London.'[43] It was not true. Most unfortunately Nelson was never painted by any of the *great* portrait painters of his day: Reynolds, Lawrence, Zoffany, Romney, Gainsborough, or Madame Le Brun. But thanks to the scholarship of Richard Walker, much more information is now available in one place on the Nelson portraits, and about the lesser artists of his day who did paint him.[44]

If all we are looking for is an exact and lifelike representation, when an image of a sitter is created by any artist, even the greatest, many hindrances to accuracy may occur. The artist may have something wrong with *his* eyes. The materials he uses may alter in colour with the passage of time. For example, many of Joshua Reynolds portraits appear deathly pale because the carmine he used has now faded out completely.[45] A dirty painting covered in thick, old or repeated layers of varnish may have the subtle colours in the picture altered, and only after proper cleaning and restoration will the artist's original coloration reappear. Dirty yellow varnish can change an original blue- or grey-coloured eye to a green or brown colour until the old varnish is removed. Artists make mistakes: Hoppner made Nelson's *left* eye very obviously the abnormal one.[46] Artists copy one another. Andras copied Hoppner[47] so that the mistake was perpetuated. The viewer himself may not record correctly what can be seen in a portrait. For example, Walker notes nothing wrong with the pupils of the National Portrait Gallery copy of Abbott's portrait of Nelson[48] whereas, quite clearly and measurably, the right pupil is larger (dilated) by comparison with the left. Nor does Walker comment on the dilated and slightly irregular right pupil of the National Maritime Museum Abbott portrait[49] although he does note the pterygium.

If we are looking to judge the accuracy of the various portraits, Nelson himself did not give too many clues. The only time he appeared to refer to the colour of his eyes was in a letter to Fanny written after his right eye injury at

Calvi, when he wrote of his right eye: 'The pupil is nearly the size of the blue part, I don't know the name' (note 15.) He is describing his enlarged pupil, comparing its size with the coloured part of his eye, the name of which (iris) he does not know. So in all likelihood he was blue-eyed.

From the point of view of medical evidence it is fortunate that not only was Nelson depicted by artists throughout his adult life from the age of 18 to two months after his death, but also in at least three instances by portraits which are, if not painted by Masters, arguably minor masterpieces: the Rigaud painting of 1777-1781, the Abbott painting of 1797 and the Beechey study portrait of 1800.

Although some evidence is conflicting, a picture of Nelson's abnormal physical signs emerges. These, when taken together with the clear accounts he gives of his own physical symptoms occurring secondary to his wounds and following constant exposure to the elements, enable diagnoses to be made across two centuries which are almost certainly accurate. Evidence of the wounds which he sustained at Calvi, Teneriffe and the Nile can be seen in Nelson's portraits. No full-length portrait shows an abdominal abnormality or swelling relating to the St. Vincent wound.

Consideration of the portraits for clinical signs produced by the two head injuries Nelson sustained (at Calvi in 1794 and at the Nile in 1798) requires the date of each to be borne in mind. This list is comprehensive. (See Appendix II for a summary of these signs, and also Chapter VI regarding the Nile head wound.)

1. The Rigaud Portrait: Started in 1777 when Nelson was 18 and finished in 1781 when he had become a young Post-Captain. A young fresh-faced man with a slightly untidy gold laced uniform coat and no physical abnormalities whatsoever.
2. The Collingwood Portrait: 1784. Nelson in profile from the right. Having his hair cut off during a fever, he is wearing an ill-fitting yellow wig. The right eyebrow is delineated fully but only the inner half is drawn normally.
3. The Leghorn Miniaturist: Painted in the autumn of 1795, it was not considered a good likeness by either Nelson or his stepson, Josiah Nisbet. The painting shows abnormal physical features from the Calvi wound: a linear scar above the outer aspect of the right eyelid and a very small curved scar on the innermost aspect of the right lower eyelid; plus a small linear scar below the outer aspect of the left lower eyelid and loss of hair from the outer half of the right eyebrow.
4. Henry Edridge: 1797. In the first pencil and ink drawing there is a scar below the outer aspect of the right lower eyelid. Both the right and left eyebrows are drawn in firmly, particularly the former.
5. Abbott: 1797. Walker listed a huge number of portraits by Abbott.[50] For the purpose of medical signs the Abbott owned by the National Maritime

Museum and that owned by the National Portrait Gallery are of particular note. Both quite clearly show a dilated right pupil. There is also a corneal abnormality in the inner aspect of both eyes in both portraits, indicated by hints of yellow colour, and this is pinguecula.

6. Lawrence Gahagan: 1778. This shows a deep indentation above and into the right eyebrow which is almost split into two parts. The outer aspect of the right eyebrow is irregular in shape when compared with the left eyebrow. It must be said Nelson sat to Lawrence Gahagan in the early months of 1798, long before he sustained the Nile head wound. Physical abnormalities in the busts by Lawrence Gahagon and his brother Lucius may not therefore be from the life *but what the artists imagined them to be.*

7. Guzzardi: 1799. This artist painted Nelson from life *after* he sustained his serious Nile head wound. Nelson's cocked-hat is tilted backwards so as to prevent the front rim of the hat from pressing on the scar and site of the missile's impact. This confirms the severity of the wound. The painting is dated 1799 so even if completed on the first day of that year it shows that five months after the wound was sustained, Nelson's head was still so painful he could not bear any pressure on the impact site. This is confirmed as the Nile scar is fully visible. The scar is not as described by surgeon Jefferson. He had said it was three inches long, with one inch of skull exposed. Guzzardi's representation is much more what one would expect from a wound caused by langridge. It has evidence of horizontal skin damage as well as vertical. The right eye appears slightly sunken but the face itself is haggard, showing evidence of weight loss and depression. The outer half of the right eyebrow is missing. Guzzardi's portrait is an artistic measure of how ill Nelson was more than five months after the Battle of the Nile.

8. Guy Head. The two portraits of Nelson by Head are medically important. The fanciful one depicting the recently wounded Nelson confirms the shortness of Nelson's amputation stump and shows a swollen right upper lip. The formal portrait – heavily criticised by historians for its historical inaccuracy – is medically fascinating since it appears to show bruising discoloration of the right cheek and moderate swelling and asymmetry of the right forehead, and a slightly sunken right eye.

9. Fuger. He painted Nelson both in and out of uniform. The angle of the head in each portrait ensures the outer half of the right eyebrow and the Nile scar do not have to be painted.

10. The Life Masks: 1800. Created in Vienna. As previously indicated, these show that the globe of Nelson's right eye was not removed after his injury at Calvi. This means the eye injury was a concussive one. The outer half of the right supra orbital crest is smooth and slightly bigger than the left, showing the absence of hair-bearing tissue replaced by scar tissue. Both worked and un-worked masks show a slightly smaller right eye. The forehead was probably worked by the artist to give a smooth non scarred effect.

11. Schmidt: 1800. Painted in October 1800 in Dresden, Nelson's forehead is powdered to cover the Nile scar. The right eyebrow is less well defined than the left, especially on the lateral aspect. The white spot of corneal highlight is very conspicuously absent in the right eye and the right pupil is 'blurred' but this could be artistic convention. The right eye itself is slightly divergent to the right, and slightly sunken within the orbit.

12. Keymer: 1801. Keymer was a local Norfolk artist who painted Nelson in March of that year. No abnormality is shown in either eye, nor is the Nile scar depicted. But the hair is very carefully placed to fall over and completely obscure the outer half of the right eyebrow. And it follows exactly the line of the keloid scar portrayed by Andras.

13. Beechey: 1800. The preliminary sketch for Beechey's full-length Norwich portrait shows the right pupil to be obviously irregular and enlarged in comparison to the left. The right eyebrow is distorted and lacking in coloration, especially laterally. This is repeated (as is the abnormal right pupil) in another oil sketch Beechey made which is in Greenwich. The National Portrait Gallery sketch also shows the Nile scar, partially powdered. Both eyes have a touch of yellow in their inner aspects. The finished Norwich portrait Beechey painted from this sketch shows the Nile scar and abnormal right eyebrow, and in the copy owned by the Drapers Company, the forehead scar is stellate and has a three-dimensional aspect suggesting some part of it was keloid. The right eye is slightly sunken.

14. Hoppner: 1800. In his preliminary oil sketch and in the finished full-length portrait, Hoppner has dimmed the wrong (left) eye. Omitting the corneal highlight, or blurring the eye by painting it properly and then smudging the oil paint with a finger, is an artistic convention to indicate an eye problem. Interestingly Hoppner's preliminary painting of Nelson shows the *right* eye pupil to be slightly dilated and irregular along its lower edge. All Hoppner's oil sketches and copies of his painting by other artists (for example Bone and Andras) slavishly make the left eye the abnormal one.

15. De Koster: 1802. The right eyebrow is not nearly so clearly depicted as the left.

16. Andras: 1895–96. The Westminster Abbey wax and wood effigy was a posthumous portrait although Andras had done a left profile wax in relief from life in September 1805, just before Nelson embarked for Trafalgar. She largely based her effigy on Hoppner and so she made the right eye the abnormal one. The keloid scar on the forehead is medically important.

The Nelson iconography, if it proves anything, proves that artists can be unobservant and inaccurate.

Nevertheless, there are some further clues. It is clear from the Rigaud and Collingwood portraits that Nelson, as a young man, had more eyebrow hairs growing medially than laterally, in both his eyebrows. The

Leghorn portrait is important in that it shows the absence of the outer half of the right eyebrow five years *before* the Nile injury was sustained. The copy of the Guzzardi portrait now hanging in the Admiralty Boardroom clearly shows the separate effects of the two head wounds; a puckered raised-looking scar about one-and-a-half inches above the right eye is the Nile injury. We can conclude therefore that the injury Nelson received at Calvi and which he so clearly described to his wife in a letter of 8th August 1794, the blow which occasioned 'a great flow of blood from my head' was the one that deeply removed hair-bearing skin from the outer aspect of his right supra-orbital ridge. Writing almost five weeks after the actual injury 'the blemish is nothing, not to be perceived unless told.'[51] he must have known he could cover the scar with a lock of hair if necessary. And this is what he did, for the rest of his life. (For further medical analysis of Nelson's portraits see Appendix II.)

There was much interest and newspaper correspondence some years ago about Nelson's right eye. This was sparked off by an article headed 'Horatio Nelson never was blind: his woundings and his frequent ill-health.'[52] It was written by a retired general surgeon, Milo Keynes. In *The Times* of 4th October 1804, a paragraph about Nelson's eyes appeared in a sort of gossip column on a back page of the paper. It read:

> It is generally understood that the gallant Lord Nelson has lost 'one eye;' and a few days ago a paragraph appeared in one of the papers lamenting that his remaining eye was considerably weaker of late, and expressing an apprehension that he might altogether lose his sight. We beg leave to state, for the satisfaction of those of his Lordship's admirers who are not personally acquainted with him, that Lord Nelson 'is not blind of either eye.' It is true that he for a short period lost the sight of 'one eye,' but it has been happily restored. He has also a speck on the other eye but that he could see with 'both' at no very distant date we are assured, from the very best authority – that of His Lordship's own information, who has declared, that 'he could see best with what people called his worst eye.'

The last sentence purports to come from Nelson himself but it did not. Nelson had left Spithead on *Victory* on 20th May 1803 and did not return to England until 19th August 1805. On and about 4th October 1804 he was sailing off Toulon in the Mediterranean.

Nevertheless the article has been used as the basis for theories that Nelson exaggerated the severity of his eye injury for financial gain, although he never received any pension or monies at all in respect of his eye injury; and as ammunition to prove he was a malingerer.

Nelson at no time said or wrote subsequent to Calvi that he could see properly with his right eye. Since he was at sea when *The Times* article appeared, there was no way anyone could have had access to 'His Lordship's own information.' Because of the delay between the article appearing and Nelson returning to England (ten-and-a-half months) the article was never refuted by Nelson, who probably never even saw it. But it would be interesting to know which newspaper provoked his comment in a letter to Lady Hamilton written on 27th May 1804, when he wrote, 'Do not believe a syllable the newspapers say, or what you hear. Mankind seems fond of telling lies.'[53]

At the Battle of Copenhagen Nelson ignored an order from his commanding Admiral, Sir Hyde Parker. This order, flown as a signal late in the action from the Admiral's flagship was for *all* British ships to 'discontinue the action.' Parker had divided the British Fleet into two halves, one of which was commanded by Nelson and it was Nelson's half which was in fierce action with the Danish forces.

Nelson could not get his ships away from the situation they were in without their being destroyed by the Danish defences. So he ignored Parker's signal, and kept his own, for 'close action', flying. No contemporary source mentions Nelson putting his telescope to his blind eye, and actually saying 'I see no signal.'

Nelson *never* wore an eye patch over his right eye. He did wear a green eye shade (made by Lady Hamilton) sewn into his naval hat. The only picture of him wearing such a hat and such a shade is in the posthumous portrait by Devis. But the Westminster Abbey effigy, dressed in clothes supplied by Nelson's family, has such a hat, again with an eye shade in situ. Beatty wrote:

> His Lordship had lost his right eye by a contusion which he received at the siege of Calvi, in the island of Corsica. The vision of the other was likewise considerably impaired: he always therefore wore a green eye shade over his forehead, to defend this eye from the effect of strong light.[54]

Notes

1. Nicolas vol II p.6
2. Clarke and M'Arthur vol 1 p.109
3. ibid p.181
4. ibid
5. Nicolas vol I p.433
6. Naish p.172
7. Nicolas vol I p.434

8. ibid p.436
9. ibid p.439
10. ibid p.442
11. ibid p.452
12. ibid p.462
13. ibid p.464
14. ibid p.180
15. Naish p.119
16. Nicolas vol I p.487-8
17. Naish p.263
18. Nicolas vol I p.488-9
19. Naish p.195
20. Nicolas vol II p.2
21. ibid p.57
22. ibid. p.200
23. Nicolas vol IV p.327
24. Clarke and M'Arthur vol l p.179
25. ibid p.181
26. ibid p.182
27. Nicolas vol I p.480
28. *Nelson's Letters to Lady Hamilton* vol I p.21–2
29. Trotter, T. *Medica Nautica* 1803 Quoted in Pugh p.49
30. Nicolas vol II p.67
31. ibid p.42
32. *The Lancet* 23rd June 1984 p.392
33. Nicolas vol VI p.257
34. ibid vol V p.311
35. ibid p.462
36. ibid vol IV p.124, 130, 141, 142, 146, 156
37. Russell *Nelson & the Hamiltons* 1972 p.153 (hereafter Russell)
38. Becket, J. B. *An Essay on Electricity* 1773 p.70–4
39. Cavallo *Essay on the Theory and Practice of Medical Electricity* 1st edition 1780 p.44–5, 53–4
40. ibid 2nd edition 1781 p.72–6
41. Naish p.552
42. White, C. *The Nelson Companion* p.33
43. Foster, Lady E. *Journal* 14th *February* 1801 cited in Stuart, D. M. *Dearest Bess* 1955 p.90
44. Walker p.199–209
45. Penguin *Dictionary of Art and Artists* 4th edition 1976 p.382
46. Walker p.126
47. ibid p.175
48. ibid p.203
49. ibid p.204

50. ibid p.199-209
51. Nicolas vol I p.480
52. Keynes, M. 'Horatio Nelson never was Blind' *Journal of Medical Biography* 1998 vol 6 p.114–9
53. *Nelson's Letters to Lady Hamilton* vol 2 p.46
54. Beatty p.82

CHAPTER IV

'His Belly off Cape St. Vincent'

The severe wounds Nelson received at Calvi did not interfere with his service or force him to return home to England. He continued as Captain of *Agamemnon* and was very much involved in the Battle of the Gulf of Genoa. Under Nelson *Agamemnon* was, not surprisingly, a very 'active' ship. However, ill-health also occurred on board. Nelson wrote to Lord Hood 'Poor *Agamemnon* wants almost a new ship's company ... I have been so low with flux and fever this last cruise that I thought I shall barely get over it.'[1] A diagnosis is not possible as he gave no further details.

In March 1795 Nelson hoisted his broad pennant as Commodore. Two months later the new Commander-in-Chief in the Mediterranean, Admiral Sir John Jervis, transferred Nelson to a new ship – *Captain* – and gave him a captain of his own, Ralph Miller. For the next 11 months *Captain* was involved in blockades, occupations and evacuations in the Mediterranean. Then on 14th February 1797 she played an extremely important role in the defeat of the Spanish Fleet at the Battle of Cape St. Vincent. During this battle Nelson sustained a severe abdominal wound, the long term effects of which were to trouble him for the rest of his life.

In August 1804 Nelson wrote a list of his wounds in a letter to a friend, Admiral Sir Robert Kingsmill, Bt. He mentioned his eye, arm and head wounds, but second on the list was 'His Belly off Cape St. Vincent.' He added 'When I run over the under-mentioned wounds – I ought to be thankful that I am what I am.'[2]

At Cape St. Vincent Nelson was struck on the side of his abdomen by flying debris of some sort. The official report stated that he was 'bruised, but not obliged to quit the deck.'[3] It is not known at what point in the battle the injury occurred but at the time it in no way hampered his physical activities, which in this battle were considerable. The famous 'Nelson's Patent Bridge for boarding first rates' episode, when he boarded two Spanish ships in quick succession, involved him in much activity. He scrambled along *Captain's* bowsprit and jumped into the stern of *San Nicolas*. He traversed that vessel, boarded the *San Josef* via her main chains, then went to her quarterdeck where the captain of this second Spanish ship 'on bended knee' presented Nelson with his sword and thus surrendered his ship.

These 'acrobatics' Nelson seems to have performed with aplomb, but seventeen days after the battle, Ralph Miller, the captain of *Captain* wrote an account of the battle to his father, and in this account he says, 'My noble Commodore [who] was struck in the side by the splinter of a block and would have fallen had not my arms supported him.'[4] So a primary source shows how serious was the wound. After the battle Nelson transferred to *Irresistible,* because *Captain* was so badly damaged. Later that same day, he was able to come on board his Commander's flagship apparently without difficulty and receive Sir John Jervis' personal congratulations. And the next morning, despite his wound, Nelson went back on board *Captain* to give Miller 'a beautiful ring, a topaz set round with diamonds ... as a token of his esteem.'[5]

Nevertheless the wound was potentially severe, as Nelson at the time fully realised. The day after the battle he wrote to Sir Gilbert Elliot 'Among the slightly wounded is myself, but it is only a contusion and of no consequence, unless an inflammation takes place in my bowels, which is the part injured.'[6] He excused himself from a Court Martial in a letter dated 17th February citing '... my present state of health ... without danger of making it worse ...'[7]

Nelson wrote to William Locker on 21st February 'I was too unwell to write to you by the *Lively*'[8] – the frigate which bore official news of the battle to Britain – but gives no details.

Nelson wrote at least nine letters to his wife in the eight weeks after the battle. He did not mention his having been wounded in any of them, almost certainly because he knew she would have worried excessively.

The effects of the wound continued to bother him in both the medium and long term. In a letter to the Duke of Clarence ten weeks after the battle, Nelson wrote: 'My health is getting so indifferent from want of a few months' repose, and the pains I suffer in my inside, that I cannot serve, unless it is absolutely necessary, longer than this summer.'[9]

Clearly there was no subsequent 'inflammation of the bowels,' but Nelson was left with a permanent life-long abdominal weakness or hernia. In a letter of November 1804 to Lady Hamilton he mentioned 'My cough is very bad, and my side, where I was struck on 14th February is very much swelled; at times a lump as large as my fist, brought on, occasionally, by violent coughing.'[10]

As he was frequently afflicted with severe coughs the hernia must have been a source of considerable discomfort. But there is no record whatsoever that he ever had a bowel stoppage, so it would seem the inner opening of this hernia was a large one, enabling part of the abdominal contents to enter the hernial cavity or sac when abdominal pressure was increased by coughing, but also to leave the sac without marked difficulty and not to remain permanently trapped inside. Such pinching can lead to a reduced or cut-off blood supply – so called 'strangulation' – which, had it happened, could have killed Nelson at a later date.

The 'stoppage of the urine' is an interesting episode. In a letter to his uncle William Suckling, written on board H.M.S. *Irresistible* nine days after the battle, he wrote: 'My hurt at the moment was nothing, but since, it has been attended with a suppression of urine, but the inflammation has gone off, and I am nearly recovered.'[11]

Although there was no mention in this letter of bowel trouble Nelson must have been in severe discomfort when he wrote it. The words 'suppression of urine' suggest an abdominal cause for the symptom. It is impossible to make an accurate diagnosis, but the problem was most likely to have been either swelling of the bladder wall near the mouth of the urethra consequent upon the abdominal blow itself, or (perhaps more likely) bleeding from trauma to the inner bladder wall causing a clot of blood in the bladder cavity. This would temporarily have blocked the urethra and outflow of urine, and then un-blocked as the clot of blood 'resolved' and became smaller. In any event Nelson never seems to have suffered from urinary problems subsequent to this one episode, mentioned on only one occasion to a close relative.

What is very clear from the contemporary quotations is the fatalistic attitude Nelson took to what could easily have been an injury severe enough to cause a slow, lingering death. He fully realised the serious nature of the injury, but ignored the post-injury symptoms all his life, apart from mentioning them in letters to Lady Hamilton.

Successful open bowel surgery attempts in any numbers would not be achieved until the First World War. Photographs of the wounded and dead in earlier conflicts (for example, the American Civil War of 1861–65) frequently showed men with their belts undone and shirts and trousers disarranged. All knew, like Nelson, that a wound which penetrated the abdominal wall and intestines, or a bruising blow which caused 'morbidity of the bowels,' was almost invariably fatal. Either gangrene of the bruised intestine would set in followed by perforation and leakage of bowel contents contaminated by natural bacteria, or intra-abdominal sepsis followed perforation of the abdominal wall and intestines by a bullet. (Faecal contamination to cause complex sepsis was still being used by the Vietcong in the Vietnam War, where pits dug and camouflaged over along jungle trails were staked with sharpened bamboo pieces smeared with faeces, to cause maximum problems to those servicemen who fell into the pits.)

Nelson was extremely lucky that all he was left with was an abdominal wall weakness which does not seem to have been life-threatening. However, Dr Scott indicated that by the last year of Nelson's life the abdominal hernia was giving him much discomfort. 'He was subject to frequent pain in the side, occasioned by the stroke of a spent ball.'[12]

Lastly it must be noted that Beatty's post-mortem report on Nelson made no mention of the abdominal wall weakness; he commented upon the abdominal organs very favourably, referring to 'the sound and healthy state of the ... abdominal viscera, none of which appeared to have ever been the seat of inflammation or disease ...'[13]

Nelson was always thin with a physique which can be described as 'wiry.' He commented about himself that he never ever got fat. His height has been estimated at about 5 ft. 6 ins. (both by measurement of his clothes and from eye-witness accounts) with a waist measurement of 32 inches and a chest circumference of 38/39 inches. The myth that he was short in stature almost certainly arose because he was so thin.

Prior to his death Nelson had complained of head colds which caused bowel problems. For example:

> Although my complaint has no danger attending it, yet it resists the medicines which Dr. Baird has prescribed and I fancy it has pulled me down very much. The cold has settled in my bowels ... Dr. Baird disapproved of rhubarb and has recommended magnesia and peppermint.[14]

It seems likely that the abdominal contents of the hernia did not always return quickly to the abdomen proper but remained in the hernia causing it to be the size of a fist due to Nelson's repeated coughing. Under such circumstances the taking of aperients – mild laxatives such as rhubarb – could have made the condition worse. Baird was quite correct to recommend a soothing medicine to try to settle Nelson's bowel symptoms.

Nelson valued Baird's advice, and after the Boulogne attack he gave the doctor a silver vase for his help with the wounded: 'He deserved it for his humanity.'[15] Nelson's last letter from Deal said, '... both cough and bowels are still very much out of order.'[16]

The next day, on leave, he was back home at Merton. No more is known of bowel complaints until May 1804 when, again in correspondence with Dr. Baird, Nelson complained of many symptoms including a 'violent pain in my side.'[17]

The information that Nelson was struck on the right side of the abdomen comes from Dr. Lambton Este, who is quoted as having written, 'On joining *Victory,* in my first interview with Nelson, he complained of frequent pains in his right side, from former injuries.'[18]

Most probably, swelling due to the contusion was followed by ischaemia (lack of blood supply to the bruised area) and subsequent scarring then occurred. This led to the weakening and loss of an area of abdominal wall tissue, but not of abdominal skin. When Nelson, by coughing, raised his intra-abdominal pressure, this forced some abdominal contents into the weakened area, giving rise to the swelling. For the rest of his life Nelson was in pain and discomfort from the St. Vincent wound.

Notes

1. Quoted in Pocock p.122
2. Nicolas vol VI p.134
3. ibid vol II p.335
4. White, C. 'An eye witness account of the Battle of Cape St. Vincent.' *Trafalgar Chronicle* No. 7 1997 p.54
5. ibid
6. Nicolas vol II p.350
7. White, C. *Nelson: The New Letters* letter 226 p.191
8. Nicolas vol II p.353
9. ibid p.383
10. *Nelson's Letters to Lady Hamilton* vol II p.85
11. Nicolas vol II p.356
12. Gatty A. and Gatty M. *Recollections of the Life of the Reverend A. J. Scott D.D.* 1842 p.199 (hereafter Gatty)
13. Beatty p.83–4
14. Pettigrew *Memoirs of the Life of Vice-Admiral Lord Viscount Nelson, K.B.* vol II p.221–222 (hereafter Pettigrew)
15. ibid p.208
16. ibid p.231
17. Nicolas vol VI p.41
18. ibid p.256

CHAPTER V

'His Arm at Tenerife'

After the euphoria of the victory at Cape St. Vincent, Nelson was created a Knight of the Order of the Bath, promoted to Rear Admiral of the Blue, and transferred to a 74-gun ship, *Theseus*. Some five months later, *Theseus* assisted in a bombardment of Cadiz. On 15th July 1797, she was part of a squadron of three '74s' plus one 50-gun ship, three frigates and a cutter, under the overall command of Nelson, sent off by Admiral Sir John Jervis (newly created Earl St. Vincent) with orders to proceed to Tenerife, capture Santa Cruz, seize a Spanish treasure ship in the harbour with its cargo, and capture or destroy all other enemy vessels.

Owing to a combination of adverse circumstances the attack was a disaster, and Nelson lost his right arm. In 1806 Lady Nelson prepared for Clarke and M'Arthur's biography of Nelson, an account of the events of July 1797. Since she would have had first hand accounts from both her husband and her son, Josiah Nisbet, the account rings very true. Lady Nelson's Memorandum of the Events of July 1797 reads:

The night Sir Horatio Nelson lost his arm he called Lieut. Nisbet into his cabin, whose watch it was, to assist him in sorting Lady N. letters in order to burn them saying they would not fall into the hands of anyone. After this business was done he said 'What are you equipped for? The care of the ship falls to you.' 'The ship, Sir, must take care of herself.' 'You must not go, supposing your poor mother was to lose us both, what will she do?' 'I will go this night if I never go again.' In the act of Sir H. putting his foot over the boat he was shot thro' the elbow. Lieut. N. who was close to him saw him turn his head from the flash of the guns, say to him 'I am shot thro' the elbow.' Upon which he seated him in the boat. The sight of the blood pouring from the arm affected him. Lieut. N. took off his hat in order to catch the blood and feeling where the bones were broken he grasped the arm with one hand which stopped the bleeding, the revolting of the blood was so great that Sir H. said he never could forget it and he tied up his arm and placed him as comfortably as he could with his two silk neckerchiefs from his throat, and then found one Lovel a seaman and five other sailors to assist in rowing him off … When the boat reached the side of the ship Nisbet called out 'Tell the surgeon the Admiral is wounded and he must prepare for amputation,' upon which they offered to let down the chair, Sir H. Nelson said 'No I have yet my legs and one arm,' and he walked up the side of the ship, Lieut. N. keeping so close that in case he had slipped he could have caught him.

On getting on the quarter deck the officers as usual saluted him by taking off their hats, which compliment Nelson returned with his left hand as if nothing had happened.

Lovel took off his shirt and gave him slips to tie the poor arm round his neck.[1]

Although Fanny's account says he was shot through the elbow, and Surgeon Eshelby's records say: 'a little above the elbow,' the actual amputation was very high and it appears from paintings (especially that by Edridge) and the Westminster Abbey shirt that Nelson was left with little more than the shoulder joint and about four inches of the humerus of his right arm. This was later confirmed by Lady Nelson herself when she wrote to William Suckling, 'My husband's spirits are very good although he suffers a good deal of pain – the arm is taken off very high, near the shoulder. Opium procures him rest and last night he was pretty quiet.'[2] Several post-amputation portraits confirm the high amputation, showing high 'return' of the empty sleeve across Nelson's chest. The copy of the Surgeon's log[3] clearly shows the missile was a musket ball.

Almost all the biographies of Nelson say that he did not want to go aboard *Seahorse*, the first ship he reached when being rowed away from the shore after being wounded, while the *Seahorse's* captain, Thomas Freemantle, was still fighting on land and his fate unknown to Nelson. This was because he did not want to upset Freemantle's very young wife who was on board. But other considerations also weighed. All Nelson's gear was on board *Theseus*. And he would have known Thomas Eshelby, the surgeon, and Louis Remonier, the French royalist surgeon's mate, whereas the surgeon on *Seahorse* was a stranger to him. Nelson's first letter to his wife written with his left hand calls Eshelby 'a good surgeon.'[4]

After the amputation Remonier helped to nurse Nelson on board *Theseus* and was paid extra for this, but Eshelby left *Theseus* with Nelson when the latter was invalided home in *Seahorse* and came back to England with him, assisting in his post-operative care. Eshelby also looked after Captain Freemantle on the inward voyage. Freemantle had a soft tissue wound of his arm which did not require amputation but was very painful and slow to heal. Eshelby had further medical duties as he was also required to diagnose and treat Freemantle's wife Betsy, who was in the early months of her first pregnancy! Nelson wrote to his wife:

Theseus, at Sea August 5, 1797
My Dearest Fanny,

I am so confident of your affection that I feel the pleasure you will receive will be equal whether my letter is wrote by my right hand or left, it was the chance of war and I have great reason to be thankful, and I know it will add much to your pleasure in finding that Josiah under God's providence was principally instrumental in saving my life. As to my health it never was better and now I hope soon to return to you ... I shall not close this letter till I join the fleet having a good surgeon on board, in short I am much more recovered than any could have expected.

I beg neither you or my father will think much of this mishap. My mind has long been made up to such an event ...

August 16th: Just joined the fleet, perfectly well and shall be with you perhaps as soon as this letter.

Good Earl St. Vincent has made Josiah master and commander ....

> God bless you and my father and ever believe
> me your most affectionate
> HORATIO NELSON
>
> To Lady Nelson, Bath.[5]

It is a fascinating letter, most especially for the remarks about the 'mishap.' Nelson had been at great pains to secure his stepson's future, writing to Earl St. Vincent the night of the attack in Santa Cruz at 8 p.m. – the attack was two-and-a-half hours later:

Theseus off Santa Cruz, July 24th, 8pm
My Dear Sir,

I shall not enter on the subject while we are not in possession of Santa Cruz; your partiality will give credit, that all has hitherto been done which was possible, but without effect; this night I, humble as I am, command the whole, destined to land under the batteries of the Town, and tomorrow my head will probably be crowned with either laurel or cypress. I have only to recommend Josiah Nisbet to you and my Country. With every affectionate wish for your health, and every blessing in this world, believe me your most faithful,

> HORATIO NELSON

The Duke of Clarence, should I fall in the service of my King and Country, will, I am certain, take a lively interest for my Son-in-Law, on his name being mentioned.[6]

The Duke of Clarence had of course been chief guest at Nelson's wedding. Nelson's letter was a typical one. He took total responsibility for the result of the action he and the sailors under his command were about to undertake, entrusted his stepson to St. Vincent's patronage should he be killed and, at the same time, let him know that he (Nelson) had friends in high places who would also keep an eye open for Josiah's future should he not be there to do so.

So what of the actual wound itself? After fainting and haemorrhaging profusely from the injured artery, once Josiah applied a tourniquet and prevented him from being upset by the sight of all the blood, Nelson recovered quickly. It is known from a portrait painted that before he lost his arm that he looked young for his age – he was 39.[7] All the famous portraits were painted after 1797. The most famous, by Abbott, was first painted only three months after the loss of his arm and while he was still in the throes of the severe post-operative complications. Comparison with the later portraits shows post-operative weight loss and ageing – the clear results of prolonged pain, sleeplessness and chronic sepsis. The Abbott painting also shows the bow ties on the outer aspect of the right sleeve. It was common practice to cut the arm of a uniform after an amputation so that the stump of the limb could be eased in and out of the coat sleeve by a helper and also so that the stump could be examined and dressed without removing the coat. Three ties held the cut in the uniform sleeve together.

Having 'walked up the side of the ship,' and saluted the officers of the watch, Nelson would have been taken down to the orlop deck, but not before one of his protegés, of whom he was extremely fond, young Midshipman Hoste (who may have been left on board *Theseus* by Nelson deliberately so as to ensure his life was not endangered) gave further first-hand details of the scene in a letter home to his parents. Hoste wrote:

At two in the morning Admiral Nelson returned on board, being dreadfully wounded in the right arm … I leave you to judge my situation, when I beheld our boat approach with him, who I may say has been a second father to me, his right arm dangling by his side, while with the other he helped himself to jump up the ship's side, and with a spirit that astonished every one, told the surgeon to get his instruments ready, for he knew he must lose his arm, and that the sooner it was off the better. He underwent the amputation with the firmness and courage that have always marked his character.[8]

During battles, time becomes telescoped and watches are not always synchronised. The first sentence of Hoste's account is particularly interesting – Hoste himself may have been inaccurate – because the log of *Theseus* records that Nelson returned on board at 3.30 a.m. The expedition did not leave *Theseus* until 10.30 p.m., but it does appear that there was considerable delay in getting Nelson to the surgeon. It is probable the interval between injury and amputation was well in excess of two hours. Yet with all the physical shock of the wound, pain, haemorrhage, time spent in the open boat and amputation shock, Nelson seems to have got over the immediate ordeal rapidly.

Most important of all, for such an inveterate letter writer, he began to practice writing with his left hand. His first left-handed signature was written on a copy of the British ultimatum to the Spaniards the day after the amputation. His first full letter was to Earl St. Vincent within two days later. Not unnaturally it was depressed in content: 'Burthen [sic] to my friends and useless to my Country … when I leave your command I become dead to the world; I go hence, and am no more seen[9]… the remains of my carcass.' But the postscript was slightly up-beat. 'You will excuse my scrawl considering it is my first attempt.'[10] In between was a short note written to Betsy Freemantle: 'God Bless you and Freemantle. Horatio Nelson.' It must have already been obvious to him that he could go on writing with his left hand and that once he was recovered from his amputation, if he was well supported by servants and friends over practical matters such as cutting up his food and helping him to dress and undress, he would not necessarily have to retire from active service. The entry in the Log of *Theseus* for Tuesday, 25th July 1797 reads:

> At half past 10 the seamen and marines left the ship under the command of Admiral Nelson … At half past 3 Admiral Nelson returned on board wounded in the right Elbow which occasioned his Arm to be cut off …[11]

Later Nelson sent to Earl St. Vincent a 'list of killed, wounded, drowned and missing of his Majesty's ships under-mentioned, in storming Santa Cruz on the Island of Tenerife on the night of the 24th July 1797.' The first on a list of five 'Officers wounded' was 'Rear-Admiral Nelson, his right arm shot off.'[12]

Why did Nelson's arm have to be amputated? Modern surgery would have been able to save the arm using X-rays and treatment including removal of compromised tissue lacking proper blood supply, the bullet and any bone splinters, insertion of a rod or rods into the fractured bone(s) for internal fixation, antibiotic cover, prophylactic anti-tetanus injections, proper immobilisation of the affected limb, blood transfusion to combat blood loss and 'shock' – all these modern medical aids would be used as a matter of course to ensure good healing of the broken bone, and prevent infection at the site.

No such aids were available to Eshelby and Remonier. John Bell, a British army surgeon writing in the late eighteenth century noted, 'If all limbs be kept, many must gangrene, if no amputations be performed all the shattered stumps must gangrene, then the sloughing stumps and gangrene limbs ... must infect the whole.'[13] Amputation was the safest treatment for compound limb injuries – injuries where the bone was exposed – since overwhelming sepsis was the likely sequel of conservative management.[14] It was also advocated for severe macerated soft tissue disruption, vascular damage, joint injury and developing sepsis.[15] Nelson, a layman, was nevertheless fully aware of current medical practice, as was his stepson. Once they both realised the musket ball had caused a compound fracture of Nelson's right arm, they knew amputation was inevitable. The early Victorian surgeon, G. J. Guthrie's dictum, 'When a limb cannot be saved it is to be amputated without delay.'[16] was being followed 58 years before he pronounced it. In soft tissue wounds caused by small gunshot, surgeons usually attempted to remove the missile, which is why Ruspini's newly invented 'Instrument for the Extraction of Balls from Gun-shot Wounds.'[17] is so fascinating. Beatty probed Nelson's fatal wound with his finger and could not locate the ball. *Victory* clearly did not carry Ruspini's combined probe/forceps. Ruspini wrote 'the probe and the forceps hitherto in use have been found, in many instances, injurious in their operation, as they frequently still further lacerate the part, and often bring away some of the integuments along with the ball.'[18] Even with the advent of Listerian antiseptic surgical principles in the 1870s infections continued to occur. In pre-antibiotic days any infection could spread and kill the patient but the one infection dreaded above all others was gas gangrene – a form of infection caused by the anaerobic organism, *Chlostridium welchii*, which flourishes especially in torn tissues with impaired blood supply and consequent poor oxygenation. Once it gains a hold in such tissues *Chlostridium welchii* infections spread rapidly along tissue 'planes' causing local tissue death, toxicity and all too often a rapid, overwhelming spread of the infection and then the death of the patient.

The severe pain and infection associated with the second ligature which was so slow to come away at Nelson's amputation site was not due to gas gangrene; if it had been, he would have died. It is not possible now to diagnose the causative bacteria which was associated with an external sore area the size of a shilling. But a degree of toxicity was present, judging by the effect the wound had on Nelson before the ligature came away and the whole began to heal. He clearly lost weight, and was prevented from sleeping properly for months by the pain of the wound, to such an extent that opium had to be prescribed for him. Fortunately, as we shall see later, those involved procrastinated when the possibility of a second operation upon the right arm was mooted. Any further surgical 'tinkering' with the wound, especially in the presence of the pre-existing sepsis, would have almost certainly caused nothing but harm to Nelson, and might well have killed him. (The author, as a clinical medical student, witnessed the death of a patient from a fulminating gas gangrene infection, in 1961. Despite intensive antibiotic medication the spread of the infection was remorseless, and has never been forgotten.)

The actual amputation was done by Thomas Eshelby with Louis Remonier assisting, holding the wounded arm. Nelson would probably have been made to lie on sea chests placed together to make a temporary operating table, with two other assistants to hold him still, although none are recorded. There is no record of analgesics (painkillers in the form of alcohol or opium, which would have been available to the surgeon) being given to him before the operation. The time taken for the amputation was probably about ten minutes. Other assistants would have had to be present holding candle lanterns as the amputation was performed in the middle of the night. The actual operation done by Eshelby was in the usual form of a circular, guillotine method, to cut through soft tissue, followed by the surgeon using a saw for the humerus bone itself. Remonier would have held the arm above the amputation site and pulled hard upwards towards the shoulder while another assistant held the hand and lower arm. Pulling hard upwards on the soft tissues would have ensured that after the amputation there would be a pad of soft tissue available to cover the stump of bone. Bleeding was controlled with a screw tourniquet round the uppermost part of the arm. The large brachial artery would have been ligated (tied off) first and then the tourniquet would have been slowly released, with smaller blood vessels identified and tied off as they bled. It is known Nelson had two main ligatures in his wound and the silk thread used for these was left long, protruding from the amputation site. The wound itself was not sutured; the edges were probably taped together.

Oozing points may have been dusted with flour. Flour particles (although probably containing weevils) would have clogged together with fluid from the oozing surfaces and almost certainly have contained less bacteria than the bandages and rags available in the orlop deck of *Theseus*. As an aid to stop oozing from open wounds and prevent bacteria gaining entrance to traumatized flesh, it was probably extremely efficacious provided the clogged flour could be kept in position on the wound. Crumplin says amputees found the most painful parts of the operation were 'the skin incisions and the taking up of the artery, which often included perivascular tissues, and was described as a powerful burning sensation,'[19] but the cutting of the arm muscles themselves must also have been very painful for Nelson. Two days later he wrote to Jervis 'I am in great pain.'[20]

After amputation Nelson was asked if he wanted the amputated arm for embalming, prior to being sent home for burial. He was totally unsentimental about what had happened. 'Throw it into the hammock with the brave fellow that was killed beside me.'[21]

After the amputation was finished Nelson was given 3 gr. Pil Opii. This amount of opium was probably equivalent to 30 mg. Morphine – a large oral dose. By this time he was somewhat 'collapsed' and complained of (and remembered vividly) the coldness of the instruments used upon him. Years later he instructed the then surgeon of *Victory*, George McGrath, always to have buckets of warm water in the cockpit to warm up his instruments prior to use.

As a post-amputation patient Nelson was put on a liquid or semi-liquid diet of sago. One ligature came away readily. The other did not. It is not possible to give a reason. John Charnock, who wrote a very early biography of Nelson, recorded:

> In the very great hurry and confusion … some mistake was made in taking up one of the arteries, in consequence of which the Admiral suffered the most excruciating torture for several months.[22]

Nelson thought a nerve had been taken up with the ligated artery and on 6th October 1797 wrote to Earl St. Vincent from London:

> My poor arm continues quite as it was, the ligature still fast to the nerve, and very painful at times. The moment I am cured I shall offer myself for service – and … shall press to return with the zeal, although not with all the personal ability, I had formerly.[23]

Others thought it might have been a ligament taken up with the artery which would be even slower to separate. For example, St. Vincent wrote to Nelson, after the second ligature came away: 'My dear Admiral, I congratulate you, Lady Nelson and your Country most heartily, on your being released from the torment of the ligament.'[24]

The night-time operating conditions on board *Theseus* must have been extremely difficult. In all probability, while one ligature was secured only to an artery and soft tissue, as was the custom, the other, when tied, included a ligament or a nerve as well as the artery. The medical log clearly says Nelson sustained a 'Compound fracture of the right arm by a musket ball passing through a little above the elbow, an artery divided.'[25]

The principle of ligating an artery was that it stopped the arterial blood loss, and gave the artery behind the tied off, cut, end, the chance to block off and heal as the wound healed. Once this had happened, the ligature sloughed away and could be pulled out of the wound. In pre-antibiotic times, as long as the ligature stayed within the wound it was a potential source for infection, since serous oozing from the wound site contaminated the ligature material (usually silk) and offered a pathway for bacteria to enter deep into the wound.

So one of Nelson's ligatures came away quickly and easily within 25 days of the amputation, but the second did not. Although one cannot be certain, obviously, if the ligature was taken up with a nerve or a ligament, the sloughing process would have been much more delayed than if only an artery with soft tissue was tied off. Nelson was advised by his brother that an incorporated nerve might be the main cause of all his pain. But deep sepsis associated with the persistent ligature was almost certainly another factor shown by a septic area the size of a shilling piece on the outer part of the amputation site which was very slow to heal.

Later annotations in *Theseus's* Medical Journal showed that 26 days elapsed between the amputation and Nelson's transfer to the *Seahorse*. Post-operative reports indicate that he 'rested pretty well and quite easy.' with the help of opium pills.[26] These induced constipation and on at least three occasions he was treated with two aperients: Senna and Jalup. He was also given cinchona which suggests he had a recurrence of malaria while in the immediate post-operative state. The first ligature must have come away within three weeks of the amputation since its coming away is recorded before Nelson was 'Discharded [sic] on board the *Seahorse* on 20th August.'[27]

The very last 'symptoms and treatment while under cure' report from on board *Theseus* recorded 'Continued getting well very fast. Stump looked well. No bad symptom whatever occurred.' But there was a sentence in the Remarks Column which contained the merest hint that all was not going completely to plan. It read 'the sore reduced to the size of a shilling. In perfect good health. One of the ligatures not come away.'[28] At one point after Nelson's arrival in London the possibility of a second operation was mooted, presumably to try and relieve the severe pain at the amputation site that had developed and which was causing him sleepless nights only relieved by the taking of opium. Fortunately, Nelson was seen and examined by three very eminent medical practitioners. Sir James Earle was son-in-law to Sir Percival Pott – probably one of the greatest surgeons of the age – and himself a Master of the Surgeons Company, and for 32 years a surgeon at St. Bartholomew's Hospital in London. John Rush was a senior army surgeon and Inspector-General of Hospitals. Thomas Keate was Surgeon to the Prince of Wales, a surgeon at St. George's Hospital, and Surgeon-General to the Army. Their wise councils prevailed, and a 'wait and see' policy was pursued. Further operative interference would have undoubtedly introduced more bacteria on the reopening of the wound.

After the amputation of his arm, Nelson experienced phantom limb pain. Phantom limb pain is the unpleasant perception of the presence, totally or in part, of the lost part of the body. That Nelson experienced this is not so surprising. Some 60% of patients may have phantom limb pain in the months following amputation[29] and the incidence of pain persisting after about two years is at least 50%.[30] The only confirmation that Nelson experienced the phenomena came from a letter from his brother William written to Nelson some thirteen weeks after Eshelby had amputated his arm. William wrote:

> I conclude and hope you are doing well even tho' it is but slowly. I this day met with Bayly, a Swaffham surgeon and esteemed a very good one. I mentioned particularly the apparent pain in your right hand. He said it was a sure sign of a nerve being taken up with the artery, indeed he says it is hardly possible to avoid it, as there are so many and such small ones that you must now have patience and all will do well, but he thinks the ligature had better not be forced too much.'[31]

William Nelson's letter clearly proves that 18th-century surgeons knew about the phenomenon of phantom limb (even local surgeons in a small town in Suffolk), that they were aware the symptoms eventually cleared up – and were prepared to give medical advice without recompense! Typically, in a good, well-healed amputation, the 'memory' of the lost part of the body gradually disappears, and this is what seems to have happened with Nelson. The exact mechanism of phantom limb is still not known for certain. One theory is that cells in a part of the brain, the somato-sensory cortex, which once received signals from the nerves in the now amputated limb, 'fire' excessively when this normal input ceases.[32] This may give rise to the feeling that the amputated part is still attached, which Nelson seems not to have experienced. An alternative theory is that an 'image' of the lost limb may be created in the brain by spontaneous nerve (neural) activity so that sensation of a phantom limb may arise from incoming signals from the cut nerve end.[33] 'A single, simple mechanism is unlikely to account for the phantom limb experience.'[34]

Whatever the cause, William's letter was the only mention of phantom limb problems. The story that Nelson once told a friend that his phantom limb pain had confirmed his belief in the immortality of the soul now appears to be apocryphal. Despite extensive recent searches by several Nelson experts, and the author, no primary source for this account has been found.

Another important point must be made. Once on the way to proper recovery Nelson continued to behave in a completely characteristic fashion with regard to the loss of his arm. A note was sent to the Vicar of St. George's, Hanover Square, saying: 'An Officer desires to return thanks to Almighty God for his perfect recovery from a severe wound, and also for many mercies bestowed upon him.'[35] When Nelson was pain-free, and found that he could still write; that with a servant's help, he could dress; and with the aid of Lady Spencer's gift of a fork-knife he could feed himself; then he was almost completely independent, and there was nothing to stop him from returning to active service. (One example of the fork-knife was lot 173 in the Christie, Manson, Woods sale of 'Old English silver and silver-gilt, etc, formerly in the possession of Admiral Viscount Nelson,' on 12th July 1895, described as 'Gold with a steel edge, engraved with an 'N' and a baron's coronet, and presented to Nelson by Countess Spencer.' It sold that day for the then very high price of £260. A different example, a fork with an ivory handle and an attached blade, to convert it into a fork-knife, is in the Nelson Gallery at the National Maritime Museum, Greenwich.) Nelson set sail in *Vanguard* from Spithead on 29th March 1798. With Nelson, events always moved fast. His arm had been amputated on 25th July 1797, and he had arrived back in England on 1st September. The same year in late November the second ligature came away and the arm began to heal. So just over nine months after the catastrophe of Tenerife, he was back at sea. He rejoined Earl St. Vincent off Cadiz, and was at once sent into the Mediterranean in command of a detached squadron to seek out a large French expeditionary force assembling at Toulon. One year and six days after losing his arm, Nelson and his 'band of brothers' smashed the naval part of this expeditionary force at the Battle of the Nile, and changed the course of history.

The long-term effects of the loss of his right arm upon Nelson were that firstly, the stump ached when there was going to be a change in the weather, and Nelson used this symptom as a sort of personal 'barometer.'[36] He named the very short stump of his right arm his 'fin' and he took to expressing inner anger and irritation by over-activity of the stump, and shipmates who observed the 'fin' being moved excessively warned each other to avoid talking to him until he had calmed down. On one occasion he identified himself thus: 'I'm Lord Nelson – see here is my "fin".' Nelson also made a play on words relating to the loss of his arm on at least two occasions.

Nelson must be the most famous person ever to be forced to change from using the favoured to the less favoured hand. Examples of his handwriting, from both right and left hands, and how it altered over the years, and with the effect of the Nile head wound, are on pages 116, 136, and 264.

Patients on whom amputation is performed of course always experience mental effects as a result of the operation, and Nelson was no exception; but there appear to have been no morbidly depressive reactions by him to the loss. In the short term he was undoubtedly reactively depressed, and as has been mentioned, quoted a passage from the order for the Burial of the Dead, from the Book of Common Prayer, in his first post-amputation letter to St. Vincent. Clarke and M'Arthur recorded that his words on being shot, as heard by his stepson, were 'I am shot through the arm; I am a dead man.'[37] Murray Parkes & Napier, in their paper on 'Psychiatric Sequelae of Amputation' state: 'Grief is the universal reaction precipitated by crises of loss,'[38] and go on to quote Fisher: 'The reaction to loss of a limb ... is grief and depression.'[39]

A.W.F. English, writing on the subject of 'Psychology of Limb Loss' wrote: 'Psychologically the loss of a limb may closely parallel the death of a loved one, and the amputee may experience many of the same emotions that accompany bereavement.'[40]

Murray Parkes & Napier considered in depth the loss involved in amputation, and how it was perceived by the victim, together with examination of the deprivation caused by the loss of a limb, whether the amputee had to alter his role in life and whether family and friends might consider the patient less of a person for having an altered body, and body image. They acknowledged that the amputee could lose not only the limb and its functions, but also feel himself less of a person. They also wrote: 'How he [the amputee] reacts will depend on the nature of the experience, his personality and previous life experience, his expectation of disability both conscious and unconscious and his appraisal of the problems created, as well as the resources provided by his family and by society.'[41]

Nelson, apropos the observations of Murray Parkes and Napier, seems to have coped with his arm loss very well. He began to adapt very quickly after the amputation, writing with his left hand within two days. His first letters *were* depressive: to St. Vincent – 'A left handed Admiral will never again be considered as useful;'[42] to his wife – 'I shall not be surprised to be neglected and forgot, as probably I shall no longer be considered as useful,'[43] to his Uncle William – 'Till I can find a hut to put my mutilated carcass in;'[44] and to St. Vincent again – '… I have suffered great misery.'[45] But in a way Nelson had been 'lucky' for the loss was not the sudden appalling shock it might have been. As mentioned he had written to his wife: 'My mind has long been made up to such an event.'[46] He then quickly rationalised the loss in patriotic terms: in a letter to a friend, 'I regret not the loss of my arm in the cause it fell from me.'[47] and to the Duke of Clarence, 'I assure your Royal Highness that not a scrap of that ardour with which I have hitherto served our King has been shot away.'[48]

He wrote to his wife, post-operatively, 'I am so confident of your affection…'[49] He knew she would not reject him, whatever he looked like. In the event, neither did 'John Bull' or Nelson's Commander-in-Chief. Earl St. Vincent took all the responsibility for the defeat at Tenerife, and Nelson was now singled out by the populace as a successful naval commander, severely wounded in his country's cause. By the sixth post-operative week, Nelson's jocular sense of humour was beginning to return. Writing from Bath to Dixon Hoste, the father of his midshipman protegé, William Hoste, he wrote:

As to myself, I suppose I was getting well too fast, for I am beset with a Physician, Surgeon, and Apothecary, and, to say the truth, am suffering much pain with some fever, but time I hope will restore me to tolerable health.[50]

It was not until mid-December when he left Bath and went up to London that the second ligature came away and the arm began properly to heal.

A list of the 'expenses attending the amputation of his wound,' which were kept by Nelson, make it completely clear that it was Thomas Eshelby who amputated his arm and Louis Remonier who assisted. Messrs. Rush, Earle & Keate were the three surgeons who advised non-interference when the wound refused to heal.

Below is an account of Admiral Nelson's expenses attending the cure of his wound from the 25th July 1797 to the 13th December:

Paid Lewis Remonier for assisting in amputating
my arm and for attendance from 25th July
1797 to 17th August following during which time
he sat up 14 nights.   £25 4/0d

Paid Thomas Eshelby for amputating my arm,
quitting the *Theseus* and attending me to England
in the *Seahorse* frigate from the 25th July to
3rd September.   £36

Paid Mr. Nicholls at Bath for dressing my arm
and attendance from the 3rd to 18th September.   £12

Paid Mr. Spry for medicines at Bath   £2
Dr. Faulkner for advice   £1 1/0d

Paid Mr. Cruikshanks for 30 days' attendance   £31 10/0d

Paid Messrs. Rush/Earle/Keate for advice   £3 3/0d

Paid Michael Jefferson for attendance from
19th October to the 13th December 1797   £24 3/0d

Paid for sick quarters from 3rd September
to the 13th December 1797 being 102 days.   [illegible]

SEQUENCE OF EVENTS AFTER
THE AMPUTATION OF NELSON'S ARM

Date	Event
25.7.1797	Arm amputated on board *Theseus*
From 25.7.1797	On board *Theseus*, receiving treatment from Eshelby and Remonier
?26.7.1797	Writes first brief note with left hand
27.7.1797	Writes first proper letter to Earl St. Vincent
20.8.1797	Transferred to Seahorse with Eshelby
1.9.1797	*Seahorse* back in England at Spithead
3.9.1797	Goes to Bath, reunited with wife and father
8–18.9.1797	In Bath attended by: a) Mr Nichols who dresses his arm and is paid £12 b) Dr Faulkner – attends once for advice Travels to London. Treated by: Mr. Cruikshank (cost £1 per day) for 30 days Writes to a Mrs Robinson, 'I feel great pain at times from my wound.'
6.19.1797	Writes to Earl St. Vincent 'My poor arm continues quite as it was, the ligature still fast to the nerve.'
12.10.1797	First attendance at Private Court of Examiners, Lincoln's Inn Fields, with regard to his eye. Sees the following examiners: John Gunning, Charles Hawkins, Isaac Minns, Samuel Howard, William Lucas, James Earle, Joseph Warner
19.10–13.12.1797	Michael Jefferson takes over the care of the wound and is paid 23 guineas
19.10.1797	Sees surgeons about his arm: James Earle, Thomas Keate, John Rush
4.12.1797	Second ligature comes away
8.12.1797	Wound begins to heal: sepsis resolves
13.12.1797	Thanksgiving message at St George's Church, Hanover Square
mid-Dec 1797	Nelson pronounced fit for service again. Nelson arranges for Michael Jefferson to be appointed to *Vanguard*
19.12.1797	Nelson hoists his flag on *Vanguard* actively preparing to sail to rejoin St. Vincent

1.3.1798	Nelson again before Court of Examiners who agree his medical expenses are reasonable. He sees James Earle, William Long, William Lucas, William Cooper, Charles Hawkins, Joseph Warner, Samuel Howard, George Chandler
29.3.1798	Nelson sails on *Vanguard*
30.4.1798	Rejoins St. Vincent off Cadiz
1.8.1798	Battle of the Nile – one year and six days since Nelson had lost his arm

Notes:

1. Naish p.374
2. Nicolas vol II p.441
3. *Log of HMS Theseus* 27th May to 18th August 1791 P.R.O. ADM 123/2
4. Naish p.333
5. ibid p.332–3
6. Nicolas vol II p.421
7. Walker p.8, 191
8. Nicolas vol II p.423
9. Psalm 39 v.13 *Book of Common Prayer* Order for Burial of the Dead.
10. Nicolas vol II p.434–5
11. Power, Sir D'A. 'Amputation' *British Journal of Surgery* vol 19 no. 75 Jan 1932 p.355
12. Nicolas vol II p.424
13. Bell, J. Quoted in Chaloner et al 'Amputation at the London Hospital 1852' *Journal of Royal Society of Medicine* vol 94 August 2001 p.411 (hereafter Chaloner)
14. ibid
15. Crumplin, M. K. H. *Journal of R.S.M.* 1988 vol 81 p.40
16. Guthrie, G. J. 'Military Surgery in the Crimea.' *The Lancet* 1855 vol 1 p.417 Quoted in Chaloner p.411
17. Ruspini, J. B. 'A brief Description of a newly important Instrument, for the Extraction of Balls from Gunshot Wounds.' *Medical & Physical Journal* vol XV No. 85 p.456
18. ibid
19. Crumplin, M. K. H. *Journal of R.S.M.* 1988 vol 81 p.40
20. Nicolas vol VII p.ccxxvi
21. Quoted in Oman p.244

22. Charnock, J. *Biographical Memoirs of Lord Viscount Nelson with Observations critical and explanatory* 1806 p.104
23. Nicolas vol II p.448
24. Clarke and M'Arthur vol 2 p.49
25. A.D.M. 101/23/2 p.9
26. ibid p.10
27. ibid p.16
28. ibid p.15
29. Katz, H. 'Phantom Limb Pain' *The Lancet* vol 350 1997 p.1338
30. Stannard, C. F. 'Phantom Limb Pain' *British Journal of Hospital Medicine* 1993 vol 50 No. 10 p.583 (hereafter Stannard)
31. Naish p.375
32. Carter, R. *Mapping the Mind* 1998 p.126
33. Stannard p.583
34. ibid p.584
35. Nicolas vol II p.455
36. Beatty p.82
37. Clarke and M'Arthur vol 2 p.35
38. Murray Parkes, C. and Napier, M. M. *B.J.H.M.* November 1970 p.610 (hereafter Murray Parkes and Napier)
39. Fisher, S. H. *Archives of Physical Medicine* 1960 vol 41 p.62
40. English, A.W. F. 'Psychology of Limb Loss' *B.M.J.* vol 299 November 1989
41. Murray Parkes and Napier p.610
42. Nicolas vol II p.435
43. ibid p.436
44. ibid p.439
45. ibid p.445
46. ibid p.436
47. ibid p.442
48. ibid p.441
49. Naish p.332
50. Nicolas vol II p.442–3

CHAPTER VI

'His Head in Egypt'

Once the amputation site of Nelson's right arm began to heal he was anxious to return to sea, and did so as soon as possible; but 'Traumatic brain injury causes an almost limitless range of troubles.'[1]

He left England on *Vanguard* and in mid-March 1798 joined St. Vincent off Cadiz. St. Vincent's orders from the Admiralty were either to go into the Mediterranean with his whole fleet (in which case he ran the risk of allowing the Spanish Fleet in Cadiz to put to sea) or to send a detachment of part of his fleet into the Mediterranean to seek out the French Fleet from Toulon. The Admiralty's orders included:

> When you are appraised that the appearance of a British Squadron in the Mediterranean is a condition on which the fate of Europe may at this moment be stated to depend, you will not be surprised that we are disposed to strain every nerve and incur considerable hazard in effecting it.[2]

St. Vincent was told by the Admiralty:

> If you determine to send a detachment into the Mediterranean, I think it almost unnecessary to suggest to you the propriety of putting it under the command of Sir Horatio Nelson whose acquaintance with that part of the world as well as his activity and disposition seem to qualify him in a peculiar manner for that service.[3]

Consequently Nelson was seconded from the main British Fleet by Earl St. Vincent, with a command of his own of twelve ships of 74 guns and three smaller vessels. Sailing in his flag-ship *Vanguard*, he embarked upon a grand chase back and forth across the Mediterranean in pursuit of the French Fleet escorting Napoleon's grand army for the defeat of Egypt. Almost a year to the day after the defeat at Tenerife, Nelson finally cornered the French ships at Aboukir Bay and blew them out of the water.

Nelson himself sustained an extremely severe head wound during the battle, which the author believes altered his emotional stability for at least two years.

At the Battle of the Nile the opposing ships were in very close proximity. The battle was fought in dusk and darkness and an immense amount of high-velocity material would have been flying about. Nobody would have any warning of being struck. When the head is struck a glancing blow by a large piece of heavy debris, a major effect is the rapid rotation of the head on the neck immediately upon impact. All parts of the brain are connected to one another and since the living brain has the consistency of blancmange, and since the brain is enclosed in a solid hard unyielding box, the skull, which has internal projections, it is obvious that shock waves from the blow go through the semi-solid brain tissue and at the same time rotational forces come into play and physical damage to the brain results. This today is measurable electronically. Electro-encephalograms (EEGs) are most commonly used to measure the abnormal electrical activity of the brains of patients with epilepsy. But tracings from such machines can show a typical type of abnormality after a concussive injury such as Nelson received. Taking serial EEGs over a period of (say) two months, shows objective improvement in the EEG, representing the injured person's symptomatic improvement. It has also been reported that deeper brain structures – not just those nearest to the point of impact – are abnormal after head injury; as one would expect, given the web of brain connections.

That Nelson was concussed and then suffered what is called post-concussion syndrome, can be confirmed using an accepted symptom description from 1998 and relating it to Nelson's behaviour during and after the injury.

About forty-five minutes after the battle commenced, Nelson was struck on the right side of his upper forehead by a piece of langridge (pieces of irregularly-shaped iron, tied with rope and fired from cannon to cause maximum damage to sails and rigging). He was lucky. An inch or so lower and it would have destroyed his face. Despite wearing a thick naval hat Nelson's forehead was deeply cut down to the bone. The cut may have been diagonal so that a flap of skin obliterated his good left eye, but it is more likely that pouring blood blinded him. Nelson already had a lot of scar tissue around his right eyebrow so the bleeding from the second head wound was probably even more difficult to control, as scalp and forehead wounds always gape badly and traumatized scar tissue can bleed profusely, and can be very difficult to staunch.

Nelson collapsed into the arms of Captain Edward Berry. His apocalyptic comment 'I am killed! Remember me to my wife!' might be *the* emotional dividing line of his life. As Pugh remarked, it was the last time he expressed such sentiments![4] Thinking he was dying concentrated Nelson's mind wonderfully. Notwithstanding the mistress he had kept at Leghorn, it was of his wife that he thought when he believed he was *in extremis* in 1798, just as when he lay dying in *Victory's* cockpit in 1805, it was to Lady Hamilton and Horatia that his thoughts turned.

Nelson was carried off the deck and down below. Michael Jefferson, the surgeon, brushed aside Nelson's request to take his turn amongst the wounded as was normal procedure in the Navy at the time. He examined Nelson's head, probed the wound and assured him that although the clinical findings were a cut three inches long with over an inch of skull exposed, it was not serious and he was not going to die. The edges of the wound were brought together and strips of adhesive (the forerunner of Elastoplast) kept the skin in place, so the wound was not stitched.

Typically, once he knew he was not mortally wounded, Nelson contacted Captain Louis of the *Minotaur* to thank him for his support of the *Vanguard* in the battle. Then the changes wrought by the head injury began to manifest themselves. Marked irritability and atypical unkindness occurred towards two subordinates, his secretary and his chaplain. The former, himself also wounded, was shocked and of no use so was dismissed out of hand and later out of Nelson's personal service. This act cannot have helped Nelson to deal with all his vast post-victory correspondence commitments.

The Chaplain of *Vanguard* was also found wanting. So Nelson composed the Nile dispatch and wrote it himself, apparently unaided.[5] This is important as it illustrates to perfection the maintenance of Nelson's intellectual powers whilst his emotional behaviour was deteriorating.

In the middle of this work Berry came down to tell Nelson that the French flagship *L'Orient* was on fire. Disobeying doctors' orders Nelson clambered back up on deck to view the 'most grand and awful spectacle' and the battle-stopping explosion. By now Nelson was closely conforming to the criteria for concussion. He was very irritable, could not settle and could not sleep.

Next day, Berry's letter to Captain Ralph Miller of *Theseus* continued to give medical information: 'Sir Horatio I believe to be out of danger tho' his wound is in the head. He has been sick.' On 3rd August, Berry wrote 'He is now more easy than he was this morning, the rage being over.'[6] A 17th-century meaning of 'rage' is 'to be impatient, or furiously eager.' It is in this way that one should look at Berry's use of the word. He almost certainly means what we should now call 'irritable.'

In pathological terms the impact of the missile caused a three-inch cut on Nelson's forehead with profuse bleeding and there was exposure of the skull for more than one inch. Possibly there was a skull fracture. The impact also caused rotation of the head on the neck and the brain within the skull. The impact and rotation in turn caused post-injury swelling of the brain with widespread microscopic injury to many of its nerve fibres and cells. This injury was of a shearing and stretching nature, in turn causing the following symptoms for variable lengths of time:

1. Prolonged severe headaches
2. Vomiting
3. Increased irritability
4. Some degree of disinhibition
5. Reduced tolerance to alcohol
6. Depression
7. Reduction in emotional control

That Nelson was expressing marked depressive ideation and complaining of being almost blind and worn out twelve months and more after the date of his head injury attests to the persistence of many of his symptoms – a serious sign. Michael Jefferson's report on Nelson's wound in the medical journal of *Vanguard* was started on the day of the battle:

Sir Horatio Nelson, K.C.B. etc. Rear-Admiral of the Blue. Aged 40.

Put on the sick list.

Statement of case: Wound on the forehead over the right eye. The cranium bared for more than an inch, the wound three inches long.

Symptoms and treatment while under care:

1st Brought the edges of the wound together and applied strips of Emp. Adhesive. Pil. Anodyn ii nss. [The wound edges were brought together with adhesive strips, not stitched, and opium pills were to be given as necessary]

2nd Mist. Pargarus Pil. Anodyn repd. [As with the arm amputation: opium pills were given for the pain and an aperient given to counteract the constipating side effect of the opium]

3rd Saline solution applied

4th Sticking plaster removed and replaced together with lint

5th and 6th Wound dressed

7th Wound dressed. Pil. Anodyn as necessary. Further aperient given

8th to 31st [Daily dressing entries]

At the end of the report under 'other remarks', Jefferson wrote:

The wound was perfectly healed on the 1st September but as the integuments [the outer skin] were much enlarged applied (every night) a compress wet with a discutient [designed to disperse swellings and tumours] embrocation for nearly a month which was of great service.[7]

Nelson was discharged from Jefferson's sick list on 1st September. Jefferson did not record any leakage of cerebro-spinal fluid, but then neither did he comment on the degree of bruising, which must have been severe. Clearly Nelson was in a lot of pain initially, which required the prescription of opium, but the complaints of his symptoms in his letters are not accompanied by parallel treatment by Jefferson. It is interesting that marked skin swelling occurred at the impact site as this could account for the obvious scarring which can be seen in the post-Nile portraits and possibly have predisposed to the formation of the keloid scar noted and reproduced by Catherine Andras.

The comments in 'Other Remarks' are slightly ambiguous: it may be that Nelson's forehead required wet compresses with the discutient embrocation (probably a lead lotion, a popular soothing preparation of that time) *after* he had been officially discharged from the sick list, and he could have been under Jefferson's care for soft tissue swelling of the forehead until *Vanguard* got into Naples on 22nd September 1798.

As well as looking after Nelson post-battle, Jefferson and his assistants looked after and treated 76 wounded men. Three arm amputations were performed, one wounded man lost an eye and another had a compound fracture of a leg. Jefferson diagnosed a fractured skull, and a 'contused' arm was differentiated from 'wound of arm' which eight casualties experienced. The total number killed on board *Vanguard* was given as 30. The complement of *Vanguard* was 589 men at the start of the battle. The vanquished suffered far more than the victors. The French Fleet was estimated to have lost 3,000 killed and wounded out of a total of 9,828 men, while the British Fleet was said to have suffered 218 killed and 678 wounded out of a total of 7,985 men. Since none of the British ships were lost, their figures would be expected to be more accurate – for example it would be difficult accurately to estimate the complement, or the killed and wounded, on *L'Orient* after she blew up and sank at the height of the battle.

Winning the Battle of the Nile gave Nelson the international heroic status he had always craved, so one would expect his post-battle correspondence to be joyous, optimistic and upbeat. However, Nelson's letters for at least fourteen months after the head wound show that he was seriously unwell during this time, experiencing many symptoms, mainly relating to his head, but his letters to especially close friends also show how depressed he was in spirit. This is demonstrated in the following excerpts from his letters which are to be found in Nicolas vols III and IV, and Charnock's *Biographic & Memories of Lord Viscount Nelson*.

1798

8th August – Sir William Hamilton: 'My head is so indifferent I can scarcely scrawl this letter'

9th August – H.E. The Governor of Bombay [a muddled letter]: 'If my letter is not so correct as might be expected, I trust your excuse, when I tell you that my brain is so shook with the wound in my head that I am sensible I am not always so clear as could be wished'

10th August – Earl St. Vincent: 'My head is ready to split and I am always so sick: in short if there be no fracture, my head is severely shaken'

19th & 29th August – Earl St. Vincent: 'My half head …' and 'My head is so wrong, that I cannot write what I wish in such a manner as to please myself'

21st August – The Hon. William Wyndham: 'My health from my wound is become so indifferent'

29th September – Earl Spencer [at end of a rambling and disinhibited letter]: 'Pray excuse this short letter, and abuse of the Marquis de Gallo'

30th September – Earl St. Vincent [somewhat disinhibited]: 'I am very unwell, and the miserable conduct of this court [Naples] is not likely to cool my irritable temper. It is a country of fiddlers and poets, whores and scoundrels.'

4th October – Earl St. Vincent [somewhat disinhibited]: 'I am writing opposite Lady Hamilton therefore you must not be surprised at the glorious jumble of this letter. Were your Lordship in my place I much doubt if you could write so well: our hearts and our hands must all be in a flutter: Naples is a dangerous place and we must keep clear of it'

9th October – Earl Spencer [disinhibited quotation]: 'to fly to Egypt, clap the Turks on the back and put matters in the best train'

9th November – Earl St. Vincent: 'My mind I know is right, but alas, my body is weak'

29th November – Earl Spencer: 'I occasionally write too freely – I will be active as long as I can but my strength fails daily – [Psalm 38 v.20] therefore pray make allowances for me'

6th December – Commander Duckworth: 'Nor is my present state that of ease; and my health, at best but indifferent, has not mended lately'

10th December – Edward Berry: 'I shall never forget your support for my mind on 1st August'

11th December – Lady Nelson: 'Lord St. Vincent is in no hurry to oblige me now' [Nicolas noted: 'morbid irritability of temper … suspicion of the motives and conduct of his best friends a sufficient … cause is the severe wound in the head which he received at the Nile, of the effects of which he so frequently complained.']

30th December – Earl St.Vincent: 'Under these circumstances I entreat, that if my health and uneasiness of mind should not be mended … permission to leave this command.'

1799

1st January – Earl Spencer: 'I trust I shall not be thought hasty in asking permission to return to England for a few months, to gather a little of that ease and quiet I have so long been a stranger to'
25th January – Earl St. Vincent: 'My health is indeed very indifferent. …There is no true happiness in this life, and in my present state I could quit it with a smile'
31st January – Admiral Goodall: 'Soon, very soon, we must all be content with a plantation of six feet by two and I probably shall possess this estate much sooner than is generally thought'
13th February – Earl St. Vincent: 'As to myself, I see but gloomy prospects look which way I will'
About the end of February – Alexander Davison: 'My only wish is to sink with honour into the grave … I shall meet death with a smile. Not that I am insensible to the honours and riches my King and Country have heaped upon me … yet I am ready to quit this world of trouble, and envy none but those of the estate of six feet by two'
20th March – Earl St. Vincent: 'I am at times ill at my ease … here I am writing from morn to eve: therefore you must excuse this jumble of a letter'
9th April – Captain Ball: 'I am tired to death'
17th April – Earl St. Vincent: 'I am almost blind and worn out and cannot in my present state hold out much longer'
12th June – Earl St. Vincent [The entire 10-line letter is very disinhibited]: 'If you are sick I will fag for you and dear Lady Hamilton will nurse you with our most affectionate attention … We all love you … Your attached, faithful and affectionate, Nelson'
14th July – Ewan Nepean: 'I am writing in a fever, and barely possible to keep out of bed'
27th July – Captain Ball: 'As to myself I have been long sick and tired out'

The structure of the brain must be considered in order to understand what happened to Nelson. The human brain can be divided vertically and horizontally. Vertically, it consists of three parts:

1. The lower-brain is the least complex concerned with very basis functions such as breathing.
2. The mid-brain, simplistically, is the site of the emotions.
3. The upper-brain is divided into two apparently mirror image parts, the left and the right cortex. Each cortex operates in different ways. For most people the left side is concerned with processing logical sequential conscious thoughts – thinking. It is the side of mathematics, language and step-by-step problem solving. The right side is more concerned with feelings, images and intuition, and with creativity.

Another important difference is that the left cortex tends to break problems into constituent parts and handles things one step at a logical time. The right cortex treats things as a whole and handles issues in parallel. The left cortex is capable of so-called convergent thinking which tends to home in on correct solutions to problems. The right cortex performs divergent thinking – considering lots of possibilities, but diverging in any direction to get the best possible answers. The last, fascinating difference is that the left side is more associated with conscious thought and the right side with unconscious thought – concepts not always controlled, day-dreams and feelings – a person's 'state of mind.'

It is contended that when Nelson was struck on the right side of his forehead, his whole skull and brain were rotated so that he sustained alteration in the function mainly of his mid- or emotional brain and his right cortex or 'state of mind' brain.

Nelson appears to have exhibited almost all the symptoms of post-concussion syndrome (P.C.S.) immediately following his serious head wound. From his own accounts we can tell that symptoms persisted for more than six weeks, which again emphasises the seriousness of his wound. On average only thirty-three percent of patients with P.C.S. still have significant symptoms six weeks after an injury,[8] whereas Nelson's letters suggest symptoms persisting for many months. His age at the time of the injury was also against him. Patients with persistent symptoms tend to be older at time of injury. Chronic social difficulties are on average twice as common amongst those with persisting symptoms. So medically, perhaps the coming together of Nelson and Lady Hamilton was an 'accident' waiting to happen.

The anxious, over-worked, severely concussed man who arrived at Naples seven weeks after the battle had informed Earl St. Vincent he would only be staying there five to six days. However, in the face of a situation he had never before experienced – volatile praise from the Italians, overwhelming displays of approval, some of it royal, and the 'matronly' sexuality of Lady Hamilton – Nelson seems, in effect, to have emotionally collapsed. He did not collapse intellectually, but as we have seen above a degree of disinhibition appeared in his letters, and subsequently in his obedience to orders, and his judgments became less accurate. He seemed to have sensed rapidly what was on offer in closely linking himself with the Hamiltons. On the one hand was friendship with Sir William, a highly intelligent 18th-century father figure with whom he could talk freely of the world, politics, the arts, history. On the other hand a warm, loving and highly sexual relationship (which had so far escaped him in his marriage), which Lady Hamilton would offer him, together with unqualified praise, and the possibility of children. An outcome that a brain-damaged man of nearly 40 might find hard to resist.

We can deduce from his letters that the only major symptoms of P.C.S. he does *not* seem to have experienced were concentration and memory difficulties, and dizziness. But Nelson was unwell, the Nile head wound of 1st August 1798 was severe and its effects remained with Nelson for months and in all probability, years. That assumption can be backed up. Not only does the Guzzardi portrait of 1799 show a man with depressive facies wearing a hat which must be tilted back on his head because he cannot bear the pressure of the hat on a five-month-old injury, but third party witnesses wrote descriptions of Nelson ten months and more after the head wound which indicate weight loss, anhedonia, (loss of any feeling of pleasure) and evidence of ageing. Most importantly, in October 1799 (fourteen months after the Battle of the Nile) Lord Elgin, on his way to become British Ambassador in Constantinople, had noted all the above on meeting with Nelson at Palermo, writing 'He has pains pretty consistently from his late wound in the head … His countenance is without animation.' – a comment strongly suggesting continued depression.[9]

The impact of the missile on 1st August 1798 would have knocked Nelson to the deck had he not been caught by Captain Edward Berry. There is no record of a period of unconsciousness and of course no mention or assessment of pre- or post-traumatic amnesias. But the irritability ('rage'), vomiting, and weakness after the injury were noted clearly by others. Significantly, these symptoms persisted. Post-concussion syndrome is a 'cluster of symptoms following on mild head injury.'[10] These symptoms include headache, dizziness, fatigue, memory and concentration difficulties, irritability, labile (fluctuating) emotion, depression and anxiety. Nelson's head injury was interesting in that significantly in his case, some symptoms persisted for many months so that, although he seems *not* to have been knocked unconscious by the impact of the langridge, nevertheless the effects of the impact were severe.

P.C.S. usually lasts for a few weeks or months, but a substantial minority of patients exhibit persistent and troublesome symptoms six months or even one year later.[11] Nelson appears to fall into this latter category, which is said to be about one third of cases diagnosed. It was found in McClelland *et al*'s study that age at time of injury was relevant, older persons having a greater likelihood of prolonged P.C.S. Nelson, at just 40 years of age, fits into the older person category. McClelland performed serial E.E.G. studies on different parts of patients' brains, most especially the brain stem and two parts of the cerebral hemispheres, the temporal and parietal regions. A large amount of diffusely distributed abnormal slow wave activity was a universal finding and these objective abnormal E.E.G. results improved parallel to the clinical improvement of the patients in their care. The primary cause of P.C.S. is diffuse brain cell and small blood vessel injury caused by rapid movement and then cessation of movement within the brain. This is precipitated by the concussive impact on the skull. Obviously none of the above medical information would have been available to Nelson or his doctors. Medically, the most extraordinary fact is that he was able to function at all, let alone that for weeks after the battle he functioned very well intellectually. Experiencing, day after day, a persistent severe headache must have been debilitating for Nelson, especially when there is no contemporary evidence that he was given any treatment for it, after Jefferson discharged him. Judging from his letters he had to struggle on with a very considerable work load for months after the battle. According to Lord Elgin's comments, Nelson's post-traumatic headache persisted a very long time. Nelson's own letters indicate severe depression persisting for at least fourteen months. and for even longer he made comments to colleagues and friends about how unwell he was (alas, with no description of symptoms).

It was almost two years after the Battle of the Nile that Nelson finally struck his flag and left the Mediterranean, going home with the Hamiltons overland via Prague, Dresden, Vienna and Hanover. By this time he had seduced or been seduced by Lady Hamilton and she was pregnant with his child. For a brain-damaged man the period between 27th September 1798 when he reached Naples and was instantly exposed to the fervour on hand there and 13th July 1800 when he left the area had been one of extraordinary activity and complexity. He had watched while the Sardinians, the King of the two Sicilies, and his General, Mack, had first captured Rome and then been routed by the French. Nelson had saved the King and his family and the Hamiltons by taking them from Naples to Palermo. He had become embroiled in local politics and been directly involved in executing opponents of King Ferdinand. He had been upset by the appointment of the mutually antipathetic Lord Keith, replacing as Commander in Chief Earl St. Vincent, to whom Nelson was very attached. Emotionally he must have been aware that his marriage to Fanny was doomed and that the problems to be faced on his return home were almost insurmountable. There must also have been considerable guilt in knowing he had cuckolded and betrayed his friend, Sir William Hamilton, of whom he was very fond.

It seems extremely likely that all the above was accompanied by persistent headache and marked depression. The following descriptions of Nelson by people who met him on his journey home are really just confirmation of the persistence of his symptoms. A Lutheran pastor named Kosegarten described him as 'one of the most insignificant looking figures I ever saw in my life. His weight cannot be more than seventy pounds. A more miserable collection of bones and wizened frame I have never yet come across ... he hardly ever smiles.'

When he was talking with Lady Hamilton, Kosegarten also noted that Nelson 'twisted his mouth into the faint resemblance of a smile.' Nelson was also described thus: 'His face is pale and sunk, with the hair combed onto the forehead ... a small thin man.'[12]

Nelson returned to England in early November 1800. He was about to be reunited with a wife he had only lived with for seven months in the last seven years, and with whom he can have had very little in common. He had become renowned throughout Europe, and had met with and was on talking terms with a King, a Queen, a Prince, an Elector, an Archduke, numerous Lords and Ladies, and the great composer, Joseph Haydn. Fanny inhabited a different world altogether, and with no children to unite them, by this time their marriage was certainly doomed; though Fanny's loyalty to her husband would prove to be, by any measure, extraordinary.

On his last leave in August 1805, Nelson 'sat' for portraits by Catherine Andras and Robert Bowyer. Andras, a wax modeller, was born in 1775 and was the niece and adopted daughter of Bowyer, who was a miniaturist. Their relationship explains why Nelson joked that they were 'attacking him port and starboard,' when he sat for them both simultaneously.[13] Bowyer's miniature of Nelson distinctly shows the abnormal outer third of the right eyebrow and has a small rather odd lock of hair transecting the right eyebrow, running exactly parallel to the keloid scar in the Andras model.[14]

After Nelson's death he was buried in St. Paul's Cathedral and this fact ensured that the public flocked there to look at his tomb. By way of competition, Westminster Abbey ordered a lifesize wax and wood model of Nelson and commissioned Andras to model the head and left hand. Genuine clothing belonging to the late Admiral was donated by his family and the 5 ft. 5½ in. figure was put on display in early 1806. Andras was able to work swiftly because she had so recently sculpted Nelson in a wax relief.[15]

The Westminster Abbey figure of Nelson shows a keloid scar above his right eyebrow.[16] Keloid scars are nodular skin overgrowths on the sites of scars. The pathogenesis (cause) of keloid scarring is not known, although there is often a positive family history of such nodular overgrowths developing after skin injury or surgery.[17] No family history is known in Nelson's case.

Unless such a scar had been definitely present on Nelson's forehead there would of course have been absolutely no reason for Andras to portray the lesion in a posthumous portrait. But Andras had sculpted Nelson in life so the keloid scar on the Abbey figure is important.

If Nelson had such a scar on his forehead, as noted earlier, it explains why the many portraits were posed as they were, and why Nelson altered his hairstyle. Other portraits (most especially the Beechey study and the Guzzardi portrait) show marked forehead scarring but no overgrowth. This was possibly to flatter the sitter. The posthumous (1807) Beechey portrait owned by The Drapers' Company has an almost three-dimensional star-shaped scar.

In other respects the Andras Abbey portrait must be considered an excellent likeness. Walker states that Nelson's nephew, George Matchum, son of his favourite sister Catherine, 'always said that the Abbey wax effigy was far more like him than any of the portraits' and quotes in full the story of Lady Hamilton's visit in 1806 very shortly after the figure, wearing Nelson's clothes, went on show.

Lady Hamilton was said to have been escorted round the Abbey by an Artillery Officer who wrote about this visit some thirty years after it occurred.

> Horatia, the late Lord Nelson's adopted daughter, was very anxious to visit Westminster Abbey; accordingly Lady Hamilton and our two selves went thither. After going through the usual routine, the guide, little guessing whom he addressed, said, 'Perhaps, Madam, the young folks would like to see the waxen image of the late Admiral Nelson; it has only been put up these two days.'
>
> Her Ladyship was much agitated but bowed assent; the man led the way to a glass case in which stood the effigy of her idol and the nation's pride. Tears flowed down her lovely face; she stood gazing intently upon this very faithful portrait; and when her emotions permitted her to speak she told the man that the likeness would be perfect if a certain lock of hair was disposed in the way his Lordship always wore it; this she offered to arrange. The guide refused to let anybody touch the figure.
>
> 'I am sure,' she said, with the bewitching grace with which she was pre-eminently gifted, 'when I tell you that I am Lady Hamilton, you will not refuse me.'
>
> The man fixed his gaze upon her. 'Lady Hamilton,' he repeated; 'What! Lord Nelson's Lady Hamilton! Oh Madam, who would refuse you. He hastened to open the case, the lock of hair was adjusted; she would have kissed the lips, but like the cautious Paulina, the guide assured her the colour was not dry.'[18]

The Times of 22nd March 1806 commented that the Abbey figure had 'a very striking resemblance to the late Lord Nelson... modelled from a smaller one for which his Lordship sat ... a strong and exact representation of the features and person of our late departed hero.'[19]

In the post-Nile adulation Lavinia Spencer, the wife of the 2nd Earl Spencer, First Sea Lord, wrote to Nelson on hearing of the result of the battle: 'Joy, Joy, Joy to you brave gallant immortalized Nelson!' The rest of the long letter included phrases such as 'My heart is absolutely bursting' and 'I am half mad and I fear I have written a strange letter ...' But to be fair to her, she did ask after Nelson himself: 'How anxious we shall be to hear of your health!' She gave very astute advice to her husband about Nelson's propensity to overwork:

... he will be a longer time useful by a well timed respite than he can possibly be by working him to death ... he is exactly like the thoroughbred Mail coach-horses that one hears of now and then that go on drawing till they drop down dead having lost shoes, hoofs and everything.[20]

Sir Peter Parker's wife, Margaret (Sir Peter had been Nelson's Commander in the West Indies years before), was about the only person with any sense. Addressing a letter to 'my dear and immortal Nelson,' which reached him almost six months after he had been wounded, she at first wrote 'I have not yet come to my senses' which sounded just like the rest of the 'Joy, Joy, Joy' brigade. However, halfway through her letter she gave some common-sense advice which, alas, nobody acted upon. From the medical point of view she deserves to be quoted:

I am very uneasy about the wound in your head and would have you quit a station that must retard your recovery. Quiet is the only remedy for a blow on the head, and it is impossible for you to enjoy a moment's rest while you remain in your present station. A few months relaxation and a cold climate will soon fit you for another enterprise but should you continue in constant exertions of both body and mind, years, not months, will be required for your recovery. Take this advice from one that always had your welfare at heart. Sir Peter and I ever regarded you as a son.

Your affectionate
MARGARET PARKER[21]

In all the letters Nelson received it is the only one which really considered his needs as a person and not a national symbol, although St. Vincent actually wrote two months after the battle, 'Tell Lady Hamilton I rely on her to administer to your health at Naples.'[22] Advice he must subsequently have regretted.

Nelson's reply to Margaret Parker's letter was written exactly six months to the day after the battle. It was obviously the writing of a man in a deep depression: it was unrealistic – 'I have few friends' – utterly pessimistic and fatalistic. He wrote: 'my health is such that without a great alteration I will venture to say a very short space of time will send me to that Bourne from whence none return.[23] But God's will be done. After the action I had nearly fell into a decline. I am worse than ever. I shall never leave this country, although I know nothing but the air of England, and peace and quietness can perfectly restore me.'[24]

Nelson's work load at this time, quite apart from being a full-time Admiral and being embroiled in local Neopolitan politics, included 21 long letters to a host of people, the Duke of Clarence and the Speaker of the House of Commons among them. Written in the seven days around 1st

February 1799, many of these letters were thanking important people for significant honours, which in former times would have thrilled him.

The author believes that this letter to Margaret Parker was from a man with severe and prolonged post concussion syndrome. The rest of the letters showed a sharp intellect still at work and in only two of them did he briefly mention his head wound and his depressions. They contained not a hint of self-pity or intellectual alteration.

Eventually Nelson did recover from his head wound, but it is contended that the wound was responsible to a significant degree for much of his extraordinary behaviour in the two years after the Nile. Nelson wrote freely of his symptoms: 'My head is ready to split and I am always so sick. In short, if there be no fracture, my head is severely shaken.'[25] These words were written ten days after he sustained the wound.

The diagnosis, over two hundred years later, is of severe concussion to the brain, which altered for at least two years his mood and his emotional stability, whilst leaving him intellectually intact. The severity of Nelson's Nile head wound has hitherto been greatly underestimated by his biographers.

As always, Nelson had insight into his condition, writing 'My spirits have received such a shock,' although it was part of his severe post-traumatic depressive ideation at the time that he went on, 'I think they cannot recover.'[26]

One last extraordinary side effect of Nelson's Nile head wound must be mentioned. Dr Colin White, when researching his excellent book, *The New Nelson Letters*, of necessity examined a very large number of examples of Nelson's handwriting. He had noted 'the handwriting itself changes quite markedly in this period, becoming flatter, tighter and less flowing post Nile, and only opening up again into the broad script we know so well, around the latter half of 1800.'[27] An example of this 'flat' writing is given on p. 264 taken from a letter written at the beginning of February 1799, six months after Nelson's head wound. The difference in the writing compared with that before the Battle of the Nile and also months before he was killed, is very obvious, and Dr White's opinion that the writing reverted to normal some two years after the date of the wound coincides with the reduction in head symptoms complained of by Nelson in his letters at that time.

Perhaps this is a physical sign as yet not fully investigated: that handwriting in patients can change in form after closed head injury, and revert to normal as the effects of the injury recede. Many medical papers have been written about the changes in *content* after head injury. Without a doubt, Nelson's handwriting altered in parallel with his other post-injury symptoms of depression, disinhibition, and headache.

Notes

1. *Journal of R.S.M.* vol 97 August 2004 p.408
2. *Spencer Papers* vol II p.437 Quoted in Vincent E. *Nelson Love and Fame* 2003 p.236 (hereafter Vincent)
3. ibid
4. Pugh p.24
5. Nicolas vol III p.56
6. ibid p.66–67
7. Keevil, J. J. *The Cockpit of HMS Vanguard* August 1st 1798 p.128–30
8. Appleby, L. et al (eds) *Post Graduate Psychiatry* 2nd edition 2001 p.244–7 Nelson does not seem to have suffered from Dysexecutive ('frontal lobe') Syndrome. This condition reflects a clinical description without specific anatomical lesions and is common after frontal lobe injuries. The patient experiences lack of ability to plan ahead, poor self-monitoring, poor problem solving and difficulties in carrying out two tasks at once.
9. Russell p.146
10. McClelland et al. *Journal of R.S.M.* vol. 87 Sept. 1994 p.508
11. ibid
12. Blumel, T. 'Nelson's overland Journey' *Nelson Dispatch* vol 7 part 3 p.166
13. Walker p.150
14. ibid p.138
15. ibid p.151
16. Harvey, A. & Mortimer, P. (eds) *The Funeral Effigies of Westminster Abbey* 1994 p.185
17. Bayat et al. *Journal of R.S.M. v*ol 96 November 2000 p.554
18. Walker p.173
19. ibid p.172
20. British Library: Althorp Papers G292. Quoted in Vincent p.305
21. Nicolas vol III p.83
22. ibid p.85
23. reference to 'The undiscover'd country from whose bourn/No traveller returns', *Hamlet* act 3 sc. 1 lines 77-8.
24. Nicolas vol III p.248
25. ibid p.100
26. ibid p.112
27. Colin White: personal communication to the Author.

London ~~fet.~~ March 4th 1793.

My Dear Fanny

Never a finer night was
seen than last night and I am not the
least tired. I have taken my place in
the Chatham Coach for one ollock. I write
this in Mr. Rumseys office. I have not seen
my brother. Yours most affectionately

Horatio Nelson

An example of Nelson's mature right-handed writing.

CHAPTER VII
Nelson and Women

The examination of Nelson's everyday life cannot be made without a consideration of his relationships with women. Equally, his head injuries almost certainly had some bearing on those relationships. Therefore it can be argued that the following deserves to form part of this book.

Considering how much of his short life was spent at sea Nelson came into contact with a considerable number of women. Always markedly heterosexual, Nelson appears to have enjoyed their company and the final romance of his life with Emma Hamilton, the wife of his best friend Sir William Hamilton, was so public an affair as to ensure that he and she became two of the most famous adulterers of all time. Recent research and the emergence of many new primary sources in the last four years have given historians a better picture of Nelson's marriage and better illuminated the rather shadowy figure that was Fanny Nisbet, his wife of 19 years. Nelson's sisters, female friends, married women friends, his mistresses and his daughter are also considered here.

In the normal scheme of things, a boy child relates, if they are available to him, with his mother, elderly female relatives such as grandmothers and aunts, and his sisters. As an adolescent and young adult, outside the home environment, he is gradually exposed to potential girlfriends and often to older married women friends who may or may not initiate him into the ways of sex. Marriage is the next stage, followed by, in the normal course of events, the birth of offspring. Some situations (absence from the wife for one being the most germane here) can encourage the acquisition of mistresses. Given survival to mature adulthood and old age, the circle of female acquaintances widens again to include on the one hand the wives of friends and married work colleagues, and on the other hand, girlfriends of daughters, and acquired daughters-in-law. Only the last stage was, by his premature death, denied to Nelson. Mother, grandmothers, sisters, girlfriends, mature married women friends, wife, mistresses, wives of married colleagues and finally a daughter; he never seems to have had difficulty, as some men do all their lives, in relating to women.

Nelson's mother has been discussed in Chapter I: the effect Catherine Nelson had upon her sixth child, in respect of her influential opinions and her untimely death, seems to have had a strong impact on Nelson for his whole life.

Nelson had three sisters: Susannah three years older, Anne two years younger, and Catherine who was nine years his junior. Anne died when Nelson was 25, having named him (with their father) as executor of her will. Susannnah and Catherine, with their spouses Thomas Bolton and George Matcham, and their large families, were essential parts of Nelson's life when he was in England.

Susannah contributed small, significant pieces of information about Nelson's mother – that she 'hated the French' and that she had 'bred herself to death.'[1]

Catherine seems to have been Nelson's favourite sister. Mahan says he confided in her the story of the gypsy Nelson had consulted as a young man when in the West Indies, who had predicted he would rise to the head of his profession by the time he was forty, but she could see no further into his future. Catherine came to see Nelson off at Portsmouth on 14th September 1805. As they were parting, he reminded her 'Oh Katty! That gypsy!'[2] And it was the Matchams who looked after Horatia when she returned to England from France in 1815, after Lady Hamilton died.

Mary Simpson was Nelson's first love. In September 1782 Nelson was almost twenty-four, but already a much-travelled veteran. Stationed in the East Coast of North America, he sailed into Quebec with a crew badly affected, like himself, with scurvy. A proper diet rapidly made him feel 'Health, that greatest of blessings' in 'Fair Canada,'[3] and he seems to have met Mary Simpson at a ball shortly after his arrival. He fell instantly in love. She did not. She was only sixteen and already, owing to her beauty, surrounded by admirers. Nelson hoped the arrival of winter weather would ensure his ship was trapped by ice so that he could continue courting her. On 13th October 1782 his ship was ordered to escort troopships to New York. During his stay in Quebec, Nelson had found time to meet a man ten years older who was to become a lifelong friend, Alexander Davison. He was a Scotsman, in Canada acting as a Naval Agent for replenishing British ships. Two days later, quite by chance, Davison saw Nelson coming ashore in his ship's boat. To Davidson's horror, Nelson said to him 'I find it impossible to leave this place without waiting on her whose society has added so much to its charms and laying myself and my fortune at her feet.' Davison replied 'Your utter ruin ... must inevitably follow.' Nelson rejoined 'Then let it follow, for I am resolved to do it.' Davison was emphatic in turn, 'I positively declare that you shall not.'[4] He got Nelson to go back on board his ship. Davison was of course correct, but the whole episode is a fascinating glimpse of the depth of emotion of which young Nelson was so capable, but which he never seemed to have shown to his wife.

A year later there was peace throughout Western Europe and Nelson, back in England and aged 25, went to France with a fellow naval captain, ostensibly to learn French. He found much in France to compare poorly with England. Poor inns, bad roads, chaises without springs, 'rats of horses,' but he quickly noted the richness of the land and the pretty agreeableness of his French landlady's daughters. Alas, they spoke no English and as he wrote to a friend 'The French goes on but slowly.'[5] It was easier by far to talk to a few of the visiting English in St. Omer where he was staying and especially to an English clergyman and his three daughters. Within twelve days of meeting them, Nelson was writing to his brother William: 'I must take care of my heart.'[6] and he used exactly the same phrase in a letter to William Locker written two weeks later. Very shortly he was head over heels in love with one of the three: Elizabeth, aged 21. He wrote to his brother, William:

> My heart is quite secured against the French beauties: I almost wish I could say as much for an English young lady, the daughter of a clergyman, with whom I am just going to dine, and spend the day. She has such accomplishments, that had I a million of money, I am sure I should at this moment make her an offer of them. My income at present is by far too small to think of marriage ...[7]

In the same letter he went on to talk of lottery tickets! Some days later desperation pushed him further and he appealed for financial aid to Uncle William Suckling. 'The whole of my income does not exceed £130 a year. Will you, if I should marry, allow me £100 a year until my income is increased?' Later on in the same long letter 'If nothing is done ... life is not worth living without happiness and I care not where I may linger out a miserable existence.'[8] William was willing to help but Elizabeth Andrews turned Nelson down. Despite the comments to his uncle, he seems to have got over the rejection without too much difficulty and he later took her brother onto his next ship as a young midshipman. These examples show a young man susceptible to a pretty face and the prospect of marriage.

The married woman in young Nelson's life was Mary Moutray, the wife of the Commissioner to the Dockyard at English Harbour, Antigua, West Indies. She was a woman of charm and kindness and entertained naval officers who came ashore there. She knew Nelson's friend, Cuthbert Collingwood well and when Nelson – the young captain of the *Boreas* – arrived, he was introduced to the Moutrays. Mrs Moutray was 32 and her husband 61. Nelson stayed at their house while his ship was refitting. He himself was suffering from another bout of fever (probably malaria) and had had all his hair shaved off. He wore an ill-fitting yellow wig. Mary Moutray persuaded Nelson and Collingwood to draw one another; Collingwood's picture of Nelson in the wig is in the National Maritime Museum. Nelson seems to have fallen for Mary. She was kindness itself and unattainable. He wrote to a friend 'Were it not for Mrs. Moutray who is very, very good to me, I should almost hang myself in this infernal hole.'[9] Not long afterwards the Moutrays returned to England.

It is clear from his letters about her that Nelson was a fervent admirer 'My dear sweet friend,' and 'Her equal I never saw.'[10] He even, wrote about her in eulogistic tones to a new female friend, Fanny Nesbit.

Nelson's wife was born Fanny Woolward, the daughter of a judge, whose wife was the sister of the President of the Council of Nevis, John Herbert. Both her parents were dead before she reached the age of 19, and she lived with her uncle, the most important man on the island of Nevis.

At the age of 21 she married a Doctor Nesbit and a year later had a son, Josiah. Left a widow when her husband died soon after, she returned to Herbert's house to act as his hostess.

Fanny has often been treated badly by Nelson's biographers. Many male biographers have found Lady Hamilton much more interesting. But Fanny had a quiet charm and innate dignity. She was first heard of in a delightful vignette at Nevis. She was not present at a dinner party which Nelson attended. Fanny's cousin wrote to her 'We have at last seen the Little Captain of the *Boreas*.' She went on to describe a man 'much heated … very silent' and exhibiting 'taciturnity'. Clearly something, it is not known what, had put Nelson out of countenance and he was not prepared to be sociable even though Fanny's correspondent 'endeavoured to rouse his attention by showing him all the civilities in my power, but I drew out little more than 'Yes' and 'No'. If you, Fanny, had been there we think you would have made something of him, for you have been in the habit of attending to these odd sort of people.'[11]

At his next visit to Fanny's house, Nelson was found playing under a dining room table with her five-year-old son – behaviour guaranteed to warm a young widow's heart. Not long after their first meeting, Nelson proposed and was accepted, subject to the consent of Fanny's Uncle Herbert, who Nelson had described in a letter as 'very rich and very proud.'[12] Herbert could, and did, promise some monies to Fanny but in the event she received nothing like as much as the young couple had hoped for. Her uncle also wanted them to wait two years so that Fanny could go on serving as his hostess at Nevis until he retired. But the arrival in the area of Prince William Henry, second son of King George III and an old acquaintance of Nelson's, speeded the nuptuals a little. Prince William arrived in the Caribbean in December 1786 and asked Nelson in effect to be his aide-de-camp while he carried out official visits to British islands there on behalf of his father. He then insisted that he should be present at Fanny and Nelson's marriage. So this was expedited and the young couple were married in early March 1787. Prince William, the future King William IV of England, gave the bride away.

Nelson's time in the West Indies was coming to an end and about a month later he returned to England in his frigate while Fanny and her son crossed the Atlantic in a merchantman. Then things seem to have started to go wrong. The young married couple moved around Southern England visiting friends and relatives as they had no home of their own. Fanny hated the fogs of London which made her very 'chesty' and when they finally got to Norfolk, the metamorphosis from tropical flower to wilted bloom seems rapidly to have been completed. Fanny had been young, gay, vivacious and bridal but under cold English skies she seems to have become droopy, depressed, sisterly and prematurely aged.

The letters of Lord Chesterfield to his son were published in 1774. One wonders if Nelson ever read them. Probably not. In his political career in the early 1740s Chesterfield had been the Leader of the Opposition to Walpole (Nelson's great-uncle) in the House of Lords and was instrumental in Walpole's downfall in 1742. The letters have been described as being full of elegant wisdom and keen wit. They contain one aphorism Nelson could usefully have noted 'To take a wife merely as an agreeable and rational companion will commonly be found to be a grand mistake.' Examination of Nelson's letters to his wife show that this was the basis of his choice.

However, perhaps the biggest 'mistake' in Nelson's marriage was the lack of children. To such a man at such a time, arguably the duties of father-hood might have muted the siren voices of Naples and Lady Hamilton.

As it was, when he met Lady Hamilton in September 1798, in his post-Nile brain-damaged subconscious, she became for him a series of first and second chances: a chance to recapture his youth (he was almost forty when he met Lady Hamilton); a second chance to try for the genetic immortality assured to those who have children; a first chance to have a physical rela-tionship with a woman at once motherly and sexual; and a second chance to prove he was fertile.

Why was Nelson's marriage infertile? Fanny had proved to be rapidly fertile with her first husband. They married in June 1779 and Josiah was born a year later. It may be that Fanny only had the one child in her first marriage because her husband was too sickly to father another: he is said to have died insane.[13] It may have been that Fanny had such a difficult delivery, having Josiah, that she was frightened of further pain and refused intercourse, although this seems unlikely. By the time she married again perhaps Nelson himself was ill, but it is unlikely this state of affairs lasted throughout his five years 'on the Beach.' It may be that due to a chemical problem within Fanny, so-called 'cervical hostility,' no conception took place despite physical rela-tions between Nelson and his wife. It may be that Fanny had developed an infection after Josiah's birth which made her the infertile partner. An exact diagnosis is not possible. In any event, until the conception of Horatia in 1799, Nelson had no confirmation in his life that he was capable of fathering a child and as he had suspected himself of having venereal disease in 1781 that must in all probability have been deeply disturbing.

In 2001, with the discovery of a large cache of letters sent by Fanny to Alexander Davison during the (for her) awful time when Nelson returned to England with the Hamiltons and their marriage was in the process of disintegrating, it is now possible to make a more accurate account of their separation, unclouded by fictions put in place by Lady Hamilton at later dates.

Thanks to the letters it is now known that between January and December 1801 Fanny made repeated attempts to save the marriage, and she forbore to publish the very harsh letters Nelson sent to her as he rebuffed each of her attempts. Throughout this time, although not unnaturally anxious that Nelson, on whom she was financially dependent, might withdraw some or all of his monetary support, she managed to maintain her social position as his true wife. She also kept hoping for the reconciliation which never came, and which it must be said could never come, given that Nelson now had a child by Emma, and he was writing to the latter as 'my own dear wife, for such you are in my eyes and in the face of heaven.'[14]

Above all Fanny maintained her dignity. She continued close links with Nelson's father, who was extremely distressed by Nelson's public flouting of the seventh Commandment. She attended at Court, as she was entitled to do as Nelson's wife, and she 'kept the way open for reconciliation.'[15]

Finally, on 18th December 1801 Fanny wrote an abject but carefully composed letter: 'Do my dear husband let us live together. I can never be happy until such an event takes place. I assure you again I have but one wish in the world, to please you. Let everything be buried in oblivion, it will pass like a dream.'[16]

Fanny sent the letter to Alexander Davison's London house for him to pass it on to Nelson. She did not send it to Merton, where Nelson was now living openly with Emma and Sir William Hamilton. It was her final attempt at reconciliation with the husband she had married fourteen-and-a-half years before, but actually lived with for only about six years of that time. She had hardly altered; he had changed out of all recognition. Even so, that was no excuse for the despicable way he treated her at this time. Although he must have recognised the handwriting, Nelson got Davidson to send it back to Fanny with the dreadful superscription: 'Opened by mistake by Lord Nelson but not read. A. Davison.'[17] It was utterly cruel but it had the desired effect. Fanny never again attempted a reconciliation with her husband.

Fanny died in 1831, outliving Sir William, Nelson and Emma herself by many years. In the immediate aftermath of the marriage break-up, Fanny continued to look after Nelson's father and even nursed him in his final illness. As Nelson advanced in the Peerage, so did Fanny, becoming a Baroness in 1798 and Viscountess Nelson in 1801. Only in financial matters was Nelson fair to his wife. He seems to have allowed her about half of his annual income, but this may have been done not with contrition but for calculated, selfish reasons, since he wrote to Davison in April 1801:

You will at a proper time, and before my arrival in England signify to Lady Nelson that I expect, and for which I have made such a very liberal allowance for her, to be kept to myself, and without any inquiries from her ... my mind is as fixed as fate ...[18]

His last letter written directly to her some seven weeks previously, contained the awful words 'my only wish is to be left to myself'.[19]

The affair between Nelson and Emma Hamilton has been called 'Extremely destructive as well as highly romantic.'[20] However, perhaps the most important aspect of Nelson's love affair with Emma was that it was a fertile union. In one of his last letters to Emma, Nelson held out to her the possibility of more children, whereas in 1799 in *Sketch of My Life* he had summed up his marriage to Fanny in one line – the stark phrase 'by whom I have no children.'[21] It was a fatal and insurmountable flaw in a marriage 'founded upon the principles of reason but also upon the basis of mutual attachment,' as Nelson wrote in his first letter to his future wife.[22] Nelson's relationship with Emma was never, ever founded upon the principles of reason. Nelson signed almost all his letters to Fanny in a slightly variable but consistent way. 'Your most Affectionate Husband,' 'ever your most Affectionate Husband,' and in the early days of his courtship, he could be more effusive 'I am with the most pure affection ever your most sincere Horatio Nelson,' or 'I am in the fullest sense of the word most affectionately.' The signature may change 'Horatio Nelson,' 'Bronte Nelson,' 'Bronte Nelson of the Nile,' but it is always accompanied by 'Ever your most affectionate,' even the last oh-so-brief, direct, letter written in March 1801 is signed 'Believe that I am, your affectionate Nelson.' But from 'Leghorn' or *Agamemnon* at sea, having just left Leghorn' came four letters signed 'ever your most faithful and affectionate husband,' and one uniquely signed 'Your faithful husband'. It is around this time that we know Nelson was unfaithful to Fanny with a mistress, Adelaide Correglia, born in Genoa but then living in Leghorn. A fellow captain called her 'Nelson's dolly,' commenting that Nelson 'makes himself ridiculous with that woman,' and that the food at their table 'was very bad indeed'.[23] Nelson paid her rent and possibly used her to glean for him information respecting affairs in Leghorn. Fanny never knew of her existence. The relationship went on for at least fifteen months, and was even known about by Nelson's Commander-in-Chief, Admiral Sir John Jervis. 'Faithful' is an interesting Freudian slip, Nelson *only* using the word to Fanny during the time he was committing adultery with 'la Belle Adelaide.'[24]

Lady Spencer, wife of the then First Lord of the Admiralty was in the habit of having naval officers to dinner without their wives. Nelson, about to return to duty after having lost his arm, asked if he could bring his wife. 'He said she was beautiful, accomplished, her care alone had saved his life.' Lady Spencer reported after the dinner 'His attentions to her [Lady Nelson] were those of a lover. He handed her in to dinner and sat by her saying he was so little with her that he would not voluntarily lose an instant of her company.'[25] Lady Spencer having noted that Fanny cut up his food, later gave Nelson a combined knife/fork to enable him to be more independent with regard to eating.

On his return to London after the Battle of the Nile and the Naples episode, Lady Spencer had Fanny and Nelson to dinner again and noted the terrible change. She wrote that Nelson treated his wife with every mark of dislike and even contempt. At the end of what must have been a nightmare meal with Nelson in a sour and silent mood, he pushed aside a glass of walnuts Fanny had shelled for him so vigorously that the glass broke and Fanny burst into tears.[26] Others criticised Nelson very forcibly, condemning his conduct toward Lady Nelson, as in his infatuation with Lady Hamilton he was publicly wounding his wife's feelings when he knew very well she had done no wrong.

Emma Hamilton was born Amy Lyon, the daughter of a blacksmith, in Cheshire. The exact date of her birth is not known. She was brought up in Wales and then went to work in London as a maid. She moved in series through several houses and then became an attendant 'Goddess' at the Temple of Health and Hymen, an establishment run by the quack doctor James Graham, to assist fertility in sterile couples by a variety of questionable means.

James Graham was born in Scotland in 1734 and studied Medicine at Edinburgh University. He may never have qualified, nevertheless he travelled to America in 1772, practising as a doctor in Philadelphia and studying the electrical experiments of Benjamin Franklin. Twenty years before, Franklin had opined that static electricity might be used in the treatment of cases of paralysis and blindness. Graham returned to England in 1774 to find that electrical treatments for illness were now available from, for example, preachers such as John Wesley who had advertised in a prospectus that after purchasing an Electrical Machine 'any person may be electrified gratis, from nine to twelve every day except Saturdays and Sundays.'

Graham worked in Bristol from 1774 where he advertised 'wonderful cures' and then in Bath, in 1777, where he was using 'Electrical Applications and Influences' on patients. A year later he went to Paris, where he must have gained knowledge of the 'treatments' of Anton Mesmer which centred around theories of 'animal magnetism' and which were successful as early forms of hypnotism, most especially treating 'hysterical' symptoms. Back in London later the same year, Graham opened 'The Temple of Health' in the Adelphi. It seems to have been a large emporium. It had several rooms, at least one of them extremely large, plus a lot of equipment – including a magnetic throne and a bath through which currents of electricity were said to pass. Graham became a fashionable and expensive quack.[27]

Other equipment in the Temple of Health included static electrical machines, Leyden jars, insulated glass pillars and chemical apparatus. Music was played, and perfumes wafted, and Graham advertised publicly for so-called 'Goddesses' of youth and beauty. These young women were then 'displayed,' and said to represent the examples of physical perfection others could achieve if they followed Graham's precepts for healthy living. Emma Hart, as she was now known, became one of these 'Goddesses' and she, aged fifteen-and-a-half, must have been in her youthful element. Some of Graham's recommendations were in fact excellent and ahead of their time. He was much in favour of frequent washing and personal cleanliness and strongly advocated fresh air and exercise. He was also aware of the adverse effects of alcohol upon the body as well as on sexual performance. Some of these (to us) common-sense ideas seem to have brushed off on Emma and since the pervading 'culture' of the Temple of Health was Classical (one part of the Temple was called 'the Great Apollo Apartment' and 'Templum Aesculapius Sacrum', Sacred Temple of Aesculapius, was above the main doorway) one can see where the first glimmering of ideas for her later 'Attitudes' (see below) must have originated.

The main attraction of the Temple was the 'Celestial Bed'. This was twelve foot by nine foot, had a double frame which enabled it to tilt in several directions, and was supported on forty pillars of glass. Music, spices, odours, essences and two live turtle-doves were useful additions, as was 'the exhilarating force of electrical fire'. Graham described the principle feature of the Bed to be 'artificial lodestones ... About fifteen hundredweight of compound magnets are continually pouring forth in an ever flowing circle ...' It was said to 'infallibly produce a genial and happy issue' for those whom sterility or impotence had rendered infertile.[28]

Emma seems to have worked at the place for some ten months; surely an important period in her life. When working for Graham, or while under the 'care' of later 'protectors,' she was never either a prostitute or promiscuous.

One year later Emma was set up in a cottage near Uppark in Sussex by the owner, Sir Harry Fetherstonhaugh. Uppark is now owned by the National Trust, and a table upon which Emma said to have danced, naked, is still on view in one of the grand rooms. It was at Uppark that Emma met Charles Greville, nephew of Sir William Hamilton, and to Greville she appealed when Sir Harry tired of her. Greville, as Mahan quaintly put it, 'took her up,' when she was not yet seventeen and she fell in love with him. In turn he educated her, not only in the ways of a hostess in semi-polite society but also in such basics as her spelling. It was while she was living with Greville that George Romney painted her so often. Sir William

Hamilton first met her in 1784 when he had been two years a widower. In England only for a short time he returned to Naples alone but Greville had noted his uncle's fancy. By now seeking to divest himself of Emma in order to try to restore his fortune by marrying an heiress, he sent her out to Naples with her mother, having led her to believe he would join her there. Realising slowly that he never would come, she resigned herself to the situation and began further to develop her capabilities with Sir William as her new, elderly tutor. She proved an apt pupil and later, on a short visit back to England, they married in 1791. She was 26 and he 61. As well as being beautiful with spectacular auburn hair and a wonderful face, she was highly intelligent and a good linguist; but also impulsive, possessed of a terrible temper and capable of being wildly extravagant. Again, at the Neapolitan Court, renowned for its laissez-faire attitudes, no hint of sexual scandal was ever attached to her name.

Emma was very musical and had a singing voice which must have been better than good. When she later sang songs with Joseph Haydn at the piano, a Hungarian newspaper reported on her 'clear, strong voice with which she filled the audience with such enthusiasm they almost became ecstatic. Many were reminded of the Goddesses Dido and Calypso.'[29] This is a particularly interesting comment as Sir William had also encouraged her to develop a group of dumb show movements associated with the manipulation of silken scarves, in which she re-created classical poses – her so-called 'Attitudes'. When Goethe saw her perform these movements in 1787 he wrote 'The spectator can hardly believe his eyes. He sees what thousands of artists would have liked to express realised before him in movements and transformations. She has a hundred ways of turning the folds of her veil into a headdress.'[30] Others were equally enthusiastic.

All his adult life Nelson longed for people to give him deserved recognition. He was also a stickler for ensuring other people got their just deserts. He was fully prepared to fight and argue with powerful people if he thought he and the deeds of his fellow comrades in arms were not rewarded. After the Battle of Copenhagen he refused to dine with the City of London because of its failure to recognise the importance of the battle and the bravery of his men.[31] He may have looked like a Christmas tree when wearing all his medals and orders but he had written to heraldic and government authorities to make quite sure he was entitled to wear them all. To his logical mind he had won them, was entitled to them and could and would wear them. Overt recognition and reassurance were things Lady Hamilton would provide.

Nelson had met Lady Hamilton for the first time in 1794. He was then Captain of the *Agamemnon* and the visit to Naples was brief. He got on very well with Sir William, achieving an instant rapport, and Lady Hamilton had taken some of his midshipmen, including his stepson, Josiah Nisbet, sightseeing in Naples. The trio did not meet again for four years.

After the Battle of the Nile it took Nelson 53 days to reach Naples from Aboukir Bay. While at sea he wrote to St. Vincent, 'As for myself I know I ought to give up for a while. My head is splitting at this moment.'[32] It took him three attempts to write the word 'splitting'.

When Nelson met Lady Hamilton for the second time she was running to fat but still possessed of beautiful features, raven hair and boundless energy. Almost at once the Hamiltons organised a vast party for his birthday. He wrote to Fanny 'The preparations of Lady Hamilton for celebrating my birthday are enough to fill me with vanity.'[33] One wonders who paid for it all since over 1700 people were entertained – the whole, as Nelson wrote 'conducted in a style of elegance as I never saw, nor shall again probably.'[34] Poor Fanny; on exactly the same day, hundreds of miles away in Suffolk she was writing 'We have had much rain. The season was particularly unfavourable for preserving fruit.'[35] But the husband she was writing to was gone forever. 'Our hearts and hands must be all in a flutter,'[36] wrote Nelson in that letter to Earl St. Vincent, marked by extraordinary disinhibition, the result of his head injury. He had moved Lady Hamilton into his heart and as far as he was concerned she never left there, for the remaining eight years of his life.

There is evidence that Nelson never intended to stay long in Naples. 'I hope not to be in Naples more than 4–5 days – these times are not for idleness'[37] he had written in a letter to Sir William sent on before his arrival. When his crippled ship arrived, Sir William and Emma were early visitors. Nelson wrote to Fanny 'Lady Hamilton fell into my arm more dead than alive. Tears however soon set matters to rights.'[38] Further evidence of Nelson's besottedness and emotional collapse is seen the extraordinary letter to his Commander-in-Chief quoted earlier, on p. 106: 'I am writing opposite Lady Hamilton, therefore you will not be surprised at the glorious jumble of this letter.'[39] St. Vincent must have been appalled to get this missive, another example of Nelson's disinhibition, due to the head wound.

By November 1800 Nelson regarded Sir William as a father figure, and he had not only embarked on a physical relationship with Lady Hamilton and made her pregnant, but he continued utterly besotted with her in every respect. Many first-hand accounts record this. An English lady in Dresden, who saw them when they were coming home overland wrote: 'It is plain Lord Nelson thinks of nothing but Lady Hamilton who is totally occupied with the same subject. Lady Hamilton takes possession of him, and he is a willing captive – the most submissive and devoted I have ever seen.' This same witness hit upon a crucial part of the dynamic: 'Lady Hamilton puffs the incense full in his face but he receives it with pleasure and sniffs it up very cordially.'[40] This was a major reason for Lady Hamilton's success with Nelson. She was an expert flatterer and she went on telling him until the day he was killed, that as far as she was concerned he was the greatest man in the world. In one of the few extant letters from her to him, because he burned all her letters, and only in existence because he was killed before it could be delivered and so it was returned to her, she had written 'Oh, Nelson, how I do idolise you the dearest husband of my heart, you are all in this world to your Emma.'[41] The existence of her actual husband and Nelson's real wife never stopped Emma from behaving like she did, and as he wanted. In 1802 a very old friend of Nelson's had met the ménage and wrote to his own wife, 'She goes on charming Nelson with trowelfuls of flattery which he goes on taking as quietly as a child does pap.'[42]

One thing difficult to forgive Lady Hamilton for is her treatment of her children. Her first daughter, born in 1782, possibly as a result of a liaison with an earlier naval captain, was known of by both Charles Greville and Sir William Hamilton, who helped in series with the child's up-keep. Nelson was never aware of her existence. He wrote two letters to Emma on 1st March 1801, just one month after Horatia's birth. The first was one of the erotic ones: 'Would to God I had dined alone with you, what a dessert we would have had.'[43] But the second letter, the famous one beginning 'Now my own dear Wife for such you are in my eyes and in the face of Heaven,' went on to say, 'I never had a dear pledge of love 'til you gave me one, and you, thank my God, never gave one to anyone else.'[44] In this he was mistaken. Lady Hamilton's first daughter, Emma Carew or Anne Connor (she was known by both names) had been brought up in Wales with her cousins. When she came to London in 1806 to try to meet with her mother, Emma deliberately disowned her.

Emma was not a doting mother to Horatia either. Many of Nelson's letters indicate that he wished for Horatia to stay at Merton, the house Lady Hamilton purchased for him in September 1801. For example 'I hope she [Horatia] is at Merton Fixed.' he wrote on 29th September 1804,[45] and 'How is my dear Horatia. I hope you have her under your guardian wing, at Merton?'[46] And as a doting father he requested '... as my dear Horatia is to be at Merton, that a strong netting about three feet high, be placed round the Nile [the title he and Lady Hamilton gave to the Wandle river which ran through the grounds of Merton] so that the little thing may not tumble in,'[47] and 'My earnest wish is that you should take her to Merton.'[48] Within a week of her birth, Horatia had been left in the care of a Mrs Gibson at her house in Marylebone, and whenever it suited Emma she was placed back there for long periods. She had even been staying with Mrs. Gibson when Nelson returned to England in August 1805 and she had to be hastily collected so she could be with all the other members of Nelson's family during his last leave at Merton.

Today Sir William Hamilton is remembered only as the elderly husband of Emma. This is unfair. Highly intelligent, after some years in the army, he was appointed British Envoy Extraordinary and Plenepotentiary at the

Court of Naples, and he stayed there for 36 years. However, Sir William should best be remembered as a pioneer vulcanologist, making many ascents of Vesuvius and witnessing and describing two eruptions. He was elected a Fellow of the Royal Society, at 36 years of age. Sir William's other sphere of influence was as an archaeologist and collector of classical arte-facts. His two collections (of vases, terracotta, coins, bronzes and Roman glass) were brought back to England and sold in large part to the British Museum, where they still form the basis of the classical collection.

Josiah Wedgewood, the celebrated British potter and innovator, was much influenced by an account of Hamilton's collection published in four illustrated volumes in 1766 and 1767; so that Hamilton's taste came to be incorporated in the most widespread manner, in the houses of everyone who purchased Wedgewood pottery. This influence has lasted even up to the present day.[49] It is easy to understand why Nelson should have become friendly with this highly intelligent father figure. It is also important to emphasize that no hint of scandal was ever attached to the marriage of Hamilton and Emma until Nelson arrived in Naples after the Battle of the Nile.

Hamilton was genuinely very fond of Nelson, and this was recipro-cated. He also retained the affection of his wife. After the extraordinary journey with Nelson and with Emma overland through Europe which lasted six months, the party arrived back in England. Thereafter, in retire-ment, Hamilton lived mainly with Nelson (and Emma) in Nelson's house at Merton, south of London. But the three friends also undertook one last journey in order to visit Hamilton's estates in Wales. This turned into a triumphant tour for Nelson, and also an incredibly important one for the history of England.

While near the Forest of Dean, Nelson had one or more meetings with local businessmen who had formed themselves into a cartel controlling the supply of wood for warships. He appears to have mediated between that cartel and the Admiralty so that wood became available for proper repairs to be performed on ships of the fleet, including *Victory* herself, thus enabling them to be correctly refurbished before the Battle of Trafalgar came to be fought. It is doubtful if Nelson would have journeyed to that part of England had it not been for Hamilton wanting to visit his estates.

Eventually, in his 74th year, Hamilton (who had all his life been a man of great mental and physical activity) became ill. He left Merton, and returned to his London home, where he died in Emma's arms, with Nelson holding his hand.

Nelson seems never to have written an erotic letter to his wife, even when separated from her for months or years, either before or during their marriage. A relationship 'founded on esteem' appears to have been lacking in sexuality and Nelson's youngest sister, Catherine, described Fanny as 'cold'.[50]

Nelson's erotic letters to Emma have been compared to those of James Joyce to Nora Barnacle[51] (though some of Joyce's letters are far more obscene than anything Nelson wrote or could conceive of). Nevertheless, it is as if Nelson changes almost two hundred years in his style over a period of less than twenty months, from the formal epistles to Fanny to the overt sexuality of his letters to Emma.

These letters are at times very explicit. Many of them were published in 1815, which did not help Emma's attempts to get a state pension. Reading the letters confirms what Nelson wrote in August 1803: 'To say I think of you by day, night and all day and all night, but too faintly express my feelings of love towards you.'[52] In a much earlier letter to his wife he said that he knew she wished to hear from him frequently; but it was Emma who received up to four letters a day: 'Your utmost stretch of fancy cannot imagine more than I feel towards my own dear Emma.'[53] To make the point perhaps more forcefully than is strictly necessary, frequent requests to Fanny to buy a cottage in the country to which they could retire when his naval service was over was not at all the same as requesting that Emma: 'Have the dear thatched cottage' ready to receive him (18th-century slang for female genitalia).[54]

Perhaps *the* most extraordinary result of Nelson and Lady Hamilton's fame as lovers occurred only in December 2003 when a private buyer was prepared to pay £117,000 for the first erotic letter Nelson is known to have written to Emma, even though the whole text of the letter had already been printed in 1995. This letter included the words 'I kissed you fervently and we enjoyed the height of love. Ah Emma, I pour out my soul to you ... no love is like mine towards you.'[55] and that statement continued to be true from 29th January 1800, when it was written, until the day Nelson died.

The more Nelson felt he could trust the carrier of his letters to Lady Hamilton the more 'open' the letters he wrote were. For example, via a not very safe carrier, he wrote:

> This letter my dearest, beloved Emma, goes – although in Mr. Marsden's letters – in such a roundabout way, that I cannot say all that my heart wishes. Imagine everything which is kind and affectionate, and you will come near the mark.[56]

When he was first parted from her after they returned to England, he wrote by a safe route:

> What must be my sensations at the idea of sleeping with you? It sets me on fire, even the thoughts, much more would be the reality. I am sure my love and desires are all to you and if any woman were to come to me, even as I am at this moment from thinking of you, I hope it might rot off if I would touch her even with my hand.[57]

The last sentence is something of a gift to the cod-Freudians.

There is an incredible feeling of immediacy about Nelson's writings to Lady Hamilton. In one, from *Victory* on 13th October, 1804 he wrote:

> I should for your sake, and for many of our friends, have liked an odd hundred thousand pounds; but, never mind. If they give me the choice of staying a few months longer, it will be very handsome; and, for the sake of others, we would give up, my dear Emma, very much of our own felicity. If they do not, we shall be happy with each other, and with dear Horatia. The cutter returns with my answers directly; therefore, my own Emma, you must only fancy all my thoughts and feelings towards you. They are everything which a fond heart can fancy … I have not a moment; I am writing and signing orders, whilst I am writing to my own Emma … My life, my soul, God in Heaven bless you! … Kiss our dear Horatia a thousand times, for your own faithful Nelson. I send two hundred pounds, keep it for your own pocket money.[58]

One can visualise the scene on board *Victory* – a constant stream of secretaries and naval officers coming and going to his main cabin with letters for Nelson as Commander-in-Chief of the British Fleet to read, act upon, sign; or relaying to him information about the movements of other ships, asking for orders, and all the time he is writing to the love of his life, urgently and secretly, so as to catch the cutter.

Unfortunately Nelson destroyed almost all Lady Hamilton's letters to him. 'I have read all, all your kind and affectionate letters; and have read them frequently over and committed them to the flames, much against my inclination.'[59] Later he wrote 'All your letters, my dear letters, are so entertaining! And which paint so clearly what you are after, that they give me either the greatest pleasure or pain. It is the next best thing, to being with you.'[60] It is known from Emma's two letters that Nelson never received because he was already killed, that she was as exuberant a correspondent as she was in her person. Nelson wrote 'you have that happy knack of making everything you write interesting.'[61]

How did Lady Hamilton manage to fool almost everyone over the pregnancy? Horatia was a twin, so Lady Hamilton's size, in the last month of the pregnancy, must have been almost impossible to hide. Somehow she managed it, and the delivery was also achieved in total secrecy.

The other child, another girl, was apparently sent to the Foundling Hospital and Nelson never knew of her survival. He and Lady Hamilton employed a rather silly arrangement, at the time of the birth, whereby they pretended Nelson was writing on behalf of a mythical member of his ship's company, one Thompson, to Mrs Thompson, known only to Lady Hamilton. Hearing of Horatia's birth, Nelson wrote from on board ship, in an ecstasy: 'I believe poor dear Mrs Thompson's friend will go mad with joy. He cries, prays and performs all tricks yet dare not show all or any of his feelings.'[62] Shortly to set sail for the Baltic, he snatched three days away from his ship to see a baby he described as 'in truth a love begotten child.'[63]

Horatia was born at the same time that he was writing the first awful dismissal letter to Fanny 'My only wish is to be left to myself.'[64] He provided well for Fanny financially but once he had what he called 'a dear pledge of love'[65] by Emma, Fanny was totally abandoned.

It is not always realised how little Nelson saw of Horatia. He was away at sea for most of her young life. Despite his writing at least twice to Emma 'I hope Horatia is at Merton fixed.' this was not the case and, as has been said, Emma frequently left Horatia with her foster mother, Mrs Gibson, in London for weeks at a time, while she gadded about in London and visited friends in the Home Counties.

With Lady Hamilton as her mother, Horatia had a very peripatetic existence and it is amazing, given the utter instability of her first 14 years, that she grew up so well-balanced. Physically, she very much resembled her father. Nelson constantly mentioned her in his letters to Emma; dreamed about her – 'She called me Papa'[66] – bought her presents whenever he could, and wrote delightful letters to her. For example: 'As I am sure that for the world you would not tell a story, it must have slipped my memory that I promised you a watch,'[67] and he sent her one 'to wear when she behaves well and is obedient.'[68]

He obviously adored her. And as he was extremely good with children, giving them his undivided attention, by his untimely death Horatia was deprived of one who would have been the very best of caring and loving fathers.

From the moment Nelson was shot at Trafalgar, he was sure he was going to die. Just as at the Battle of the Nile when he collapsed into the arms of Captain Berry crying 'I am killed, remember me to my wife,'[69] so, when he was shot at Trafalgar, his mind instantly reverted to the two most important living females in his life. Thoughts of his mistress and his daughter ran like a thread through his reported speech of the last two-and-a-half hours (see chapter X).

Initially he feared he would die quickly and poured out a torrent of words to Reverend 'Doctor' Scott, his chaplain and secretary, even as he was being laid on the Orlop decking, stripped of his clothes and examined by the surgeon. 'I am gone, I have to leave Lady Hamilton and my adopted daughter Horatia as legacy to my Country.'[70] Later he returned to this theme when Hardy visited him the first time. 'Pray let my dear Lady Hamilton have my hair and all other things belonging to me.'[71] Later again, he said, 'What would become of poor Lady Hamilton if she knew my situation?'[72] He even put Lady Hamilton into the care of Hardy at the second visit, asking him to 'Take care of my dear Lady Hamilton.'[73] When Hardy left him, he spoke in a low voice to Scott, who was something of a father confessor to him, 'I have not been a great sinner. Remember that I leave Lady Hamilton and my daughter Horatia as a legacy to my Country. Never forget Horatia.'[74] The names of his little daughter and his beloved mistress were almost the last coherent words of his life.

Notes:

1   Nicolas vol V p238; Morrison vol 2 letter 700
2. Mahan p.690
3. Nicholas vol I p.67
4. Clarke and M'Arthur vol 1 p.52
5. Nicolas vol I p.89
6. ibid p.88
7. ibid p.92
8. Nicolas vol II p.47
9. Nicolas vol I p.110
10. ibid p.124
11 Clarke and M'Arthur vol 1 p.78
12. Nicolas vol I p.145
13. Sugden, J. p.310
14. Morrison vol 2 letter 532 p.123
15. Lincoln, M. & White, C. *History today* vol 53 No.11 2003
16. Naish p.xxviii
17. ibid
18. Nicolas vol VII Addenda ccix and Naish p.586–587
19. Naish p.580
20. White, C. *Nelson Encyclopaedia* 2002 p.188
21. Nicolas vol I p.12
22. Naish p.16
23. Freemantle, A (ed) *The Wynne Diaries* 1952 p.255
24. Naish letters 116, 117, 119, and 120 all end with the words 'believe me ever your most faithful and affectionate husband, Horatio Nelson.' The first two were written from Leghorn, the second two from *Agamemnon* off Minorca. It is letter 127 that ends 'Your most faithful husband.'
25. Edgcumbe, R. (ed) *The Diary of Lady Frances Shelley* 1912 p.77–80 Quoted in Oman p.272
26. ibid p.410

27. Rowbottom & Susskind *Electricity and Medicine: History of their interaction* 1984 p.20
28. *Dictionary of National Biography* 2004
29. Blumel, p.15
30. Quoted in Fraser *Beloved Emma* 1986 p.121
31. Quoted in Oman p.496 and Nicolas vol V p.33
32. Nicolas vol III p.113
33. ibid p.134
34. Naish p.404
35. ibid p.450
36. Nicolas vol III p.145
37. ibid p.117
38. ibid p.130
39. ibid p.144–145
40. Blumel, p.21–4
41. National Maritime Museum (hereafter N.M.M. NWD/9594 Quoted in Hibbert p.356
42. Minto, Countess of *Life and Letters of Sir Gilbert Elliot* (1st Earl Minto) from 1757 to 1806. 1874 vol 3 p.242. Quoted in Fraser p.295
43. Morrison vol 2 letter 531 p.123
44. ibid letter 532 p.123
45. Nicolas vol VII p.384
46. ibid
47. ibid p.382
48. Morrison vol 2 letter 779 p.239
49. See *Dictionary of National Biography* for an account
50. Quoted in Oman p.492
51. White C. (ed) *The Nelson Companion* 2005 p.156
52. *Nelson's Letters to Lady Hamilton* vol I p.175
53. ibid vol II p.95
54. Morrison vol 2 letter 528 p.121
55. White, C. *Nelson: The New Letters* 2005 letter 47 p.43–4
56. *Nelson's Letters to Lady Hamilton* vol II p.84
57. Morrison vol 2 letter 532 p.123
58. *Nelson's Letters to Lady Hamilton* vol II p.80–1
59. ibid vol I p.34
60. ibid p.135–6
61. ibid p.155
62. Morrison vol 2 letter 504 p.110
63. *Nelson's Letters to Lady Hamilton* vol I p.36
64. Naish p.580
65. Morrison vol 2 letter 532 p123
66. ibid letter 778 p239
67. N.M.M. N.N.D/9594/16 Quoted in Gerin. 1970 p.69

68. Morrison vol 2 Letter 742 p.223
69. Mahan p.300
70. Beatty p.37
71. ibid p.42
72. ibid p.45
73. ibid p.48
74. ibid p.49

PS I pray give my best respects to my Old School fellow H. Hammond

Dear Brother

Your Affectionate Brother

Horatio. Nelson

An example of Nelson's mature handwriting.

1 John Francis Rigaud portrait, 1781, of the young Captain Nelson, (aged 22). The portrait shows no abnormalities, but X-ray indicates Nelson had a much fuller face as a young lieutenant when the picture was started three years earlier. (National Maritime Museum)

2 & 3 Aschoff & Koch article, 1919. Examples of scurvy symptoms. They show *(left)* effects of scurvy on bone: sub-periostial bleeding and *(below)* effects of scurvy on teeth and gums: swelling and bleeding.

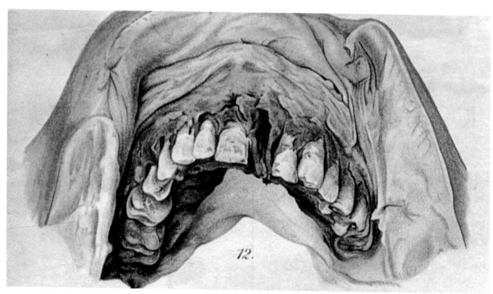

4 Lemuel Abbott, 1798; Nelson hatless. The portrait shows the dilated right pupil, and a slightly sunken right eye. (National Maritime Museum)

5 Matthias Ranson's 1800 life mask. It shows scarring around the outer aspect of the right eyebrow, the presence of the globe of the right eye and the right eye as slightly smaller than the left eye. (Royal Naval Museum)

A N

E S S A Y

ON THE

THEORY AND PRACTICE

O F

MEDICAL ELECTRICITY.

BY

TIBERIUS CAVALLO, F. R. S.

LONDON:

PRINTED FOR THE AUTHOR.

M.DCC.LXXX.

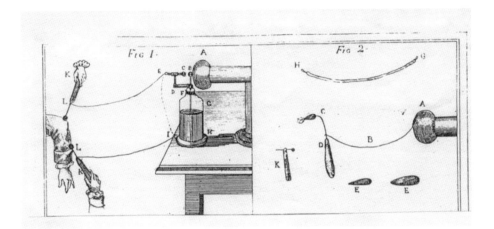

6 & 7 *Left and Above:* Tiberius Cavallo's book, 1781; a Leydon Jar and apparatus for producing static electricity. Figure 2(c) and (d) show the type of instrument probably used on Nelson's right eye at Palermo. (The Wellcome Trust)

8 Drawing of an arm amputation, 1778, from Laurence Heister's *System of Surgery*.

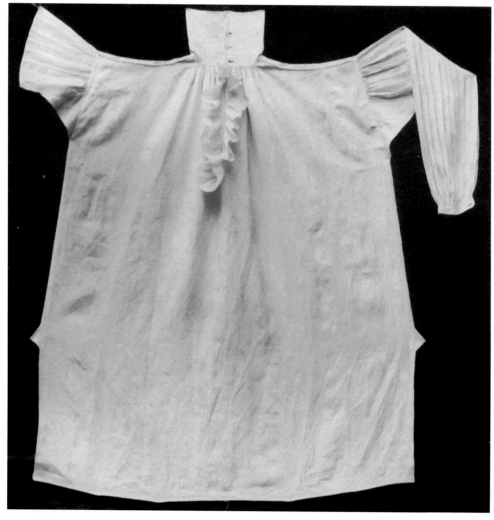

9 Nelson's shirt, given by the Nelson Family to clothe the Westminster Abbey effigy, shows how high was the amputation. The left sleeve is 21½ inches long, the right sleeve is 6½ inches long. (© Westminster Abbey Dean & Chapter)

Page 7"			July 25th		
Mens Names, Ages and Qualities.	When and where put on the Sick List.	Statement of the Case when put on the List.	Symptoms and Treatment while under Cure.	When discharged to Duty, Died, or sent to the Hospital.	R E M
Admiral Nelson	25 July	Compound fracture of the right arm by a musket ball passing thro' a little above the Elbow an Artery divided the Arm was immediately Amputated, and the following give him ℞ Opii ℈ij ℔Pil statim s. Rep Pil Opii ℈j Rep Pil Opii ℈ij horas. s.			
Jas. Holden Sea⁰ Aged abt 27 Yrs	25 July	A Wound of the breast and Compound fracture of the right Arm close to the Shoulders by a Musket Ball passing			

10 The *Theseus* medical log recording the amputation of Nelson's arm, dated 25th July 1779. (The National Archives of the United Kingdom, ADM/101/123/2)

11 *Above:* Nelson's fork/knife; silver, ivory and steel. (National Maritime Museum)

12 *Right:* Daniel Orme, Lady Nelson, 1800. (National Maritime Museum)

13 *Left:* Johann Heinrich Schmidt, Lady Hamilton, 1800. (National Maritime Museum)

EXPERIMENTAL PHILOSOPHY.

14 *Above:* L.Foy, 'Experimental Philosophy.' A cartoon showing an electric shock passing along a line of people from an electrostatic source on the right. Just one finger makes the connection from figure one to figure two. A cat connects figure six to figure seven. (The National Trust)

15 Arthur William Devis, William Beatty as Physician to The Fleet, 1807.

16 Peter Drury's picture of the dramatic damage done to Nelson's body by the path of the musket ball. (Courtesy Professor Leslie Le Quesne)

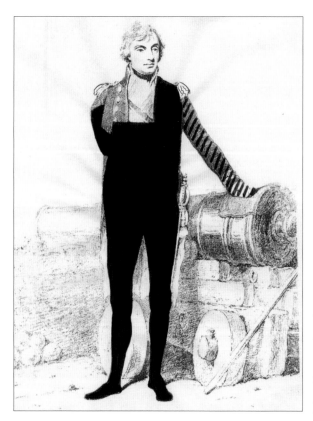

17 Henry Eldridge, the Death of Nelson. The final awful picture: total paralysis below the level of thoracic vertebra 6 and non functioning left chest and lung. (Royal Naval Museum)

18 Arthur William Devis, Death of Nelson. Reverend Scott rubs Nelson's chest. Servant Chevalier pushes forward a pillow while Purser Burke supports Nelson's chest. Surgeon Beatty takes Nelson's pulse. No bullet entry wound is shown. (National Maritime Museum)

19 Leonardo Guzzardi, 1799, enlargement of Nelson's face slightly widened by computer technology. The naval hat tilted backwards shows that the head wound of 1st August 1798 was still painful at least five months after Nelson was wounded. The outer half of the right eyebrow is less well delineated. The face shows depression. The right pupil is dilated.

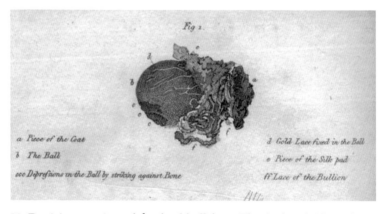

20 Devis' engraving of the fatal ball from *The Authentic Narrative*, Beatty's book.

21 *Opposite:* Frontispiece of William Beatty's book, *The Authentic Narrative*. (Author's collection)

AUTHENTIC NARRATIVE

OF THE

𝕯eath

OF

LORD NELSON:

WITH

THE CIRCUMSTANCES PRECEDING, ATTENDING, AND
SUBSEQUENT TO, THAT EVENT;

THE

PROFESSIONAL REPORT

ON HIS LORDSHIP'S WOUND;

AND

SEVERAL INTERESTING ANECDOTES.

BY WILLIAM BEATTY, M.D.

Surgeon to the Victory in the Battle of Trafalgar, and now Physician to the Fleet under the
Command of the Earl of St. Vincent, K.B. &c. &c. &c.

LONDON:

PRINTED BY T. DAVISON, WHITE-FRIARS;

FOR T. CADELL AND W. DAVIES, IN THE STRAND.

1807.

22 Posthumous portrait from Beatty's book by Devis, 1807, engraved by Scriven. This is the only representation of Nelson wearing one of the eye shades he asked Lady Hamilton to make for him.

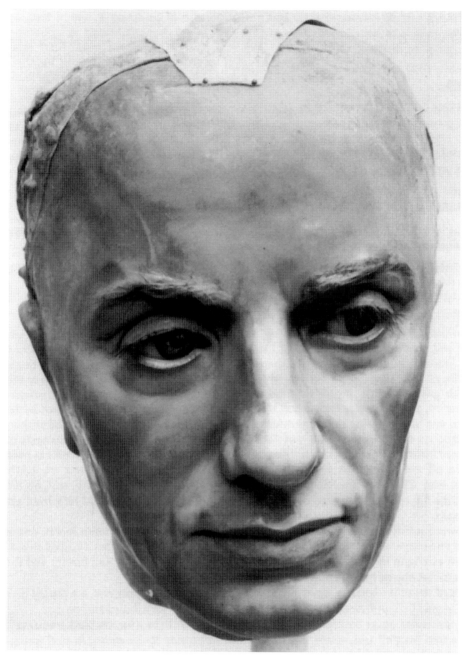

23 Catherine Andras wax effigy, 1806. The wax head shows a keloid scar above the right eyebrow and scarring around the outer aspect of the eyebrow. (National Maritime Museum)

24 Detail from Devis' Death of Nelson showing a trickle of blood from the right side of the mouth.

VIII

Character and Personality

In the late 1990s, when the National Maritime Museum was putting together a new Nelson Gallery, fifty-four people on site were asked to describe in one word Nelson's personality. There were surprisingly few repetitions. Forty-six different adjectives from Ambitious to Xenophobic were used as an attempt to 'explain' Nelson; a hard task. Even in his lifetime he was considered unique. As Earl St. Vincent wrote: 'There is but one Nelson'[1], but because he had such an impact upon everyone he met, it is possible to describe the man using the words of his relatives and friends, enemies and contemporaries, professional colleagues and intimates; and of course Nelson's judgement of himself.

The chief characteristics and personality traits of successful military leaders were discussed in Professor Norman Dixon's book, *On the Psychology of Military Incompetence*. He listed:

1. Achievement, and motivation towards professional excellence.
2. Greater occupational and intellectual competence.
3. A good memory for unfinished tasks, and a predisposition to finish tasks once begun.
4. A preference to choosing for working partners successful strangers rather than unsuccessful friends.
4. Greater activity in the institution or community of which they are a member.[2]

That Nelson was highly motivated towards professional excellence and then succeeded in attaining it, is self evident. What tends to be forgotten is how comparatively young he was when he was killed and also how much he had already achieved, working up ship after ship, and then fleet after fleet, and leading them to almost universal success against their enemies, whether in major naval battles or minor ship-to-ship or ship-to-shore engagements. This could only have been achieved by extraordinary intellectual competence.

Nelson never shirked work, physical or mental. He seems never to have left tasks unfinished however busy he was. Despite a good secretariat, in the last weeks of his life, he was often writing six to eight hours a day. In a letter to Emma on 13th October 1805 he gave some idea of his *modus operandi*: 'I am working like a horse in a mill, but never the nearer finishing my task, which I find difficulty enough in getting and keeping clear from confusion, *but I never allow it to accumulate.*'[3] (Author's italics.) He also seems to have been a superb delegator and managed almost always to get the best out of subordinates by the use of excellent man management skills. Very few people let him down, and he led by example: he himself let very few people down. Captain Duff of the *Mars*, (later killed at Trafalgar) wrote to his wife 'He is so good and pleasant that we all wish to do what he likes, without any kind of orders,' and added later, 'He certainly is the pleasantest Admiral I ever served under.'[4] It is a fact that Nelson always looked for efficient strangers to work with rather than inefficient friends. The warmth of his character and personality was much appreciated, easily understood and greatly welcomed. He gave praise whenever possible, showed confidence in subordinates and issued them clear orders. He somehow changed almost everyone he came into contact with into a friend. From the highest in the land (the King's third son who was chief guest at Nelson's wedding), to the lowliest – he on one occasion was rebuked by his sailor servant publicly for drinking too much and accepted the reprimand – all were friends.

Nelson's unstinting activities in the community of which he was a member are everywhere recorded in this book. His high intelligence was an enabling factor, as was his sleep pattern: but there was a price to pay. There were frequent times when anxiety and stress caused marked weight loss.

Casual acquaintances and even strangers who turned up unannounced at his home, Merton, were talked to, or entertained. He seems to have been the most warm and loving member of his very extended family. Only to his wife and his stepson did his affections alter in a most terrible way, as has been discussed earlier. Even then, when he reacted so wickedly (no other word for it) towards both Fanny, who had never ceased to love him, and Josiah, who had helped to save his life at Tenerife, he did not change the financial provisions made for his wife when he left her.[5]

Nelson helped to put his nephews and nieces through school, he kept 'open house' afloat and ashore. There are many examples of Nelson's practical, financial generosity. The upshot was that he died leaving very little money and in debt to his old friend of many years, Alexander Davison. His generosity was frequently spontaneous. In January 1801, more than two years after the Battle of the Nile, Nelson went to Plymouth to board the *San Jose*. He travelled via Honiton where he invited to breakfast with him the widow and daughter of Captain George Wescott, of the *Majestic*, who had been killed at the Nile. He asked Mrs Wescott if she had received her late husband's gold medal to which all Nile Captains, Nelson's original

'Band of Brothers', had been entitled. She replied she had not yet received it and Nelson took his own Nile medal from around his neck and gave it to her there and then. 'It was my duty to show them respect.'[6] he wrote to Lady Hamilton. But, since we know his medals, ribbons and decorations meant a lot to him, it was a gesture of real generosity.

Nelson was always generous with his money. When his older brother, Maurice, died, it was discovered he had never married the lady he had been living with for years. Nevertheless, Nelson regarded her as his sister-in-law, paid her debts and gave her an annuity of £100 a year. He also invited her to Merton exactly as one of the family. When he heard of Maurice's death, Nelson wrote to Alexander Davison 'I hope he (Maurice) has left her well provided for, if not I beg you will take the trouble to arrange a proper and simple subsistence, and I will make it up.'[7] Three days later he wrote again to Davison 'I beg you will be everything generous towards her for she shall ever be by me considered as his honoured wife.'[8] In a codicil to his will of 10th May 1803, he wrote 'I desire that the sum of £100 … may be annually paid into the reputed widow of my brother Maurice Nelson … to be paid quarterly as it is paid at present.'[9]

George Matcham, eldest son of Nelson's favourite sister, Catherine, described Nelson's caring nature in 'Notes on the Character of Lord Nelson' published in *The Times* over 50 years after Nelson's death:

> Lord Nelson in private life was remarkable for a demeanour quiet and unobtrusive, anxious to give pleasure to everyone about him, distinguishing each in turn by some act of kindness, and chiefly those who seemed to require it most … He delighted in quiet conversation, through which occasionally ran an undercurrent of pleasantry not unmixed with caustic wit.[10]

As well as knowing how to lead seamen in battle, on active ships at sea, and in blockade Nelson was also adept at influencing the Great and the Good on shore.

In the 18th century young men were 'brought out' (that is, left home for employment) young, and grew up quickly. Nelson was lucky in his early naval mentors. They taught him at a young age to be master of his craft of captaining a King's ship, and to take responsibility for the men under his command. He never seems to have had any difficulty in exercising authority, leading by example so that men under his command were prepared to follow him into battle, accepting the risk that they might be killed or wounded whilst so doing. In early 1797, having been promoted to rear admiral, he raised his flag on *Theseus*, captained by Ralph Miller. In April and May of the same year the Spithead and Nore Mutinies broke out in the British Fleet, and *Theseus* was not unaffected. But Nelson, when he took over the ship, had brought with him officers and men from his two previous ships, the extremely successful *Agamemnon* and *Captain*. 'All her [*Theseus*] key posts were put in the hands of proven followers.'[11] A new regime of fewer floggings was instituted by Miller. Improved pay and provisions were instituted by the Admiralty. These were the precursors of modern management 'reward systems'.[12] They resulted in a paper being dropped on the quarter deck one night, which read:

> Success attend Admiral Nelson. God bless Captain Miller. We thank them for the officers they have placed over us. We are happy and comfortable, and will shed every drop of blood in our veins to support them, and the name of the *Theseus* shall be immortalised....
> Signed: Ship's Company.[13]

Nelson seems always to have been able to exercise authority over his men whilst at the same time ensuring that he was captain of a team to each member or group of which he had clearly designated and delegated relevant tasks. It is evident from even the most cursory glance at Nelson's letters that he was an extraordinarily able communicator. He would have set goals at meetings, made decisions after discussion, ensured that everyone knew his role.

Vitally important was his ability to motivate men. Initially this was on a one-to-one basis to the officers in a single ship command, and through those officers to the men they in turn directed. Latterly, as he rose through his profession he motivated increasingly large numbers of ships and their ships' companies in the fleets he commanded, until his well-deserved reputation went before him. As a young captain, his paternalistic attitude to his midshipmen was brilliantly described by Lady Hughes, the wife of Admiral Sir Richard Hughes, who was to be Nelson's Commander in the West Indies. In April 1784, Nelson in *Boreas* sailed from Portsmouth, taking Lady Hughes across the Atlantic to join her husband. He also had on board some 30 midshipmen, most of whom were going to join other ships once they reached Barbados, where Sir Richard was stationed. Some 21 years later she wrote the following account of Nelson's leadership where the midshipmen were concerned:

> I can only be a judge of those things that I could comprehend – such as his attention to the young gentlemen who had the happiness of being on his quarter-deck. It may reasonably be supposed that among the number of thirty, there must be timid as well as bold; the timid he never rebuked, but always wished to show them he desired nothing of them that he would not instantly do himself: and I have known him say 'Well, Sir, I am going a race to the masthead, and beg I may meet you there.' No denial could be given to such a wish, and the poor fellow instantly began his march. His Lordship never took

the least notice with what alacrity it was done, but when he met in the top, instantly began speaking in the most cheerful manner, and saying how much a person was to be pitied that could fancy there was any danger, or even anything disagreeable, in the attempt. After this excellent example, I have seen the timid youth lead another, and rehearse his captain's words. In like manner, he every day went into the school-room, and saw them do their nautical business, and at twelve o'clock he was the first upon deck with his quadrant. No one there could be behind-hand in their business when their captain set them so good an example.[14]

Nelson's single ship-board leadership was gradually replaced by a reputation second to none as an extremely successful battle fleet leader, fully appreciated even by those who had never served under him. 'Send us Lord Nelson, O ye men of Power!'[15] wrote Captain Codrington, of the *Orion*, who had never met Nelson when he made the appeal, just before the battle of Trafalgar.

The first time Codrington and Nelson met was at the second of Nelson's famous pre-Trafalgar dinners. Codrington wrote to his wife 'the signal has been made this morning for all of us who did not dine on board *Victory* yesterday, to go there today.' He noted '… the superiority of Nelson in all these social arrangements *which bind his captains to their Admiral.*' (Author's italics). Codrington was even more touched when Nelson personally handed him a letter from his wife, saying that as it had been entrusted to him (Nelson) by a lady, he was making a point of delivering it personally.[16]

What Mahan calls 'the same genial sweetness of manner, the outcome of an unaffected cordial goodwill to all,'[17] was shown to (almost all) those who came in contact with him, so that Captain Duff wrote of Nelson to his wife just before Trafalgar: 'He is so good and pleasant a man, that we all wish to do what he likes, without any kind of orders.'[18]

Nelson analysed problems and issued clear cut goals. He was happy to discuss objectives with other officers in the fleets he led. By maintaining open communication with all his captains he ensured on the one hand that all their possible good contributions to the overall aim of victory were taken into consideration while at the same time knowing that *his* plans were understood by those he commanded. Perhaps the single most vital aspect of Nelson's leadership, aside from his innate command of warfare, was that throughout his life he gave praise, rewarding real merit openly, but never appeared to have any favourites.[19]

A good example of Nelson's quickness to praise occurred in a letter he wrote to William Marsden at the Admiralty in August 1804 from *Victory* at sea in the Mediterranean:

I herewith transmit you a copy of a contract entered into by Doctor Snipe, Physician of the Fleet, and Mr. Gray, Surgeon of the Naval Hospital at Malta, with Mr. John Broadbent, Merchant at Messina, for supplying thirty thousand gallons of lemon juice, for the Sick and Hurt Board, which you will please to lay before the Lords Commissioners of the Admiralty for their information, as it appears to me, from the low price contracted for, to be an object of great consideration in the Victualling Department, and by which immense sums might be saved by that Board in their future purchase of this article, which I understand from the Physician of the Fleet, may be had in any quantity.

I must here beg to observe, that Doctor Snipe went from Malta (where he was on service) to Messina, for the purpose of accomplishing this contract: and when it is considered that lemon juice in England (if so it may be called) costs eight shillings per gallon, and in the contract before-mentioned only one shilling for the real juice, it will, I am sure, entitle Doctor Snipe to their Lordships' approbation for his conduct and perseverance on the occasion; and I understand from him, that Mr. Broadbent's profits are still very fair.[20]

It is not known if he informed Dr Snipe that he had written to the Admiralty about him but, shortly after his considerable achievement in obtaining the lemon juice at such a cheap price, Dr Snipe died and Nelson wrote again to Lord Barham, First Lord of the Admiralty in support of Snipe's widow. He reiterated how clever Snipe had been and commented that he had probably caught the illness that killed him while so employed.[21]

Captain Keats of the *Superb* must have been delighted to receive a letter from his Admiral written from *Victory* on 19th May 1805 when the British Fleet were in hot pursuit of Villeneuve's French Fleet, out in the Atlantic. Nelson wrote:

My dear Keats, I am fearful that you may think that the *Superb* does not go so fast as I could wish. However that may be, (for if we all went ten knots, I should not think it fast enough,) yet I would have you be assured that I know and feel that the *Superb* does all which is possible for a ship to accomplish; and I desire that you will not fret upon the occasion.[22]

Superb clearly had a foul ship's bottom from being a long time at sea. This meant she would find it very difficult to keep up with the rest of the fleet due to the 'drag' of many yards of seaweed and marine animalculae attached to her keel. Nelson had written to the Admiralty about *Royal Sovereign* three months previously when she had a similar problem. *Royal Sovereign* was re-coppered before Trafalgar which meant that she, leading the half of the British Fleet commanded by Collingwood, out-sailed every ship in the fleet and was subjected to fire from several enemy ships at once without support at the beginning of the battle. There was nothing that Keats could do about his ship, lagging behind the rest of the British Fleet out in the Atlantic. But the reassuring letter from his Admiral must have made a considerable difference to the morale of Keats and his crew.

The following story of Nelson and the coxswain's letter must have travelled from ship to ship to ship in the British Fleet. The account comes from Mahan, and was told to him by a descendant of Lieutenant Pasco:

> Just before Trafalgar, 'Word had been passed through the fleet that a mail was about to start for England, which would not improbably be the last opportunity of writing home before the enemy came forth. The letters had been collected as usual, the bags were all on board the departing vessel, and she herself, under full sail, had got already some distance away, when Nelson saw a midshipman come up and speak to Lieutenant Pasco, the signal officer, who, upon hearing what was said, stamped his foot in evident vexation, and uttered an exclamation. The admiral, of whose nearness Pasco was not aware, called him, and asked what was the matter. 'Nothing that need trouble your Lordship' was the reply. 'You are not the man to lose your temper for nothing,' rejoined Nelson. 'What was it?' 'Well, if you must know, my Lord, I will tell you. You see that cockswain,' [sic] pointing to one of the most active of the petty officers; 'we have not a better man on board the *Victory* and the message which put me out was this. I was told that he was so busy receiving and getting off the mail-bags, that he forgot to drop his own letter to his wife into one of them, and he has just discovered it in his pocket.' 'Hoist a signal to bring her back,' was Nelson's instant command; 'who knows that he may not fall in action tomorrow. His letter shall go with the rest,' – and the dispatch vessel was brought back for that alone.' In telling the story, Pasco used to say it was no wonder that the common sailors idolized Nelson, since he was always thinking about them, and won their hearts by showing his own.[23]

Lastly, Nelson the leader was a visionary. A vision needs to be expressed as a statement that communicates a clear understanding of the long term aims and the principles underlying it. Vision and mission wording should be kept brief, clear and prescriptive, and visionaries 'can see the benefits of change, and have the courage to carry out change despite obstacles.'[24] Nelson's Trafalgar battle plan – 'It was new, it was singular, it was simple'[25] – and the way he explained it in the two 'master' dinners he organised as soon as he arrived off Cadiz in September

1805, established amongst the captains of all the ships under his command the vision he had of complete annihilation of the combined French-Spanish Fleet. An innovative battle plan had been circulated, discussed, evaluated, 'it must succeed,' and then utterly simplified: 'But in case signals can neither be seen or perfectly understood, no captain can do very wrong if he places his ship alongside that of an enemy.'[26] It is the author's opinion that never before – *or since* – 21st October 1805 has any British military force ever entered into a major contest with an enemy more sure of exiting from the contest utterly victorious.

In her book *The 7 Keys of Charisma*, Kozubska argues that great military leaders combine the skills of being excellent at planning with running the 'business' of controlling their men: that is, analysis and leadership.[27] Nelson was an archetypal example of a person having these two skills. He was adept at controlling the overall practical considerations necessary to achieve a first-class finely-tuned fleet while at the same time planning for the successful fleet actions which ensured that it was always victorious. This is why Dr. Gillespie's letter (see p. 245) is so relevant as it is contemporaneous proof from an intelligent witness of how Nelson achieved extraordinary levels of fitness and high morale amongst the many ships and thousands of men he commanded.

Admiral Sir Michael Layard K.C.B., in a speech in 1994, talked of 'the four 'T's' and then applied them to Nelson's Fleet at Trafalgar. The first 'T' was *Technology*: the guns of the British ships and their rate of fire, were superior. But the other three 'T's: *Training, Tactics* and *Trust* were very much under the control and leadership of Nelson. Layard pointed out that training at sea gave the British an enormous advantage; that Nelson's tactics, cutting the enemy fleet at right angles, were risky but brilliant, dividing as they did a superior enemy force into manageable pieces; but that above all victory was ensured due to the trust he engendered among his two fellow admirals and the captains of the ships he commanded, by his frequent personal briefings. It must not be forgotten that it was not only at Trafalgar, but also in his other battles that Nelson's wide-ranging leadership skills were manifest.

Layard made other very important points. He considered Nelson to be self-confident, brave, a master of his profession and a proven winner, who showed charisma, charm, and generosity of spirit mixed with genuine concern and liking for people.[28]

To draw a parallel with the medical profession, a 2003 article by Galloway[29] was concerned with modern Medical Leadership Programmes. Skills required were said to include vision, motivation, communication practice and hard work. Medical Leadership Programmes examine and teach members collaborative working, self awareness, self-belief and self management together with effective and strategic influencing, and empowering of others. The more Nelson is examined in terms of his leadership skills the more modern he appears.

In June 1797 Nelson wrote two letters to Sir John Jervis about two men who were on board *Swiftsure,* suspected of pretending to be mad in order to obtain their discharge:

> ... even the sight of the two poor men in irons on board her has affected me more than I can express; if Mr. Weir would look at them, I should be glad. The youth may, I hope, be saved, as he has intervals of sense, his countenance is most interesting. If any mode can be devised for sending him home, I will with pleasure pay fifty pounds to place him in some proper place for his recovery; the other, I fear, is too old.[30]

Letter 2:

> I hope, for the poor men's sakes, that they are imposing on me; but depend on it, that God Almighty has afflicted them with the most dreadful of all diseases. They do not sham; indeed you will find I am not mistaken, and all the Commissioners in the World cannot convince me of it. For what purpose can these poor wretches attempt to destroy themselves? For what purpose can one of them have spoken to me as rationally as a person could do? Do let Mr. Weir look at them; I am sure he will think with me, from the order to represent those who are objects unfit for the service, I could not do otherwise than I did ...[31]

Dr Weir was Physician to the Fleet at the time. Nelson was not a wealthy man and the two men were not even from his ship. The offer of £50 was an extremely generous one.

In another example, written only three weeks before Trafalgar, Nelson again offered his own money, if it were needed, in a situation which was nothing personally to do with him. The letter is self-explanatory:

To Captain Sotheron, Naples   *Victory* September 30th 1805

My dear Sotheron,

> Captain ...'s son is adrift in Italy, at Naples, or Rome; we think, very probably, in prison for debt. His father is very anxious to save the lad. He was Lieutenant of the *Hydra* and ran away with an opera-dancer from Malta. Pray try, with Mr. Elliot, at Naples, and with Mr. Jackson, at Rome, to get word of Mr. ... Captain ... will pay the bills he has drawn for on England – supposed to be two or three hundred pounds – and if now a few more is necessary to liberate the youth, I will be answerable. All we want is to save him from perdition.
> NELSON AND BRONTE [32]

145

The harshness not only of living in the 18th century but also of the particular rigours of navy life make Nelson's compassion all the more noteworthy; apart from his behaviour towards his wife and stepson after the breakdown of his marriage, when there is a strong sense that Nelson's own guilt was transferred to a guiltless pair.

During his period of unemployment for five years from 1788 to 1792, Nelson lived the life of a minor squire. He shot, gardened and rode out on a pony over his father's farm land. But he also put together in December 1783 an extraordinary report on his father's local Norfolk farm labourers. During those five years, France had been in political turmoil with the storming of the Bastille, (July 1789) the unsuccessful flight of King Louis XVI (June 1791) and the success of Revolutionary France against a Prussian army (September 1792). Discontents and *agents provocateurs* had appeared in England and Norfolk was particularly affected. There were riots throughout the county. This then was the background to Nelson's social survey, which must have involved him in a lot of research and labour, and which he sent to his friend, Prince William, by then the Duke of Clarence, in December 1792.

> That the poor labourer should have been seduced by promises and hopes of better times, your Royal Highness will not wonder at, when I assure you that they are really in want of everything to make life comfortable.* Part of their wants, perhaps, are unavoidable from the dearness of every article of life: but much has arisen from the neglect of the country gentlemen in not making their farmers raise their wages in some small proportion as the prices of things increased. The enclosed paper will give your Royal Highness an idea of their situation … I have been careful that no country gentleman should have it in his power to say, I had pointed out the wants of the poor greater than they really are.[33]

> [*Nelson had originally written 'Hunger is a sharp thorn, and they are not only in want of food sufficient, but also of clothes and firing.']

Nelson then carefully itemised the earnings and expenses of a Norfolk labourer with a wife and three children. The whole report made chilling reading. Alas, it was completely ignored by the recipient.

ACCOUNT OF THE EARNINGS AND EXPENSES OF A LABOURER
IN NORFOLK, WITH A WIFE AND THREE CHILDREN, SUPPOSING
THAT HE IS NOT TO BE ONE DAY KEPT FROM LABOUR IN THE
WHOLE YEAR; DRAWN UP BY CAPTAIN NELSON

One pair of Men's shoes, 7s., one pair of Women's, 4s. 6d., one pair for each of the three Children, 10s. 6d.	£1. 1. 0.
For mending:	
Shoes and Mending	2. 3. 0.
Shirts, two	0. 10. 0.
Breeches or Jacket	0. 3. 0.
Women's and Children's clothes	1. 6. 0.
Soap, 12 lbs.	0. 8. 10.
Candles, 6 lbs.	0. 4. 0.
Coals, one chaldron and a half	1. 19. 0.
House Rent	2. 0. 0.
	8. 13. 10.

The advanced prices

From Oct. 10th to March 31st, at 9s. per week	11. 14. 0.
From March 31st to June 30th, at 8s. per week	5. 4. 0.
From June 30th to Aug. 24th, turnip-hoeing & hay harvest	3. 0. 0.
Harvest	2. 2. 0.
Woman's gleaning	1. 1. 0.
Total earnings	23. 1. 0.

Earnings	23. 1. 0.
Clothes, etc.	8. 13. 10.
For food, five people	14. 7. 2.

Not quite two-pence a day for each person, and to drink nothing
but water, for beer our poor labourers never taste, unless they are
tempted, which is too often the case, to go to the Alehouse.[34]

Reading the survey it is extraordinary that the families Nelson interviewed
should have been prepared to give him such intimate details.

Nelson was nothing if not thorough if he felt details were called for.
Two letters exist from his long last-but-one commission. William Marsden
Esq., Admiralty, must have been astonished and yet fascinated to receive
this letter of 12th August 1803 from the most famous and exalted of the
Admiralty's servants:

Victory, 12th August 1804
To William Marsden Esq., Admiralty

Sir,

You will please to acquaint the Lords Commissioners of the Admiralty, that the Diligent Transport has brought out frocks and trowsers [sic] for the use of the Fleet under my command, but instead of their being made of good Russia duck, as was formerly supplied the Seamen of his Majesty's Navy, the frocks at 4s. 8d. each, and the trowsers at 4s. per pair, those sent out are made of coarse wrapper-stuff, and the price increased – the frocks two-pence each and the trowsers threepence per pair, which makes the former 4s. 10d. and the latter 4s. 3d. I therefore think it necessary to send you one of each in order that their Lordships may judge of their quality and price; and at the same time beg to observe, for their information, that the issuing such coarse stuff to the people, who have been accustomed to good Russia duck cheaper, will no doubt occasion murmur and discontent, and may [have] serious consequences. *I therefore am most decidedly of opinion, that the Contractor who furnished such stuff ought to be hanged:* [author's italics] and little less, if anything, is due to those who have received them from him. I shall say no more on the subject as their Lordships will naturally see the propriety of this evil being remedied as early as possible.

I am, etc.
NELSON AND BRONTE

P.S. Enclosed is a letter from Captain Hardy of the *Victory*, on the subject of the frocks, and trowsers. The Malta cotton therein alluded to is sent in a box, with a sample of the Slops lately received by the *Diligent* store-ship.³⁵

One cannot help but wonder what happened to the 'Contractor ... [who] ought to be hanged'! Another letter was also full of fascinating detail:

[To the Commissioners of the Navy]
Victory at sea, 20th November 1804

Gentlemen,

In further answer to your Letter of the 25th June last, relative to my opinion of the Guernsey jackets of a new manufacture, as therein mentioned (which were issued to the Seamen on the 14th October) and what further supply of them may be necessary for the Squadron under my command, I must beg leave to observe that the quality of the said Guernsey jackets is most excellent, but that they are considerably too narrow and short to be tucked into the Men's trowsers. It is therefore, my opinion, that they ought to be at least three inches wider, and six longer. Indeed, if they were ten inches or a foot, it would be so much better, as they shrink very considerably in washing; and when the Seamen are on the yards, reefing or furling sails, the jacket rubs out of their trowsers, and exposes them to great danger of taking cold in their loins, so that, with this alteration, which is particularly necessary, they certainly would be the best and most valuable slops that ever were introduced into the Service, and be the means of saving many a good Seaman's life. With respect to the quantity required, it would not be too many to send out one for every Seaman in the Fleet. Perhaps the Guernsey jacket, in its present state, might answer the largest of the boys.[36]

Over the centuries Britain has been for the most part fortunate in her war leaders. Marlborough, Wellington, Wolfe, Haig, Montgomery, Slim, and Churchill were all successful. But none, not even Slim, has been loved as Nelson was loved. Alexander Scott, Nelson's foreign secretary and chaplain, wrote after he was killed 'When I think, setting aside his greatness, what an affectionate fascinating little fellow he was, how kind and condescending his manners, I become quite stupid with grief for what I have lost.'[37] It is important to attempt an analysis of why Nelson was loved. Matt Ridley seems to reach the heart of what it was in his character that made his subordinates react towards him as they did. Ridley wrote:

All human beings have a taboo against selfishness whereas virtue is for the greater good of the group. The conspicuously virtuous things we praise: co-operation, altruism, generosity, sympathy, kindness, selflessness are all unambiguously concerned with the welfare of others ... Only something like glory is an ambiguous virtue because it shades so easily into vain glory.[38]

Under the command of Nelson, however, his officers and men found glory which was genuine, fighting and winning against Napoleon and his ambitions which they saw as threatening their country and their way of life. The Nile was the El Alamein of its time and Napoleon's first major setback. Trafalgar ensured that Napoleon *had* thereafter to fight a European land war and could never conquer Britain.

Sir Robert Calder was Sir John Jervis' Captain of the Fleet at the Battle of Cape St. Vincent. He is remembered in naval history for the following exchange with his leader, just before the battle started:

'There are eight sail-of-the-line, Sir John.'

'Very well, sir.'

'There are twenty sail-of-the-line, Sir John ... Twenty-five ...'

'Enough of that, sir! If there are fifty sail, I will go through them. England badly needs a victory at present!'[39]

In the battle, Nelson in *Captain*, supported only by four other ships, one of which was commanded by his friend Collingwood, had performed a very unorthodox manoeuvre in order to prevent part of the enemy fleet from escaping. He had also captured two enemy ships by the extraordinary expedient of attacking the second by launching himself and his forces from the first – Nelson's so-called 'Patent Bridge for Boarding First Rates.' Calder's reaction to this was recorded. He suggested that Nelson had acted in defiance of orders. Sir John Jervis' reply is also on record: 'It certainly was so, and if ever you commit such a breach of your orders, I will forgive you also.' Calder was knighted after the battle. One can see why Nelson and Calder were not at all close friends.

In the weeks before Trafalgar, Calder, now in command of a British Fleet squadron off Finistere, came into contact with Villeneuve's Fleet as it fled back to Europe from the West Indies. Two of Villeneuve's ships were captured, but winds were very light, nightfall intervened and the encounter was inconclusive. Calder, although he had the opportunity, failed to press home the action. The majority of Villeneuve's force escaped into Vigo and so remained a threat to the British defending the English Channel in their efforts to prevent the invasion of England by Napoleon. When Nelson landed back in England on 20th August 1805, he found that Calder was being heavily criticised for not pressing home his action in the way that the public and the popular press were sure Nelson would have done. When Nelson rejoined the British Fleet he had to give Calder orders from the Admiralty to return home to face an inquiry Calder had asked for, which would enquire into why he had not been more aggressive. Calder had little insight into feelings, both official and populist, about his failure to press home the fight against the enemy. Nelson commented to Collingwood, 'He has an ordeal to pass through which I fear he little expects'[40] and suggested to Calder that he delay his departure until after the battle which all knew was imminent. Calder refused, and also requested that he be allowed to go home in his own 90-gun flagship *Prince of Wales*, instead of leaving such a powerful vessel with Nelson and transferring to a small ship. Nelson, as an act of huge generosity, which cold reason would call foolhardy, agreed. All he asked of Calder was to wait until *Royal Sovereign*, newly coppered, arrived. When explaining his decision, Nelson wrote 'He is in adversity.'[41]

On 15th October 1805 Nelson wrote to Captain Hamond, commanding the frigate *Lively:*

Sir Robert Calder has just left us to stand his trial, which I think of a very serious nature. God send him a good deliverance.[42] [Quoting from Richard III]

There was one fascinating post-script to this story. Calder asked for three Captains of British ships to go back with him to act as witnesses for his defence. The captains of *Ajax* and *Thunderer* did so – and their ships fought at Trafalgar commanded by their First Lieutenants. Both these men survived and were made Post-Captains after the victory. The third captain – Durham of the *Defiance* – read the Admiralty Order and noted that it only said the Captains were to go home 'if willing'. Durham was not willing and so he refused, and declined to sign a public letter applying for leave to quit his ship[43] and he captained *Defiance* at Trafalgar, sailing in Collingwood's division. He, too, survived the battle. Nelson's letter to the First Lord of the Admiralty about Calder is reproduced in full as an example of Nelson's prose and of his extraordinary sensitivity:

TO LORD BARHAM, FIRST LORD OF THE ADMIRALTY

September 1805

My dear Lord,

I did not fail, immediately on my arrival, to deliver your message to Sir Robert Calder; and it will give your Lordship pleasure to find, as it has me, that an inquiry is what the Vice-Admiral wishes, and that he had written to you by the *Nautilus*, which I detained, to say so. Sir Robert thinks that he can clearly prove, that it was not in his power to bring the Combined Squadrons again to Battle. It would be only taking up your time, were I to enter more at large on all our conversation; but Sir Robert felt so much, even at the idea of being removed from his own Ship which he commanded, in the face of the Fleet, that I much fear I shall incur the censure of the Board of Admiralty, without your Lordship's influence with the Members of it. I may be thought wrong, as an Officer, to disobey the orders of the Admiralty, by not insisting on Sir Robert Calder's quitting the *Prince of Wales* for the *Dreadnaught*, and for parting with a 90-gun Ship, before the force arrives which their Lordships have judged necessary; but I trust that I shall be considered to have done right as a man, and to a Brother Officer in affliction – my heart could not stand it, and so the thing must rest, I shall submit to the wisdom of the Board to censure me or not, as to them may seem best for the Service; I shall bow with all due respect to their decision.
I am, &c.

NELSON AND BRONTE[44]

Nelson was, as Nicolas commented[45] 'ever interested in the welfare of those he regarded.' When Nelson left *Albemarle* upon her being paid off on 3rd July 1783, he wrote to the Admiralty, as was proper procedure, to 'Request I may be put upon half-pay.'[46] Within nine days he was writing to William Locker from an address in central London, that:

> My time, since I arrived in town has been taken up in attempting to get the wages due to my *good fellows*, for various Ships they have served in the war. The disquiet of the Seamen to the Navy is all owing to the infernal plan of turning them over from Ship to Ship, so that Men cannot be attached to their Officers, or the Officers care two-pence about them.[47]

It is no surprise, therefore, that Nelson wrote in the next paragraph of the same letter telling Locker that the whole of *Albemarle's* ships company 'offered, if I could get a Ship, to enter for her immediately.'[48]

It has been noted that Nelson on two occasions supported in person, as character references, former shipmates and comrades in Courts of Law, when they were being tried for extremely serious offences.

Reverend Scott wrote to a friend on 10th June 1803, shortly after he began to work as Nelson's foreign language secretary and chaplain:

> I have to communicate some pleasure to you in declaring that I am very well and very happily situated with Lord Nelson. Before embarkation, not having been to sea particularly attached to his suite a possibility arose in my mind that the hero, although very kind, might at sea in his own ship become distant and haughty. To say the truth I did not imagine this myself but it was suggested to me at Portsmouth. I am however glad to say he is quite the contrary, a man with very common abilities and a very vitiated mind may pass his time in England visit in the higher circles and be thought a superior character but in the same cabin at sea the gloss of appearance soon wears off of the man, that is his propensities and his intellect declares itself. In this manner I have observed Lord Nelson and can assure you I think him one of the purist and most disinterested beings I ever yet in life met with – I speak of him thus without either praising him for his heroism or blaming him for what the idle mob does – but I think of him as having a mind free from envy hatred and malice even of thinking evil of another of the most charitable nature, charity in its most comprehensive sense (not that of mere almsgiving by the by as the meanest part of it) which includes every good quality spiritualized. To finish with him I am convinced that he has abilities and judges the state of parties in England and the relative politics in Europe with great discrimination. With all this he is acquainted with the world which

notwithstanding his purity of mind is paradoxical and able to play a game at politics with anyone – what makes him able to do so is his honesty of mind the most refined way of doing anything nowadays and against which no rogue is upon his guard.[49]

The Reverend Alexander (John) Scott (1768–1840) was officially Chaplain of *Victory* and nothing else. Unofficially Nelson paid him £100 a year and he acted as Nelson's private secretary and interpreter. He was one of the two people (Walter Burke, purser of *Victory* was the other) in whose arms Nelson died, and he listened to his last wishes. Nelson was very fond of Scott, so it is particularly interesting to read Scott's first impressions.

Nelson's sleep pattern was unusual. Stampi, a researcher with a sleep and alertness research unit in Boston, investigated the sleep patterns of solo yachtsmen in the *Observer* Single-handed Transatlantic Race (OSTAR). He found what counted most for success on OSTAR were sailing skills, mental and physical endurance, and stamina.[50] Stampi also found certain patterns of sleep were associated with better yachtsman performance. The best racers abandoned traditional sleep patterns, taking their sleep in short naps usually of 10–20 minutes and none longer than one hour.[51] This recalls Dr. Scott's comment 'Those brief slumbers for which he (Nelson) was renowned.'[52] Beatty also recorded, 'He possessed such a wonderful activity of mind, as even prevented him from taking ordinary repose, seldom enjoying two hours of uninterrupted sleep, and on several occasions he did not quit the deck during the whole night.'[53]

Stampi noted that the better performing racers could cut their sleep time down to a total of four or five hours in 24. But when he reproduced OSTAR circumstances in controlled experimentation in the laboratory, he found they could only be maintained successfully for eight weeks at most, after which time there occurred in the laboratory subjects gradual deterioration of mood, and further continuation of the experiment produced depression, together with reduced initiative and alertness.[54]

Nelson was almost certainly in considerable sleep deficit for long periods of his active life when at sea; and one example was before the Battle of the Nile. By the time the long chase criss-crossing the Mediterranean ended, he had been eating poorly, was worried about not finding the French and, above all, stressed by the constant delays in obtaining news. He had asked his senior captains for their opinions but he was well aware the ultimate responsibility was his alone.

It must have been with a sense of immense relief that, just prior to the attack upon the stationary French Fleet in Aboukir Bay, Nelson waved his hat to Captain Hood of the *Zealous* to lead into the battle. Hood waved back and lost his hat to a gust of wind – 'There it goes for luck' – but Nelson must have crammed his own back onto his head, which almost certainly saved his life.

After the battle, instead of being able to relax and recuperate, all the local post-battle responsibilities devolved upon Nelson, now severely wounded in the head. The wound itself would have interfered with sleep, and the dawn of 2nd August revealed the extent of the crushing victory on the one hand and the parlous state of some British ships on the other. Notwithstanding the unpleasant effects of his severe concussion Nelson had a great number of decisions to make as Commander of the British Fleet – decisions involving writing dispatches, re-fitting and re-directing the British ships, destroying the most damaged French ships and writing a large number of very important letters. Nelson's own list included letters to India, the Admiralty, Trieste, Vienna, Minorca, St. Petersburg, Constantinople, Smyrna, Egypt, and to Earl St. Vincent, his Command-in-Chief. Nelson's personality and character were not wholly submerged under these responsibilities. Thanks to God for victory were at once given.[55] The Nile Dispatch was written in superb style, for all that *The Times* leader criticised it: 'The narrative of this glorious action is much too concise.'[56] And on the same page is the confirmation: 'Admiral Nelson was severely hurt by a splinter.'[57] Nelson himself, in the penultimate paragraph of his Dispatch, which in *The Times* is dated 3rd August, wrote 'I was wounded in the head and obliged to be carried off the deck.'[58]

Twenty-nine years after their meeting, Wellington recalled to John Wilson Croker the only time that he met Nelson, and Croker wrote down Wellington's account. The recollection has passed into Nelsonian folklore, apparently indicating Nelson's vanity, self glorification and self absorption. However, the account is secondhand and the recollection interval is a very long one. Also, by 1834 Wellington himself was aged 66 and may not have remembered the meeting entirely accurately. At no other time during Nelson's last leave did he behave in the manner described by Wellington in the first part of their meeting. Nevertheless, Croker's account is included for completeness. It should be approached with circumspection:

Walmer, October 1st 1834

We were talking of Lord Nelson, and some instances were mentioned of the egotism and vanity that derogated from his character. 'Why,' said the Duke, 'I am not surprised at such instances, for Lord Nelson was, in different circumstances, two quite different men, as I myself can vouch, though I only saw him once in my life, and for, perhaps, an hour. It was soon after I returned from India. I went to the little waiting-room on the right hand, where I found, also waiting to see the Secretary of State, a gentleman, whom, from his likeness to his pictures and the loss of an arm, I immediately recognised as Lord Nelson. He could not know who I was, but he entered at once into conversation with me, if I can call it conversation, for it was almost all on his side and all about himself, and in, really, a style so vain and so silly as to surprise and almost disgust me. I suppose something that I happened to say may have made him guess that I was *somebody*, and he went out of the room for a moment, I have no doubt to ask the office-keeper who I was, for when he came back he was altogether a different man, both in manner and matter. All that I had thought a charlatan style had vanished, and he talked of the state of the country and of the aspect and probabilities of affairs on the Continent with a good sense, and a knowledge of subjects both at home and abroad, that surprised me equally and more agreeably than the first part of our interview had done; in fact, he talked like an officer and a states-man. The Secretary of State kept us long waiting, and certainly, for the last half or three quarters of an hour, I don't know that I ever had a conversation that interested me more. Now, if the Secretary of State had been punctual, and admitted Lord Nelson in the first quarter of an hour, I should have had the same impression of a light and trivial character that other people have had; but luckily I saw enough to be satisfied that he was really a very superior man; but certainly a more sudden and complete metamorphosis I never saw.[59]

Nelson frequently inveighed against the French. His mother's dislike of them was one of the few things he remembered about her. The author's parents heartily loathed the French and the Germans – the former for their capitulation in 1940 and the latter for seeing them as the cause of both world wars. The influence of parental opinions on children is often underestimated.

Some examples of Nelson's anti-French sentiments:

1. To The Hon. William Wyndham in a letter written four months after the Battle of the Nile – 'Down, down with the French! Is my most earnest prayer.'[60]
2. To the Rt. Hon. Sir Morton Eden in a letter written the same day –'Down, down with the French! ought to be placed in the Council room of every Country in the World.'[61]
3. To Earl Spencer, in a letter written from Naples exactly one year after the Battle of the Nile – 'My principle, my Dear Lord, is, to assist in driving the French to the Devil, and in restoring peace and happiness to mankind.'[62]
4. To the Duke of Clarence, in a letter written from Palermo in November 1799 – 'To serve my King, and to destroy the French, I consider as the great order of all, from which little ones spring ... to obey the great order and object, to down, down with the damned French villains. Excuse my warmth, but my blood boils at the name of a Frenchman. I hate them all – Royalists and Republicans.'[63]

Behind these sentiments lay not only his mother's opinions, but also what Nelson had seen for himself – for example, the French pillaging of Italy and the awful fate of the French Royalists when Toulon was captured by the Jacobins – and he feared the political fallout. He had written to the Duke of Clarence in December 1793 'What calamities Civil Wars produce, and how much does it behove every person to give their aid in keeping peace at Home.'[64] He wrote to his wife the same day: 'Everything which domestic wars produce usually, is multiplied in Toulon ... all is horror.'[65] It was the disaffection in Norfolk that Nelson had witnessed which provoked his research into the Social Report on the agricultural labourers.

Another interesting characteristic was that Nelson was well known to be at times very irritable and on a short fuse. A peer, Lord Radstock, who knew Nelson well, wrote to his son who was a midshipman on board *Victory*, 'Lord Nelson is of so hasty a temper, that in spite of all his natural goodness ... [he] is a man of strong passions ...'[66]

Both of Nelson's most successful captains – Thomas Hardy and Ralph Miller – considered him to be impatient, and Mahan wrote 'Such readiness to flare up must needs be the defect of that quality of promptness, that instant succession of deed to thought, which was a distinguishing feature of Nelson's genius and action.'[67]

Kozubska wrote:

> If I could choose to have only one of the charismatic keys, it would be this one: the ability to communicate effectively. I'd want to have passion and enthusiasm. I'd want to be known as a person who expressed these feelings, who showed that they cared ... [to] help people share visions and intentions, collect and disseminate information, lead, manage, love, and care. [68]

For all his adult life – this was Nelson, and he knew it: 'My disposition cannot bear tame and slow measures'[69] and 'Half measures will never do when I am in command.' [70] But there was a price to pay, and Nelson knew this too: 'Disappointment has worn me to a skeleton and I am, in good truth, very far from well'[71] and 'My health is ruined by fretting.'[72]

On 9th March 1805, from *Victory* at sea, he wrote:

> If I have the good fortune to meet the French Fleet I hope they will make me amends for all my anxiety; which has been, and is, indescribable.[73]

Notes

1. Mahan p.742 (The last words of the book)
2. Dixon, N. p.241
3. Nicolas vol VII p.385
4. ibid p.71
5. ibid p.ccix
6. Quoted in Hibbert p.245
7. Nicolas vol IV p.378
8. ibid p.391
9. Nicolas vol VII p.ccxxxviii
10. *The Times* 6th November 1861
11. Sugden J. p.733
12. Heller R. *Effective Leadership* 1999 p.45 (hereafter Heller)
13. Naish p.326
14. Mahan p.39-40
15. Oman p.608
16. ibid
17. Mahan p.40
18. Nicolas vol VII p.71
19. Heller p.45
20. Nicolas vol VI p.141–2
21. White, C. *Nelson: The New Letters* 2005 p.119
22. Nicolas vol VI p.442
23. Mahan p.710
24. Heller p.60–61
25. *Nelson's Letters to Lady Hamilton* vol. 2 p.101
26. Clarke and M'Arthur vol. 2 p.437
27. Kozubska J. *The 7 Keys of Charisma* p.234 (hereafter Kozubska)
28. Layard, Sir M. *Nelson, Victory, Trafalgar* Friends of the N.M.M. 1995 p.67
29. Galloway M. 'How can Doctors learn to be great Leaders' *Hospital Doctor* 18th September 2003
30. Nicolas vol VII p.58
31. Nicolas vol II p.394
32. ibid p.395
33. Clarke and M'Arthur vol 1 p.120
34. ibid
35. Nicolas vol VI p.153–4
36. Nicolas vol VI p.275–6
37. Morrison vol 2 letter 860 p.274
38. Ridley M. *The Origins of Virtue* 1997 p.38
39. Oman p.204
40. Nicolas vol VII p.114

41. Quoted in Mahan p.705
42. Nicolas vol VII p.126
43. ibid p.84
44. ibid p.56–7
45. ibid p.35
46. Nicolas vol 1 p.76
47. ibid
48. ibid p.77
49. N.M.M. AGC/8/16
50. Coren S. *Sleep Thieves* 1996 p.281. (Hereafter Coren)
51. ibid
52. Gatty p.122
53. Beatty p.80
54. Coren p.282
55. Nicolas vol III p.61
56. *The Times* 3rd October 1796 p.2 col. 3
57. ibid
58. ibid
59. Jennings J. (ed) *Correspondence and Diaries of J. W. Croker* 1884 vol.2 p.23–234
60. Nicolas vol III p.191
61. ibid p.194
62. ibid vol III p.427
63. Nicolas vol IV p.95
64. Nicolas vol I p.344
65. ibid p.345
66. Mahan p.606
67. ibid
68. Kozubska p.102
69. Nicolas vol II p.26
70. Nicolas vol II p.64
71. Nicolas vol VI p.431
72. Nicolas vol VII p.ccvi
73. *Nelson's Letters to Lady Hamilton* vol 2 p.89

CHAPTER IX

Refuting Suicide; and Nelson's Religion

The possibility that Nelson committed suicide was first suggested in a biography published in 1930.[1] This theory was not given widespread consideration until 1969 when *The Times* published an article by a doctor, Henry Durrant, with the title 'Was Nelson a Suicide?' Durrant put forward his theory that Nelson 'determinedly planned his own death that day so that his mistress, Lady Hamilton, and their daughter Horatia could be made financially secure.'[2]

Durrant based his opinion that Nelson deliberately courted death upon evidence that can be demonstrated to be false. Nelson's possible suicide is medically relevant; it must therefore be properly refuted.

The first evidence Durrant cited was that Nelson did not put on his sword on the morning of the Battle of Trafalgar, for the first known time going into a major sea battle unarmed. Durrant believed this was because psychologically Nelson did not want to defend himself in the coming battle. It is not difficult to dismiss this claim. Tom Allen, Nelson's usual chief body servant, was not on board *Victory* to look after him because he had arrived at Portsmouth one day too late to join *Victory* when she sailed on 15th September. Chevalier, the body servant Nelson took with him put the sword out for Nelson to wear but did not help him to do so, as a one-armed man would require. The sword, a mere uniform decoration and not a genuine means of defence, was left in his cabin.

Durrant alleged that Nelson wore 'a long full dress coat with epaulettes, his full decorations were embroidered upon it ... We have to assume that contrary to all the priorities of naval warfare, the Commander-in-Chief wishes to be, and remain, conspicuous to the Enemy.'[3] But subsequent correspondents to *The Times* were quick to point out Nelson was wearing *un*dress uniform – what Surgeon Beatty called 'his common apparel.'[4] Undress uniform is much less conspicuous than full dress as it has far less gold braid upon it. It was clearly a type of uniform he frequently wore. His servant put out his ordinary clothes on the morning of the battle.

Durrant next said that Nelson refused to abandon, at the request of all the friends around him on board *Victory*, the most dangerous position in the British Fleet, thereby exposing himself to the utmost danger. But there was no more danger for Nelson in *Victory* leading one half of the attacking British Fleet than for Admiral Collingwood in *Royal Sovereign* leading the other half. Collingwood's only concession to *his* dangerous position was to urge his captain, Rotherham, to wear shoes and stockings (as Collingwood himself was) and not boots, so that any necessary surgical intervention, should he be wounded, could be more easily carried out. The crew on the upper decks of all ships at Trafalgar, be they British, Spanish or French, were exposed to a hail of small and large shot, langridge, shrapnel and grenades, and large and small wood splinters, whatever they wore, and wherever on the upper deck they positioned themselves. The whole British Fleet knew that their two senior admirals were in the two ships leading the two halves of the fleet into battle. This was a major morale factor.

Durrant alleged that Nelson was in poor health, about to go blind, very short of money and had many impecunious relatives to support, and that these 'facts' made him suicidal. Not one of these observations was true.

Surgeon Beatty asserted: 'His Lordship's health was uniformly good' and also mentioned: 'His Lordship used a great deal of exercise generally walking on deck six or seven hours a day.'[5]

Beatty believed Nelson would have gone blind (actually unlikely) but even if he had done so, such was his intellectual calibre he never forgot what he heard. Had he lived, it is extremely likely 'Doctor' Scott would have continued as his personal chaplain and secretary wherever he lived and they would have continued their daily habit of Scott reading all newspapers and relevant documents to Nelson and Nelson remembering every word of what Scott said to him. Total blindness, had it eventually occurred, would have inconvenienced Nelson, but it would not have made him suicidal.

With regard to his finances, it is true that his Merton estate had swallowed up much of Nelson's available money and he had borrowed from his friend, Alexander Davison. But he was well aware that successful fleet commanders were financially rewarded not only with superior titles but also with large sums of money. There is no written evidence that financial worries played upon Nelson's mind in the weeks before Trafalgar.

Regarding his relatives, with the exception of his late brother Maurice's 'widow' Blindy, none of them depended upon Nelson financially. They chose to accept Nelson's invitations to stay at Merton but they all had homes of their own. Nelson chose to help to pay the school fees of his nephews and nieces. He could easily have afforded to continue the practice had he survived and returned to Merton.

Durrant said in his article that the future for Nelson after Trafalgar would have been dreary and dull with long spells on shore at half pay. There is no evidence for this. Collingwood was employed at sea for a further five years after Trafalgar and died 'in harness'. Even had Nelson been retired from the Navy (which is highly unlikely) once free from money worries he could have bought a new house or stayed on at 'dear, dear, Merton.' With his extraordinary gift for friendship, his life would never have been dreary or dull.

Nelson's letters to Emma after the death of their second child strongly suggested he had hopes of having further children by her. So did one of the last letters he wrote to her before Trafalgar: 'We will look forward to many, many happy years and be surrounded by our children's children.'[6] In practical terms, should he survive the coming battle, he would be able to view his future with complete optimism.

There is no evidence that Nelson actually contemplated committing suicide, or deliberately setting out to be killed on the day of the battle. *The Times* of 7th November 1805 records that Nelson said to Captain Hardy before the battle, 'I shall probably lose a leg, but that will be purchasing a victory cheaply.'

Nelson would have been fully aware of the religious implications of suicide. A man's life and soul are not his but God's. If he takes his own life he is committing a mortal sin and is stealing something which belongs to God. His soul would not therefore go to heaven and his body could not be buried in consecrated ground. As a suicide, Nelson's soul would not be reunited with his parents in heaven. Nelson, a true believer, would never have taken such a spiritually isolating step.

It is evident in Beatty's account of the battle that anxiety was felt by others for Nelson's safety. Beatty, [with hindsight] wrote:

Several Officers of the ship now communicated to each other their sentiments and anxiety for his Lordship's personal safety, to which every other consideration seemed to give way. Indeed, all were confident of gaining a glorious victory, but the apprehensions for his Lordship were great and general and the Surgeon made known to Dr. Scott his fears that his Lordship would be made the object of the Enemy's marksmen, and his desire that he might be entreated by somebody to cover the stars on his coat with a handkerchief. Dr. Scott and Mr. Scott [Public Secretary] both observed, however, that such a request would have no effect; as they knew his Lordship's sentiments on the subject so well, that they were sure he would be highly displeased with whoever should take the liberty of recommending any change in his dress on this account; and when the Surgeon declared to Mr. Scott that he would avail himself of the opportunity of making his sick-report for the day, to submit his sentiments to the Admiral, Mr. Scott replied, 'Take care, Doctor, what you are about; I would not be the man to mention such a matter to him.' The Surgeon, notwithstanding, persisted in his design, and remained on deck to find a proper opportunity for addressing his Lordship; but this never occurred; as his Lordship continued occupied with the Captains of the frigates [to whom he was explaining his intentions respecting their performance during the battle] till a short time before the Enemy opened their fire on the *Royal Sovereign,* when Lord Nelson ordered all persons not stationed on the poop and quarter-deck to repair to their proper quarters and the Surgeon, much concerned at this disappointment, retired from the deck with several other Officers.[7]

The chief frigate captain was Captain the Honourable Henry Blackwood, a very close friend of Nelson. He, with Hardy, signed as a witness the famous codicil to Nelson's will on the morning of the Battle and his letter to his wife after the battle is reproduced (see p. 215) giving as it does a vivid feel of his emotions on that, and subsequent days. Blackwood clearly felt Nelson's appearance, 'his unfortunate decorations of innumerable stars', was part of the cause of his death. He was also sure that had Nelson accepted his offer and transferred to his ship *Euryalus,* (frigates did not enter into the main battle but skirted around, taking dismasted ships in tow or transmitting signals and orders from ships in one part of the battle to ships in another area) he would have lived. This is almost certainly true, but Nelson refused to transfer to *Euryalus* giving to Blackwood, as his reason, 'force of example.'

What happened in Nelson's mind was not the emergence of suicidal thoughts but a resurgence of the fatalism mentioned elsewhere which had long been a feature of his belief in God. There is no evidence of mental depression in the last weeks of his life – he had been shown marked evidence of regard in England by everyone from the Prince Regent to the ordinary people of Portsmouth. He 'had their hearts now' and knew it. Merton to him was paradise, and Emma 'You are all in all to me' was writing letters, 'All your letters, my dear letters, are so entertaining ... the next best thing to being with you.'[8] He knew he was going to win the battle, so he handed his life to his God. 'For myself individually I commit my life to Him who made me'[9] and 'If it is His providence to cut short my days upon earth I bow with the greatest submission.'[10]

The only time Nelson even appeared to have mentioned the possibility of suicide was during his description, thirty years before, of his feelings just before the 'Radiant Orb' experience, when he 'almost wished myself overboard.'[11] There is no doubt from time to time throughout his life he suffered from anxiety and marked reactive depression but he was never actually suicidal.

Durrant attempted to prove that Nelson, on the last day of his life, deliberately used his position on the upper exposed deck of *Victory* as the means of courting death. But Nelson's chance of being killed at Trafalgar was no greater than at any of his earlier battles when he had not only been at risk from high velocity missiles but had on three occasions been struck by them.

Nelson's letters in the last weeks before his death were warm and not introspective. In private writings, especially his last ones, he mentions the possibility of death, but this was reasonable considering he was fully aware of the high risk of death for all those exposed to the 'Pell Mell' battle that his innovative tactics would precipitate. To Lady Hamilton he was delightfully optimistic, writing to her soon after he left England, 'I entreat my dear Emma, that you will cheer up,' and he added 'God Almighty can, when he pleases, remove the impediment,' clearly holding out to his beloved mistress the picture of a future with an ultimately respectable married life, when his first wife dies! The letter finishes 'For ever, ever I am yours, most devotedly.'[12]

From a medical viewpoint, at the time of Trafalgar Nelson suffered from no conditions associated with an increased risk of self harm. He had no psychiatric illness. He was possessed of an extremely strong character and normal, not to say noble, personality. He knew, after his return from the long chase of Villeneuve and the Combined Fleet across the Atlantic, that he had helped to save Britain from invasion by Napoleon's army. He knew his contribution was fully recognised by the British Government and Establishment. Above all he knew, with a certainty which he communicated to many during his last days in England, that in the next battle he fought the fleet he commanded would defeat the enemy. If he was willing to explain his full battle plan to a junior captain who called on him at Merton on his last leave, as well as to Henry Addington, Lord Sidmouth, using a glass of port wine, his finger and a polished table, he would surely have communicated his certitude of victory to Prime Minister Pitt, colleagues, and members of the Royal Family – the Duke of Clarence and the Prince of Wales – who met with him. Once he knew where the Combined Fleet had sheltered (Cadiz harbour) he was utterly confident of defeating them whenever they emerged.

At the end his fatalism returned – how could he possibly have taken any other attitude? His last hours and days were littered with 'if onlys' (discussed in the next chapter). Once he refused Blackwood's offer to transfer to *Euryalus*, Nelson's chance of being maimed or killed increased immeasurably. But it was not *felo de se* but 'force of example' which made him take up the ultimately fatal position on *Victory's* exposed upper deck.

Amongst *The Times* correspondents responding to Dr. Durrant's 1969 article were four major Nelson biographers, Carola Oman, Oliver Warner, David Howarth, and Sir William James and two other significant historians, Mollie Hardwick and Elizabeth Longford. Not one of them agreed with Dr. Durrant.

The suicide theory brings us to Nelson's religion, which was such a vital part of his thought processes. On 4th March 1793 Nelson, the newly-

appointed Captain of *Agamemnon* fitting out at Chatham, wrote a letter to
one Doctor Gaskin:

> I have to request that you will have the goodness, to offer my solicita-
> tions to the Society for Promoting Christian Knowledge, for a dona-
> tion of Bibles and Prayer books, for the use of the ships crew under
> my command consisting of 500 men.[13]

Nelson's religious beliefs were typically erudite, and uncommon. As the
son of a clergyman, he would have attended church services every sunday
of his life from a very early age. A form of Anglican worship conducted
by the Captain of the ship was performed every Sabbath on Royal Navy
vessels. As a young naval officer Nelson would have attended many such
and conducted them himself as soon as he became Post-Captain. The
Prayer Book of 1662 and the King James Bible of 1611 would have been
part of Nelson's inmost being both in their theology and in their literary
merit, content and form. He quoted both very frequently and deliberately.
However, if being a Christian is to believe that Jesus Christ is the sole
mediator between God and mankind then Nelson appears never to have
been a Christian. The above letter is one of only five instances known of
Nelson having written the word 'Christian,' in letters asking for bibles and
prayer books for the crews of different ships, and then only because he
was writing to the Society for promoting Christian Knowledge. Religious
thought and belief were of enormous importance to him, but he never
appears to have believed in God the Son, or God the Holy Spirit. Nelson's
thoughts, as befitted a son of the Church and a man with at least nine
relatives in Holy Orders, often turned to God, but his Deity was always
God the Father.

His religious beliefs were deeply personal, and an integral part of
his background. They stressed the Oneness of God, and appear to be
committed to reason and tolerance, which are features of Unitarianism,
although it is more likely Nelson was influenced in his religious
beliefs by the Latitudinarians, a religious group whose ideas persisted through the 18th century. Their members flourished in Bath and
Nelson probably came into contact with them there. Latitudinarians
believed the essentials of faith could (and should) be expressed in very
simple religious terms. Nelson is reported on more than one occasion to
have reprimanded his Chaplain and foreign language secretary Alexander
Scott for preaching sermons which were too 'highbrow' for his congregation – the crew of *Victory*. Scott also said Nelson frequently expressed his
attachment to the Established Church, but it would appear that it was
Nelson's own version of that Church to which he was attached.

Latitudinarians believed that the harmony and order of the Universe
pointed to a Creator benevolent and good and this 'God-Father' demanded

of His children a benevolence like His own. This teaching had two simple parts: God the Father, and our duty to show a goodwill comparable to His. The religious outlook of the Latitudinarians has been described as 'reasonable and dispassionate, magnanimous and charitable,'[14] which could also sum up Nelson's own spiritual outlook. They also insisted on the primacy of moral standards – no wonder Nelson sought to rationalise his behaviour with Lady Hamilton so strongly.

During his lifetime Nelson wrote several prayers. His was a generation which did so. Hs spiritual writings, when his brain was concentrated on a matter as important to him as his relationship with God, are crystal clear; and the last prayer he wrote, on the morning of his death, is rightly considered a masterpiece of prayer and of the English language. In his personal religious beliefs, Nelson was a fatalist. He clearly believed in the action of God in freely ordaining whatever comes to pass, especially the lot and fate of all men, and resigned himself to God's will throughout his life.

The background to Nelson's own literary achievements was his deep knowledge of the Bible and Shakespeare. From his letters it can be deduced that he was familiar with the work of other authors and of painters. A letter to William Locker of 2nd November 1783 from St. Omer, France, includes this extract:

> At half past ten we were safe at breakfast in Monsieur Grandsire's house at Calais. His mother kept it when Hogarth wrote [sic] his 'Gate of Calais.' Sterne's Sentimental Journey is the best description I can give of this journey.[15]

So Nelson was familiar with the work of Laurence Sterne (1713–1768), the English novelist and clergyman and author of the inimitable comic masterpiece *The Life and Opinions of Tristram Shandy, Gentleman* (1759–). William Hogarth (1697-1764), the pictorial satirist, painted 'Gate of Calais' in 1749 and it was turned into an extremely popular print. No surprise that Nelson knew of this picture, also known as 'The Roast Beef of Old England', portraying as it does the French as cringing and emaciated! Nelson had Boswell's *Life of Johnson* in his cabin at Trafalgar. As an aside, Nelson achieved a literary 'first' in his letter of November 1783 to William Locker from St. Omer, when writing about two other English naval captains: Ball and Shephard, who he had met there. He commented that 'they are very fine gentlemen with epaulettes.'[16] This is the first known use of the word 'epaulette' in written English, although since Locker was clearly expected to know what Nelson was writing about, the word must have been current in English speech.

Colin White has pointed out that Nelson altered Shakespearean quotations so that they could be recognised but were not repeated verbatim.[17] He did the same with his Biblical quotations. It is possible to find the source of the quotation, the chapter and verse, but often the original was subtly rearranged as it passed through Nelson's brain.

The 'spread' of the quotations was wide in both Old and New Testaments; just as his knowledge of Shakespeare was not confined to the more famous plays. On occasion, a single sentence would include a multiplicity of Shakespearean and biblical references. And, unlike in this impious age, the recipients of Nelson's quotations would have been as familiar with their sources as he was. Nelson clearly had complete access to two of the mainsprings of the English language and used them to build his own literary style.

Here are some examples of Nelson's modifications of the Bible:

'I lament in sackcloth and ashes' (13th October 1796, Nelson to his wife.)[18]	'Mordecai rent his clothes, and put on sackcloth and ashes.' (Esther ch.4 v.1)
'I shall not bring with me either riches or honours' (12th September 1794, Nelson to his wife.)[19]	'I have also given thee that which thou has not asked, both riches and honours' (First Book of Kings ch. 3 v.13)
'I am endeavouring to work for good' (14th July 1799, Nelson to his Wife.)[20]	'and we know that all things work together for good to them that love God.' (St. Paul's Epistle to the Romans chapter 8 v.28)
'May God increase their confusion' (21st December 1799, Nelson to Spiridion Foresti, Corfu.)[21]	'Make haste, oh God, to deliver me … let them be turned backward, and put to confusion, that desire my hurt' (Psalm 70 v. l and 2)
'Would to God I could come and take up my abode there' (29th September 1801, Nelson to Lady Hamilton in Morrison, 1893-94.)[22]	'We will come unto him and make our abode with him' (St. John's Gospel chapter 14 v.23)

Nelson also wrote frequently about God: 'That Great Being who has so often raised me from the sick bed'[23]; 'It has ever pleased God to prosper all my undertakings.'[24]; 'Josiah, under God's providence, was principally instrumental in saving my life'.[25] (Of course, such references to the Divine came as naturally and easily as breathing to most in the 18th century.)

What is very characteristic of Nelson's writing is his *absence* of references to the Son of God.

The Reverend Scott gave an account of Nelson's devotions on board *Victory*:

> To a question put to Dr. Scott as to Lord Nelson's religious sentiments, his answer was, 'He was a thorough clergyman's son – I should think he never went to bed or got up, without kneeling down to say his prayers.' Dr. Scott also said of him ... he always had divine service performed on board the *Victory*, whenever the weather permitted. After the service he had generally a few words with the chaplain on the subject of the sermon, either thanking him for its being a good one, or remarking that it was not so well adapted as usual to the crew; the Admiral being always anxious that the discourse should be sufficiently plain for the men, and his chaplain, with the liability of a scholar, being sometimes tempted into a too learned disquisition; more than once, on such occasions, has Lord Nelson taken down a volume of sermons in his own cabin, with the page already marked at some discourse, which he thought well suited to such a congregation, and requested Dr. Scott to preach it on the following Sunday.[26]

Nelson was very much a 'son of the Church' with a large number of relatives in Holy Orders. Here are the clergyman relatives of Nelson (in all probability not a complete list) as further proof of how steeped in the religious life Nelson was:

Father	Edmund Nelson
Paternal grandfather	Edmund Nelson
Maternal grandfather	Maurice Suckling
Brother	William Nelson
Brother	Suckling Nelson
Uncle by marriage	Robert Rolfe
First cousin once removed	Edmund Nelson
First cousin once removed	William Nelson
First cousin once removed	John Goulty

Subsequently:

Daughter's husband	Philip Ward
Grandson	Horatio Nelson Ward
Great grandson	Hugh Nelson Ward

Notes

1. Edinger G and Neep E. J. C. *Horatio Nelson* 1930
2. Durrant H. 'Was Nelson a Suicide?' *The Times* : June 26th 1969
3. ibid
4. Beatty p.12
5. ibid p.79
6. *Nelson's Letters to Lady Hamilton* 1814 vol II p.97
7. Beatty p.19–22
8. *Nelson's Letters to Lady Hamilton* vol I p.135–6
9. Beatty p.15
10. Nicolas vol VII p.35
11. Clarke and M'Arthur vol 1 p.14
12. *Nelson's Letters to Lady Hamilton* vol II p.97
13. Van Der Merwe, P (ed) *Nelson: An Illustrated History* 1995 p.63
14. Cragg, G.R. *The Church & the Age of Reason* 1960 p.158
15. Nicolas vol I p.84
16. ibid p.89
17. White, C. 'Nelson & Shakespeare' *Nelson Dispatch* vol. 7 part 3 p.145 2000
18. Naish p.305
19. ibid p.122-3
20. Nicolas vol III p.411
21. ibid vol IV p.152
22. ibid vol II p.168 letter 626
23. ibid vol I p.199
24. Naish p.343
25. Naish p.332 letter to Fanny 1797
26. Gatty p.191–2

CHAPTER X

Nelson's Fatal Wounding and Death

On 16th May 1803, after an armistice lasting about two years, the war with France was resumed, and Nelson was appointed Commander in the Mediterranean. He sailed in Victory from Spithead on 18th May joining the British Fleet off Toulon on 16th July. Thereafter Nelson spent many months on blockade duty, never quitting his ship. Unfortunately, in April 1805 the enemy fleet, under Admiral Villeneuve, got out of Toulon, and gave Nelson the slip.

Passing through the Straits of Gibraltar they sailed across the Atlantic in an attempt to capture the West Indies. When he found out what had happened Nelson immediately followed, and it was a measure of the readiness of his fleet and the superb condition in which it was maintained that, although currently on blockade, it could immediately set sail for a trans-oceanic voyage. The chase lasted until July. Villeneuve's attempt failed, but Nelson could not get near enough to the French Fleet in his pursuit to bring it to battle and it once again sought sanctuary in a continental harbour, this time Cadiz. It was while Victory was returning from the West Indies to European waters that a seaman, James Bush, fell out of the rigging and gave Nelson foreknowledge of his own fatal wound.

After the blockade followed by the transatlantic pursuit, Nelson stepped on shore, at Gibraltar, for the first time in two years less ten days. Victory then sailed for home and Nelson landed at Portsmouth on 18th August. His leave lasted only until 14th September, but was quite extraordinarily busy. (See Appendix 2) He then re-embarked on Victory at Portsmouth and rejoined the British Fleet on 28th September, the day before his 47th birthday. He finally brought the combined French and Spanish Fleets to battle on 21st October and on that day he was killed, together with 56 other personnel on board Victory.

The death of Nelson is one of the most famous in British history. Notwithstanding its most familiar aspects – 'Kiss me Hardy' and 'Thank God I have done my duty' – there are many new facts to be considered and conclusions to be drawn, even though the death occurred 200 years ago. William Beatty, the Senior Surgeon on board Victory, produced a sanitised account of Nelson's last hours which has passed into British folklore, and has been repeated in every Nelson biography. Beatty was aided by the iconographic paintings of Benjamin West and Arthur Devis. From the moment 'The Hero' drew his last breath, layers of inaccuracies were put upon the death. These unrealistic descriptions must be challenged in the light of other sources which were contemporaneous with Beatty's own account and appear to have been written by persons present at Nelson's death. Although Beatty's account was medically important since it was one of the first published descriptions of traumatic paraplegia, nevertheless Nelson's death was not the almost bloodless affair Beatty described, and the artists depicted. This chapter also looks at the series of extraordinary circumstances and coincidences which culminated in the shooting of Nelson. At a time when questioning received wisdom has become the norm where Nelson's life is concerned, no biographer, not even the latest, has done more than copy Beatty's account, the *Authentic Narrative*, when describing his death. If his was the only known account of Nelson's death, one would be forced to rely upon what Beatty wrote, but it is not. The other sources, together with consideration of subtle changes in Beatty's own accounts – for he published in at least three different forms – reveal not only that Nelson's last hours were different and far more awful than Beatty described in his book, but that Beatty, and his acolyte, the artist A. W. Devis, were in large measure responsible for the written and pictorial deification of Nelson after 21st October 1805.

Beatty was an ambitious man: the 'Authentic' account of Nelson's last hours was his springboard, and he vaulted very successfully. Devis wanted to sell his picture and the prints from it. He, too, achieved a degree of fame and recognition as a result of Nelson's demise. The British Government and the British People were given their Hero. The (relatively) young leader prepared to lay down his life for his people in times of great danger is a legend as old as Man himself. Aided by Beatty and Devis (and then Benjamin West and Gillray) the gentle slipping away of the mortally wounded Nelson on board *Victory* over a period of some 2¾ hours during the Battle of Trafalgar has been set in stone: the hero dying, but still alert to danger, in control of himself and his fleet, ever mindful of his responsibilities, even to the end of his life. A death others might envy and aspire to.

Four prior events or decisions probably increased the chances of Nelson being wounded at the Battle of Trafalgar. One of these ensured that from the moment he was wounded he *knew* he was going to die and therefore all his reported words, after the wound was sustained, were in the nature of death-bed utterances.

Beatty wrote 'Lord Nelson had often talked with Captain Hardy on the subject of his being killed in battle, which appeared indeed to be a favourite topic of conversation with him. He was always prepared to lay down his life in the service of his Country, and whenever it should please Providence to remove him from this World, it was the ambitious wish of his Soul to die in the fight, and in the very hour of a great and signal victory.'[1] His stated aim of a 'Pell Mell battle' with the simple overall order, 'No Captain can do very wrong if he places his ship alongside that of an enemy,' Nelson knew would involve all upper deck personnel in extreme, unprotected danger from cannon balls, other fired missiles and wood splinters as the two fleets approached each other, and from small arms fire as well when ships were locked together in close combat. Captain Henry Blackwood's suggestion that Nelson control the battle from his ship, the frigate Euryalus, was rejected. This was the first, fatal decision. Everyone in the British Fleet on 21st October would have been aware that the Commander, Nelson in *Victory*, and the Second-in-Command, Collingwood, in *Royal Sovereign*, were each leading half of the fleet into battle as exposed to danger as their men.

The second event was an appallingly random mishap, occurring even before *Victory* broke the enemy line. Beatty reported that 'a double-headed shot struck one of the parties of marines drawn up on the port, and killed eight of them.' This shot came from *Santissima Trinidad*, (four decks, 140 guns) the biggest ship in either fleet.

Beatty continued, 'When his Lordship perceiving this, ordered Captain Adair to disperse his men round the ship, that they might not suffer so much from being together.'[2] The Marines had been gathered in a close group to oppose in a collective manner the very mast sharp-shooters Captain Lucas of the *Redoutable* had trained. Spreading the marines round the deck effectively prevented any concerted response by *Victory* at close quarters and although most of the men in *Redoutable's* rigging had been killed or wounded just about ninety minutes after the first shots in the battle had been fired, one of the last two sharp-shooters that remained aloft on *Redoutable* shot Nelson with an old-fashioned pre-Revolutionary musket at a range of about 15 yards. Captain Adair was later killed as he stood on the gangway encouraging some of his men as they repelled men from *Redoutable* trying to board *Victory*.

After he was shot, Nelson's order was clearly revoked by Marine Officer Rotely (see p. 176). At some stage Rotely also picked up the missile which killed the eight marines and kept it as a macabre souvenir.

The next person in the unfolding drama was Captain Lucas of the French ship, *Redoutable*. Approaching the crescent formation of the Combined Fleet, *Victory* at first cut through between *Bucentaure* and *Redoutable*, being fired upon not only by those two ships but also being hit by *Santissima Trinidad*, *Neptune* and *San Justo*. *Victory*'s left-sided broadside wrecked the stern of *Bucentaure*, dismounting 20 of her guns and killing more than 100 of her crew. But then *Victory*, apparently by chance, fell alongside *Redoutable*. Captain Lucas, a man of enterprise, had become convinced he could only capture a British ship by boarding, and so he trained his crew in a unique way whilst they were cooped up in Cadiz harbour. Consequently he closed his gun ports after only one broadside and while

Victory was pounding *Redoutable* so severely that she sank the day after the battle, Lucas and his men were keeping up a storm of musket fire. 'I had 100 carbines on board … The men were so accustomed to their use that they climbed halfway up the shrouds to open musketry fire.' It was as we have noted a musket ball that struck Nelson.

The whole point of a man-o'-war was to bring enormous gun power into the correct position and for that firepower to be trained on an enemy within gun range. But there were variations in approach once this had been achieved. British ships, with their vastly superior rate of fire, tended to batter the hulls of their opponents. The hull of a ship presented a more solid target from the side or bows. Otherwise, enormous damage could be done if, after manoeuvring, a ripple broadside (guns being fired one after the other and not all together) could be discharged through the less defended, and much more vulnerable stern of a wooden warship. It was easier to hit the enemy ship's hull repeatedly than to try, as the French did, to disable a ship by firing at rigging and sails and attempting to dismast the vessel.

At Trafalgar *every* person topside, in *every* ship – on either side – would have been exposed to great danger not only from the effect of cannon balls (such as killed Nelson's personal Secretary, John Scott, at the very beginning of the battle) but also from splinters of wood, langridge, grenades and small arms fire as used by Captain Lucas to such effect.

After the battle, Captain Lucas was taken to England, but by 6th May 1806 he was back in France and had an audience with Napoleon at St. Cloud. This was reported in the *Moniteur* newspaper and later in English translation:

> At the audience which took place yesterday at St. Cloud, Captains Lucas and l'Infernit, who have lately arrived from England, were presented to His Majesty. Captain Lucas commanded the *Redoutable*, in the battle of Trafalgar, and conducted himself in the most gallant manner; he attempted to board the *Victory*, Lord Nelson's ship … After an unfortunate affair, it is gratifying to acknowledge such conduct. His Majesty said to the Captains … 'If all my vessels had conducted themselves as well as those which you commanded, the victory would have been ours. I know that there are several who have not imitated your example, but I have ordered their conduct to be investigated. I have appointed you Commanders of the Legion of Honour. The captains of the vessels who, instead of boarding the enemy, kept out of cannon-shot, shall be prosecuted, and, if convicted, made a dreadful example of.

Why were Nelson's shipmates so concerned about his allegedly conspicuous attire? Certainly Blackwood's letter to his wife written within one day of the battle comments on 'his unfortunate decorations of innumerable stars.'[3] In the great shock and sorrow which followed Nelson's death, it is the author's belief that everyone looked for ways in which it could have been prevented, however unlikely. The true answer is that there were none as Nelson could just as easily have been killed by a random missile – cannon ball, musket ball, wood splinter, loosened block and tackle, langridge, or grenade – as soon as the firing commenced, whatever uniform he was wearing. But his friends began to believe immediately after the end of the conflict that if only Nelson had not worn a uniform with four stars sewn on the left breast, he would still be alive and with them.

One last card was stacked against Nelson. The *Victory* sailed into action at walking pace. Despite every possible sail being set, the ship's speed and that of the rest of the British Fleet, was a crawl. Beatty argued that 'If the *Victory's* speed had been greater, the shock of *Victory* colliding with *Redoutable* could well have dismasted the latter smaller ship. *Victory* would then, of course, have passed on to attack another ship, consequently His Lordship would not have been so long, or so much exposed to the Enemy's musketry.'[4] Beatty was no professional sailor: the comment smacks of being one he may have heard put forward by one of *Victory's* naval professionals on the long journey back to England.

What would prove to be a fatal accident on board *Victory* on 30th June 1805 assumed a particular resonance through its link to Nelson's death. A seaman on board *Victory*, James Bush, fell out of the rigging as *Victory* returned from the West Indies. He was admitted to the ship's sick quarters. The diagnosis was 'contused head and spine with slow pulse, loss of motion and sensibility of the inferior extremities ....' It was noted he was incontinent of faeces and urine and he was put on a restricted diet and local embrocation applied. Next day his mental state was assessed 'unimpaired' and he was said to be injured at the level of the 1st dorsal vertebrae, that is, high up in his spine just below his neck. He was given tincture of opium and catheterised. Bush continued 'unchanged', put up to 'half diet' and opiates were continued. On 4th July he was prescribed digitalis but there is no indication why a medicine for the heart should have been deemed necessary at that stage. By 5th July Bush was on opium three times a day and his condition worsened. Next he was reported to have 'a short cough' with impaired respiration and pulse. On 7th July he was again reported to be totally incontinent but said to be less anxious with 'appetite good' and respiration better. Ominously the report of 9th July said he 'continues without any favourable change of symptoms.' On 10th July the deterioration quickened: on 11th July 'respiration laborious with cough and small pulse:' and on 12th July 'deglutition and respiration more difficult with small pulse and further involuntary evacuation.' Opium was continued every day. On 13th July the initial report said 'unchanged as yesterday' but then this was crossed through, because it was on 13th July that James

Bush died.[5] The whole episode seems to have been a traumatic paraplegia followed by slowly developing hypostatic pneumonia and then terminal difficulty with swallowing, possible uraemia, and death.

Like many others, James Bush became famous through his association with Nelson. On 6th May 1803 Bush was pressed as an able-seaman on *Victory*. His number was 583. Bush was not the usual run of able seamen because he was quite old – 34 – when the average age of men on *Victory* was 22, he was an American, born in South Carolina and also because he had made arrangements about his pay with an attorney at Blackwall. On 18th May 1803 Nelson hoisted his flag in *Victory* at Portsmouth and she sailed for the Mediterranean; so Bush and Nelson were shipmates for over two years. But on 30th June Bush became part of the story of Nelson's death.

Beatty gave a clear account of the connection between Nelson and Bush. Hardy visited the injured Admiral, according to Beatty, about one hour and 10 minutes after Nelson was wounded. Nelson pulled no punches 'I am a dead man, Hardy. I am going fast: it will be all over with me soon ...' Hardy observed that he hoped Mr Beatty could hold out some prospect of life. 'Oh! No,' answered His Lordship, 'It is impossible. My back is shot through. Beatty will tell you so.'[6] After Hardy returned to the upper deck Beatty wrote:

> His Lordship now requested the Surgeon, who had been previously absent a short time ... to return to the wounded, and give his assistance to such of them as he could be useful to; 'for', said he 'you can do nothing for me.' The Surgeon assured him that the Assistant Surgeons were doing everything that could be effected for those unfortunate men; but on His Lordship's several times repeating his injunctions to that purpose, he left him surrounded by Doctor Scott, Mr. Burke and two of His Lordship's domestics. After the Surgeon had been absent a few minutes ... he was called by Dr. Scott to his Lordship, who said 'Ah, Mr. Beatty, I have sent for you to say what I forgot to tell you before, that all power of motion and feeling below my breast are gone; and you' continued he 'very well know I can live but a short time.' The emphatic manner in which he pronounced these last words, left no doubt in the Surgeon's mind, that he adverted to the case of a man who had some months before received a mortal injury of the spine on board Victory and had laboured under a similar privations of sense and muscular motion. The case had made a great impression on Lord Nelson: he was anxious to know the cause of such symptoms, which was accordingly explained to him and he now appeared to apply the situation and fate of this man to himself.[7]

'This man' was of course James Bush. The enterprise of the French captain; the heavy losses of the marines and the absence of their covering fire;

the past history of James Bush; the well-worn but conspicuous coat; and the slow, virtually windless approach by *Victory* to the Combined Fleet; all set the scene for one of the most famous deaths in British history.

Marine Major Louis Rotely's account of his part in the Battle of Trafalgar (where he served upon *Victory* as a young Lieutenant of Marines) is an important first-hand record as it is the only known description of just how Nelson's body was put into the leaguer barrel. Rotely also gives the reader a vivid idea of what it was like to be on the two decks of *Victory* before Nelson was shot. He gave this account on the occasion of a presentation to him of a ring by the Citizens of Swansea many years after the battle. This ring had a chamber, into which Rotely put the small lock of Nelson's hair he managed to get for himself the day after the battle – as he described in his later account (see p. 202). Rotely lived to a great age, and died at Swansea in 1861.

> Nelson's last and most decisive victory was at Trafalgar, in which I had the honour to take a part …Previous to breaking the enemy's line their fire was terrific. The *Victory* was steering for the four-decker when four ships ahead and four astern together with that huge leviathan brought their broadsides to bear upon the bows of the *Victory*. It was like a hailstorm of bullets passing over our heads on the poop, where we had forty Marines stationed with small arms. It has been stated that Lord Nelson ordered them to lie down at their quarters until wanted, but no such order was given, and no man went down until knocked down; had such orders been given many a life would have been saved, as not a man was hit below the waist. There [sic] steadiness indeed was observed by Nelson, whose eye was everywhere, and who declared he had seen nothing which surpassed it in any of his previous battles. He also made this remark during the battle, 'The young Marine is doing well,' which I have taken for my motto.
>
> This I learnt from Sir Thomas Hardy, when returning me his thanks on the quarterdeck for my conduct in the battle. The poop became a slaughterhouse, and soon after the commencement the two senior Lieutenants of Marines, and half the original forty, were placed 'hors de combat.' Captain Adair then ordered me to bring him up a reinforcement of Marines from the great guns. I need not inform a seaman the difficulty of separating a man from his gun. In the excitement of action the Marines had thrown off their red jackets and appeared in check shirts and blue trousers. There was no distinguishing Marine from Seaman – they were all working like horses. I was now upon the middle deck; we were engaging on both sides, every gun was going off. A man should witness a battle in a three-decker from the middle deck, for it beggars all description. It bewilders the senses of

175

sight and hearing. There was the fire from above, the fire from below, besides the fire from the deck I was upon, the guns recoiling with violence reports louder than thunder, the deck heaving and the side straining. I fancied myself in the infernal regions, where every man appeared a devil. Lips might move, but orders and hearing were out of the question; everything was done by signs.

With the assistance of two Sergeants and two Corporals (and in some cases by main force) I succeeded in separating about 25 men from the great guns and with this force I ascended to a purer air. The battle now raged at its greatest height, the *Redoutable* had fallen on board us on the starboard side, and the soldiers from their tops were picking off our officers and men with deadly aim. We were also engaging with the *Santissima Trinidad* and the *Bucentaure* (though at a greater distance) on our larboard. The reinforcement arrived at a most critical moment. Captain Adair's party was reduced to less than 20 men, himself wounded in the forehead by splinters, yet still using his musket with effect. One of his last orders to me was 'Rotely, fire away as fast as you can' when a ball struck him on the back of the neck and he was a corpse in a moment – and at the same time our revered Chief fell, having received his mortal wound from a soldier in the mizzen top of the *Redoutable*. The Marines became exasperated. I was now in command, and the first order I gave was to clear the mizzen top, when every musket was levelled at that top, and in five minutes not a man was left alive in it. Some Frenchmen [sic] has vaunted that he shot Nelson and survived the battle, and I have heard that a book had been published so stating, but it must be a romance, as I know the man was shot in five minutes after Nelson fell. About this time I observed the British flag on the opposite side of the *Redoutable*, which proved to belong to the *Temeraire*, and shortly after another French ship, the *Fougeux*, fell on board the Temeraire on her starboard side, so that four ships of the line were rubbing sides in the heat of the fight, with their heads all lying the same way as if moored in harbour. It consequently became a great nicety in directing the fire of the musketry, lest we should shoot our own men over the decks of the *Redoutable*. I therefore directed the fire of the Marines to the main and fore tops of that devoted ship, and but few of their men escaped.[8]

Nelson was a very organised and tidy man. He abhorred muddle and performed the day's work in the day, every day. He almost certainly prepared for death before every battle. It is known that before he fought at Tenerife he burned all his wife's letters[9] and he also destroyed almost all Lady Hamilton's letters during his life-time.[10] Just before Trafalgar he attempted to provide for the mistress he loved and the daughter he adored.

Early in the morning of 21st October 1805, Nelson asked Henry Blackwood, Senior Frigate Captain, and Thomas Hardy, Captain of *Victory*, to witness a new codicil to his will. It was an extraordinary document, and while the content has been examined many times the form has not. Nelson used the words 'King and Country' no less than five times and the word 'Country' twice more. In his terminal state Nelson was in extreme agony and shock. He was calling 'Drink, drink ... Fan, fan ... Rub, rub.' But Beatty also recorded that as he was dying Nelson spoke three complete sentences. These were:

1. 'Remember that I leave Lady Hamilton and my daughter Horatia as a legacy to my Country.'
2. 'Never forget Horatia.'
3. 'Thank God I have done my duty.'[11]

These last utterances echo, first, Nelson's penultimate dispatch, 'England expects every man will do his duty' and secondly, the codicil. 'I also leave to the beneficence of my Country my adopted daughter, Horatia Nelson Thomson, and I desire she will use in future the name of Nelson only')[12] In his terminal state this becomes 'My daughter Horatia' and 'Never forget Horatia' and at the last, 'I have done what England expected of me in return, thank God ... my Duty.'

By hopeful extension in Nelson's mind as he dies his King and Country will do what he has asked of them. 'These are the only favours I ask of my King and Country at this moment when I am going to fight their battle.'[13] The codicil to Nelson's will reads:

October the twenty first one thousand eight hundred and five, then in sight of the Combined Fleets of France and Spain, distant about ten miles.

> Whereas the eminent services of Emma Hamilton, widow of the Right Honourable Sir William Hamilton, have been of the very greatest service to our King and Country, to my knowledge, without her receiving any reward from either our King or Country; – first, that she obtained the King of Spain's letter, in 1796 to his brother, the King of Naples, acquainting him of his intention to declare War against England, from which Letter the Ministry sent our orders to then Sir John Jarvis, to strike a stroke, if opportunity offered, against either the Arsenals of Spain, or her Fleets. That neither of these was done is not the fault of Lady Hamilton. The opportunity might have been offered. Secondly, the British Fleet under my command, could never have returned the second time to Egypt, had not Lady Hamilton's influence with the Queen of Naples caused letters to be wrote, to the Governor of Syracuse, that he was to encourage the Fleet being

supplied with everything, should they put into any Port in Sicily. We put into Syracuse, and received every supply, went to Egypt, and destroyed the French Fleet. Could I have rewarded these services I would not now call upon my Country; but as that has not been in my power, I leave Emma Lady Hamilton, therefore, a Legacy to my King and Country, that they will give her an ample provision to maintain her rank in life. I also leave to the beneficence of my Country my adopted daughter, Horatia Nelson Thompson; and I desire she will use in future the name of Nelson only. These are the only favours I ask of my King and Country as this moment when I am going to fight their Battle. May God bless my King and Country, and all those who I hold dear. My relations it is needless to mention: they will of course be amply provided for.

NELSON AND BRONTE
Witness – Henry Blackwood,
T. M. Hardy[14]

The tragedy from Lady Hamilton's point of view, was that Nelson's 'King and Country' did nothing at all for her or Nelson's daughter.

Three men in particular tried to ease Nelson's final hours. These were William Beatty, the surgeon; Alexander Scott, Nelson's secretary and chaplain; and Walter Burke, the Purser of *Victory*.

Firstly, William Beatty, by virtue of his position as chief surgeon on board *Victory* at Trafalgar, became one of the most important primary sources of information about Nelson's last days. Beatty recorded Nelson's wounding at Trafalgar and the treatment he received. He also wrote about the preservation of Nelson's body after death, and performed Nelson's post mortem, writing about that in detail as well (see p. 206).

Beatty was the eldest son of James Beatty of H.M. Customs, Londonderry, and his wife Ann Smyth. His death certificate issued in 1842 said he was aged 69 when he died, making him 32 at Trafalgar.[15]

Nothing is known either of his schooling or early medical training, but his mother's brother was a medical practitioner in the Royal Navy, which may have influenced Beatty's choice of career. His first official naval appointment at the age of 20 was on 3rd December 1793 when he was warranted to *Flying Fish*. On 19th February 1795 he was examined at the College of Surgeons in London and passed as a surgeon qualified to serve in a 2nd Rate.

Beatty then served in succession on five ships between March 1795 and 14th December 1804 (the day Spain declared war on Great Britain) when he was appointed to *Victory*. It would appear the vacancy occurred because Nelson gave the previous surgeon, George Macgrath, the surgeoncy of the Naval Hospital, Gibraltar, when he became ill with gout. Beatty was one of the very first people to realise the importance of Nelson's death to the nation and his later writings upon the subject showed that he must have kept careful and very detailed notes of every aspect he considered relevant. From the medical point of view it is therefore most unfortunate that Beatty sought to gloss over the more terrible aspects of Nelson's death.

Beatty performed the post mortem on Nelson's body on 11th December 1805: he was quite correct to do one. (See p. 211-2 for his subsequent medical writings on the subject.) His account not only clearly established the cause of Nelson's death, but also indicated that had he not been shot, it was probable that Nelson could have lived to a great age like many of his close relatives.

Having removed the fatal ball from Nelson's body, Beatty gave it to Captain Hardy. Hardy had it mounted in crystal and silver and returned it to Beatty who, for a time, wore it as a pendant. It later passed into the possession of Beatty's nephew, and his family later presented it to Queen Victoria. It has been in the Royal Family's possession ever since and is currently housed in Windsor Castle.

On 28th February 1806, some seven weeks after he had attended Nelson's funeral Beatty obtained an M.D. of the University of Aberdeen. This was not a doctorate, it was a diploma. This enabled Beatty to put the initials M.D. after his name on the frontispiece of his book on Nelson's death and by the time the first edition was published in 1807 Beatty had been promoted to Physician to the Fleet. It is a measure of Beatty's talent for self promotion that he published the *Authentic Narrative* in 1807 with the following artful disclaimer:

> It was originally intended that this Narrative should be published in the LIFE OF LORD NELSON, undertaken by the Rev. J. S. CLARKE, and J. M'ARTHUR, Esq., and it will still form a part of that Work; but from the length of time which must necessarily elapse before so extensive and magnificent a Publication can be completed, the Author has been induced to print it in a separate form.[16]

Clarke and M'Arthur's monumental two-volume *Life of Admiral Nelson, K.B.* was not published until 1809. There must have been many who bought Beatty's slim volume (which ran to a 2nd edition in 1808) and did not bother to subscribe to Clarke and M'Arthur's two much more expensive tomes.

On 14th October 1817 Beatty was awarded the degree of M.D. from the University of St. Andrew's. The Minutes of the University of St. Andrew's for 14th October 1817 record, 'He (Beatty) has already a diploma from the University of Aberdeen dated some years since ...' and continued quoting a letter from a Dr Outram in London 'His (Beatty's) education, manners and character are in the highest degree respectable, and that he

(Dr. Outram) is fully convinced no one is more worthy to be granted the Degree without further delay.'[17]

In 1822 he went to Greenwich as Resident Physician. He had been appointed a Fellow of the Royal Society in 1818.[18] Beatty also became a Fellow of the Royal College of Physicians of Edinburgh in 1814, and also a Licenciate of the Royal College of Physicians of London, so his profession in the Royal Society Catalogue is correctly given as Physician and Surgeon.

Beatty was at Greenwich Hospital until 1839. After the death of King George IV on 26th June 1830, the King's brother, William, Duke of Clarence – Nelson's friend – became King William IV and it was he who knighted Beatty in May 1831.

In his last years Beatty lived in Portman Square, London, where he died of bronchitis in March 1842. He died intestate, leaving a fortune of £3,000 which went to his family. He was buried in Kensal Green cemetery. He never married.

Alexander Scott was born in 1768. A graduate of Cambridge University he was ordained priest in 1792, and became a Ship's Chaplain on board *Berwick* in the Mediterranean the year after. His natural gift for languages was noted by 1795 when he became confidential secretary to Vice Admiral Sir Hyde Parker. Scott travelled with Parker to the West Indies and then to the Baltic where he was 'lent' to Nelson to assist in the armistice negotiations after the Battle of Copenhagen. By this time Scott could speak German and had a working knowledge of Danish so he not only acted as translator but also helped to draw up the armistice documents. Because of his skills, Nelson asked Scott to join his staff, but Scott replied 'he could not bear to leave the old admiral (Parker) when he stood most in need of his company.'[19] Nelson understood such loyalty, but made Scott promise he would come to work for him when he felt he could leave Sir Hyde.

In 1802 Scott again crossed the Atlantic, but on the voyage home he was nearly killed when lightning struck the ship he was on. The metal bolts of his hammock were said to have melted and he was thrown to the cabin floor and lucky to escape with his life. He seems to have become very nervous after this episode, a state of mind which lasted the rest of his life.

In 1803 Nelson took Scott out to the Mediterranean as his Chaplain and foreign (language) secretary and paid him £100 a year in addition to his pay as Chaplain on *Victory*. Nelson frequently sent him, as though on leave, to Leghorn, Naples, Barcelona and other ports and places throughout the Mediterranean. Scott, being highly presentable and fluent in French and Spanish, gained admission to local society and was able to return to Nelson with vast quantities of local documents, newspapers and information. On one occasion Nelson used him to present church plate to a local church in Sardinia. Scott and Nelson used to sit in two identical chairs with large pockets attached on both sides with a table between them. (The three items could quickly be put together to form a day bed in which Nelson used to have the brief sleeps that Scott noted.) Scott would translate and read aloud foreign papers he had obtained, thereby saving Nelson's eyesight. The papers would be stuffed into the pockets at the sides of the chairs. Alas, when the author examined these chairs, now to be found on board *Victory*, there were no papers.

Scott was one of the persons on the upper deck of *Victory* just before the start of Trafalgar, who were said to have wanted Nelson to change his coat so as to be more inconspicuous. However he never got the chance to speak to Nelson before firing commenced and he had to go to his battle station on the orlop deck. Scott's account of the battle is on page 182.

After the battle Scott became almost unhinged with grief at Nelson's death. He also gave several illuminating and personal descriptions of Nelson, which are fascinating primary sources from a highly intelligent witness. Six days after Nelson died Scott wrote to his uncle 'What will you think of one who detests this Victory? It has deprived me of my beloved and adored friend – I knew not until his loss, how much I loved him … his last effort to speak was made at the moment of joy for victory.'[20] Scott seldom left Nelson's corpse, attending it on *Victory*, on the voyage home, in the Painted Hall at Greenwich (where he sat with it for the three days it was lying in state, and looked, so one report said, 'skeletal, like the chief mourner'[21] Then he accompanied it to the Admiralty, before the last journey to St. Paul's Cathedral.

Scott also wrote several letters to Lady Hamilton giving her solicitous details of what had happened and at the earliest opportunity he had written a personal letter of great tact to Emma's mother to warn her: 'Hasten the very moment you receive this, to dear Lady Hamilton, and prepare her for the greatest of misfortunes.'[22]

Owing to the miserliness of Nelson's brother William, the only reward Scott received for many years was a Doctorate of Divinity, granted by Royal Mandate. And he even had some of his pay as Chaplain of Victory deducted for the time he had been out of the ship on Nelson's errands. This money was only returned to him three years later. After losing his patron, Scott settled as a vicar in Southminster. He had to wait until 1816 before he was presented to the Crown living of Catterick and at the same time he was appointed Chaplain to the Prince of Wales – later King George IV. He died at Catterick in 1840. Medically Scott is interesting as, after Trafalgar, he seems to have suffered from post traumatic stress disorder. The account of Scott's experience of the carnage of a great sea battle comes from *Recollections of the Life of Rev. A. J. Scott*, written by his daughter and son-in-law. Trafalgar gave Scott nightmares and (the author believes) post traumatic stress disorder for the rest of his life.

At half past eleven, the action commenced, by the enemy firing upon the *Royal Sovereign*, and twenty minutes afterwards they opened their fire upon the *Victory*; having discharged at her as she approached, single guns, until they found she was within range of their shot, when they poured in their broadsides, maintaining an awful and tremendous fire. Before the *Victory* returned a shot, she had fifty killed or wounded. At four minutes past noon, she commenced firing from both sides of her deck on the enemy. The *Santissima Trinidad* of 136 guns, and the *Bucentaur* being on her larboard, and the *Redoutable* on her starboard side. While the *Victory* was thus engaged, her second, the *Temeraire*, fell on board the Redoutable on the opposite side and onboard of her beyond was another French ship. These four ships were lying so close to each other, that they formed a solid mass, and every gun that was fired, told. The carnage on the deck of the *Victory* became terrific. Dr. Scott's duties confined him entirely to the cockpit, which was soon crowded with wounded and dying men; and such was the horror that filled his mind at this scene of suffering, that it haunted him like a shocking dream for years afterwards. He never talked of it. Indeed the only record of a remark on the subject was one extorted from him by the inquiries of a friend, soon after his return home. The expression that escaped him at the moment was 'it was like a butcher's shambles.

His natural tenderness of feeling, very much heightened by the shock on his nervous system, quite disqualified him for being a calm spectator of death and pain, as there exhibited in their most appalling shapes. But he suppressed his aversion as well as he could, and had been for some time engaged in helping and consoling those who were suffering around him, when a fine young lieutenant was brought down desperately wounded. This officer was not aware of the extent of his injury, until the surgeon's examination, but, on discovering it, he tore off with his own hand the ligatures that were being applied, and bled to death. Almost frenzied by the sight of this, Scott hurried wildly to the deck for relief, perfectly regardless of his own safety. He rushed up the companion ladder – now slippery with gore – the scene above was all noise, confusion, and smoke – but he had hardly time to breathe there, when Lord Nelson himself fell, and this event at once sobered his disordered mind. He followed his chief to the cockpit – the scene here has been painfully portrayed by those who have written the life of Nelson; his chaplain's biographer has little to add, but that the confusion of the scene, the pain endured by the hero, and the necessity of alleviating his sufferings by giving lemonade to quench his thirst and by rubbing his body, of course precluded the reading of prayers to him in the regular form, which otherwise would have been done – but often, during the three hours and a half of Nelson's mortal agony, they ejaculated short prayers together, and Nelson frequently said, 'Pray for me, Doctor.' Every interval, indeed, allowed by the intense pain, and not taken up in the conduct of the action, or in the mention of his private affairs, was thus employed in low and earnest supplications for Divine mercy. The last words which Dr. Scott heard murmured on his lips were, 'God and my country' and he passed so quietly out of life that Scott, who had been occupied every since he was brought below, in all the offices of the most tender nurse, was still rubbing his stomach when the surgeon perceived that all was over.[23]

This rubbing seems to have been the only active treatment which afforded Nelson any relief from his extreme pain, and was a form of 'counter irritant.' Nelson's brain could register the rubbing of his skin rather than the pain of his internal wounds.

Since Surgeon Beatty was not always with Nelson nor, it seems likely, was Purser Burke, (see below) Scott must have been the primary source of a lot of the information Beatty put into his *Authentic Narrative,* although Beatty never acknowledged this.

The third man whose actions should be examined is Walter Burke who was the Chief Purser on board *Victory* at the Battle of Trafalgar. Aged 67 in 1805 he was by far the oldest member of the crew. At the time of Trafalgar he had been at sea for at least 30 years. Indeed, he had given almost his all to the Royal Navy: two of his three sons had died, by 1805, killed in action in naval engagements against the French.

The Purser on a Royal Navy ship was the warrant officer responsible for provisions and clothing. The Victualling Board, an autonomous subsidiary of the Navy Board, was responsible for the purchase, preservation and distribution to ships of all naval victuals and ship clothing, placing on board every ship, with an appointment by warrant, a purser to issue food and clothes and keep all accounts. Pursers were not well remunerated, but made up for this by a commission on the issue of the daily victualling allowance by calculating each pound weight as having only 14oz in it instead of 16oz. The purser pocketed the difference, the 2oz representing 12½ % commission. It may well have been Burke who drew Nelson's attention to the slops delivered in 1804, which provoked one of the latter's more famous humanitarian outbursts (see p. 148-9).

In 1801, having bought two houses in the Kentish village of Wouldham, on the River Medway some four miles from Chatham, Burke was officially assessed for Parish rates. He paid no rates in 1805 – his home was empty and he was at sea on the *Victory.*

Before the battle, Burke was one of those near Nelson on the quarterdeck. There are two version of what Nelson said to him: 'Go down, go down, your duty is below' or 'Burke, I expect every man to be upon his station'[24] Burke's official duty, when the ship was at action stations, was to help with the distribution of gunpowder from the magazine on the orlop deck. But, he was also available to help with the carrying of the wounded, when they reached the orlop, from other decks and it was into the arms of Burke that Nelson was delivered by the two sailors and Marine Sergeant Secker, who had brought him down from the upper deck.

Burke, possibly with the help of Surgeon Beatty, carried Nelson and placed him on the deck near the ship's side, Nelson's clothes were removed (very obviously shears were used on his trousers) and for the next some 2¾ hours, until he died, Burke helped to support him in a position of the most comfort – at a 45° angle, which was also medically the most sensible. Some authorities say Burke never moved, and a woman writer, Mrs. Newton Crosland, whose parents had known Burke well in his last years, recorded in a book written some time in the 1870s, that she was told by her parents that Burke's arm was so be-numbed by supporting Nelson that he did not recover the use of it for several hours.[25]

Burke must have been privy to all the intensely personal conversations between Nelson and Beatty (medical), Alexander Scott (spiritual) and Hardy (concerning friendship) and he also conversed with Nelson himself.

After Nelson died, and *Victory* returned to England, Burke was co-author, with Surgeon Beatty, of the first account of his death in *The Times* of 30th December 1805, published quite clearly under their joint names. (see p. 211-2). After this article Burke was 'air-brushed' out of all Beatty's subsequent reports and not mentioned as a material source in Beatty's book. But Beatty was not always near the dying Nelson and Burke was probably always with him or near him, so Beatty almost certainly recorded information in the *Authentic Narrative* which he obtained from Burke. It is also extremely likely that the fascinating extra information, much of it medical, given in the *Gibraltar Chronicle* of November 1805 and the Naval Chronicle, came from Burke, as Reverend Scott would in all probability have stayed on board *Victory* with the body. Beatty does not include this extra information in his book, but, judging by the content, it *must* have been provided by a fixed source very close to Nelson as he died and this was very probably Burke.

Burke came back to Wouldham after the battle. By 1807 he was farming there, and continued to do so until he died in 1815. He was buried in the village churchyard, near to the east door.

Nearly 110 years ago, a tradition began that children from the two local Church of England primary schools of Wouldham, and Burham nearby, should process every year on 21st October to Burke's grave. The tradition continues to this day.[26] The children leave flowers on the grave, and poems and pictures they have produced themselves. Members of the

Royal Naval Reserve are usually present with a Colour, and the Last Post is sounded. Nelson's last prayer is always read aloud to the children. All then move into the Church where a service is held and different classes give short presentations about Nelson, Walter Burke, and the Battle of Trafalgar. The service ends with a simple prayer and a Blessing, and the hymn 'Eternal Father, Strong to Save' is always included. The flowers are left on the grave. Nelson would have approved.

So, Burke and Beatty were on the orlop deck, with Scott on the upper deck, when Nelson's fatal wounding occurred. Nelson and Hardy pacing back and forth on *Victory's* quarter-deck had already had a close encounter with death when a missile passed between them, ripping the buckle from Hardy's shoe and bruising his left foot. 'This is too warm work, Hardy, to last long,' said Nelson,[27] but they continued to walk until Hardy, on turning, found Nelson had not turned with him and on looking back Hardy saw him, face forward trying to support himself with his left arm which then gave way. He fell onto a portion of the deck heavily soiled by the blood of his lay Secretary, Mr Scott, who had been one of the first fatal casualties of the action. 'They have done for me at last, Hardy.' 'I hope not.' 'Yes, my backbone is shot through.'[28]

Nelson had listened to Beatty's medical account of the fallen man and his injuries, and his helped him to make his own immediate diagnosis, that he was fatally wounded. Every action and comment he made until his death some 2¾ hours later must be viewed in the light of his own knowledge that 'It will be all over with me soon.'

Beatty says that en route to the cockpit, in the arms of two sailors and a marine, Nelson noticed the tiller ropes, shot away early in the action, had not been replaced, and asked a midshipman to go up to the quarter-deck to remind Hardy about their absence. He then 'took his handkerchief from his pocket, and covered his face with it, that he might be conveyed to the cockpit at this crisis unnoticed by the crew.'[29]

The Addenda to the Biographical memoir in the *Naval Chronicle* says 'Walter Burke on seeing him brought down, immediately ran to him. 'I fear,' he said, 'Your Lordship is wounded!' 'Mortally! Mortally!'- 'I hope not, my dear Lord, let Mr. Beatty examine your wounds.' 'It is of no use' exclaimed the dying Nelson 'He had better attend to others.'[30]

Beatty said he was confirming the deaths of two officers, when he heard the voices of other wounded men calling to him 'Mr. Beatty, Lord Nelson is here. Mr. Beatty – the Admiral is wounded.' Beatty wrote 'Walter Burke and Beatty took Nelson from the arms of the seamen. Nelson asked who was now carrying him and on being told at once said 'Ah, Mr. Beatty. You can do nothing for me. I have but a short time to live: my back is shot through.'[31]

Alexander Scott now appeared. Nelson was laid on a bed of sails, stripped of his clothes, and covered with a sheet. Nelson was talking to

Scott even as this was being done so fearful was he that he would die quickly. 'Doctor, I told you so. Doctor, I am gone. I have to leave Lady Hamilton and my adopted daughter Horatia as a legacy to my Country.'[32] He was then propped at an angle supported by Walter Burke, the Purser. Beatty actually said this was because lying at an angle was most comfortable for him. Modern treatment for patients after chest operations is in fact to nurse them at 45 degrees semi-recumbent (the so-called Fowler position). At that angle the blood supply to the lower lobes of the lungs is improved, there is the best possible air/blood mix in the circumstances, and it is most comfortable for the patient.[33] In addition modern patients have their legs elevated to achieve the maximum return of blood to the heart and lungs. But Nelson's paralysed legs were just covered with a sheet. Muscle contraction in the legs aids return of the blood from the parts of the body furthest away from the heart, back to the heart. But Nelson's legs were paralysed and no muscles in them would have contracted. A considerable amount of reduction in circulation and pooling of blood must have occurred.

This would have been made worse by low blood pressure. The injury to the spine and spinal cord at level thoracic vertebrae 6 & 7[34] would have induced hypotension in Nelson's body from that high level (mid chest) due to destruction of that part of his Automonic Nervous System (ANS) which helps to maintain blood pressure, and this would explain Beatty's comment about Nelson's pulse 'In the course of an hour, his pulse became indistinct and was gradually lost in the arm'[35] and his noting that Nelson's 'extremities and forehead became soon afterwards cold.'[36] There is, in Beatty's account, clear indication of severe and deteriorating hypotension and hypoperfusion (low blood pressure and poor circulation)[37] Beatty said he next did a brief examination but the *Naval Chronicle* is more explicit:

> Mr. Beatty now approached to examine the wound. His Lordship was raised up: and Beatty, whose attention was anxiously fixed upon the eyes of his patient, as an indication the most certain when a wound is mortal, after a few moments glanced his eye on Burke and expressed his opinion in his countenance. Lord Nelson now turned to Burke and said, 'Tell Hardy to come to me.' Burke left the cockpit. Beatty now said 'Suffer me, My Lord, to probe the wound with my finger; I will give you no pain.' Lord Nelson permitted him, and, passing his left hand round his waist, he probed it with the forefinger of his right.[38]

This rings true. Having probed the wound and not having encountered the musket ball with his fingertip, Beatty asked Nelson for 'All his sensations', i.e. his symptoms. These were, according to Beatty's subsequent record:

1. He felt a gush of blood every *minute* within his breast
2. He had no feeling in the lower part of his body
3. His breathing was difficult
4. He had severe pain about that part of the spine where he was confident the ball had struck.[39]

Later Beatty added that Nelson had 'sensations which indicated to him the approach of death.'[40] The *Naval Chronicle* Addenda also states that Nelson said he felt every *instant* a gush of blood within his breast and so does Beatty's first account in *The Times*. Beatty's second account of Nelson's fatal wound later in the *Authentic Narrative* is medically much more likely. The torn pulmonary artery Beatty found at post mortem would eject a pulse of blood against the pleura (the lining of the lungs) with every heart beat. This is what Nelson would have felt since the brain can appreciate sensations originating in or on the pleura, but not within the actual lungs themselves. Beatty says he now became convinced Nelson's case was hopeless, basing his opinion on:

1. Nelson's respiration, which was short and difficult
2. Nelson's pulse, which was abnormal, being weak, small (in volume) and irregular
3. The gush of blood within the chest
4. The other symptoms to a lesser extent.[41]

It is clear Beatty 'told' Walter Burke first, when he 'expressed his opinion in his countenance.' Beatty then arranged for Captain Hardy, 'Doctor' Scott and the two other surgeons on board – Smith and Westemburg – to be informed of Nelson's condition.

Nelson now started going into 'shock' due to severe pain, blood loss and low blood pressure, and typically became very thirsty. He also felt a need for cool air. (The orlop deck being below the waterline would have been extremely hot, airless and would have reeked of blood.) He was fanned with paper fans and given frequent lemonade and wine mixed with water to drink. He became very anxious about Hardy (fearful he too had been shot and 'destroyed') and understandably very pessimistic about his own case. Dr Scott and Burke used every argument they could suggest to relieve his anxiety, but naturally, they both failed. Burke told him 'The enemy were decisively defeated, and that he hoped his Lordship would still live to be himself the bearer of the joyful tidings to his Country.' Nelson replied, 'It is nonsense, Mr. Burke, to suppose I can live; my sufferings are great, but they will all be soon over.' Dr. Scott entreated his Lordship 'Not to despair of living' and said he 'trusted that divine providence would restore him once more to his dear Country and friends.' 'Ah, Doctor!' replied his lordship 'It is all over, it is all over.'[42]

During the 70 minutes from his own wounding to Hardy's first visit, in response to the many messages sent by Beatty to Hardy, the Captain's aide-de-camp, Midshipman Bulkley, now came below and stated that 'Circumstances respecting the fleet required Captain Hardy's presence on deck, but that he would avail himself of the first favourable moment to visit his Lordship.' On hearing him deliver this message to the surgeon, His Lordship inquired who had brought it. Mr Burke answered, 'It is Mr. Bulkley, my Lord.' 'It is his voice' replied his Lordship; he then said to the young gentleman, 'Remember me to your father.'[43]

Even in death, Nelson was punctilious and did not forget a friend. Young Mr. Bulkley's father had served with young Captain Nelson in Nicaragua 25 years previously.

The next piece of information about Nelson's last hours most probably also comes from Burke's description of what happened – it is certainly not in Beatty's account. Someone wrote in the *Gibraltar Chronicle* 'His lower extremities soon became cold and insensible, and the effusion of blood from his lungs *often threatened suffocation*' (author's italics).[44] This is exactly what one would expect with such a very serious chest wound, but it is nowhere mentioned by Beatty.

In the dust, stench and gloom of the orlop deck with *Victory's* guns firing continuously above, Nelson addressed the ship directly on one occasion: 'Ah *Victory, Victory*, how you distract my poor brain.' It was proof of the friendship and love those around him felt for Nelson that they strove so hard to hear and remember his every dying word.

Eventually Hardy came to Nelson, and Nelson at once told him 'I am a dead man ... I am going fast: it will be all over with me soon.' After Hardy left the first time Nelson sent Beatty away as well, 'You can do nothing for me.'[45] However, a few minutes later, Beatty was called by Scott to Nelson's side. Nelson told him, 'All power of motion and feeling below my breast are gone and you very well *know* I can live but a short time.' Now even Beatty's reserve broke down as he realised by the emphasis of the words, Nelson 'adverted to the case of a man who had some months before received a mortal wound of the spine on board *Victory*.' This, of course, was the American, James Bush.[46]

Beatty examined Nelson's extremities only to be told 'I am too certain of it.' Scott and Burke had already checked them. Beatty then was subjected to one of the worst things that can happen to a caring doctor: a patient of whom he is fond makes the ultimate challenge, as Nelson did. 'You know very well I am gone.' Beatty replied so well: 'My Lord, unhappily for our country, nothing can be done for you,' and as he later recorded, 'Having made this declaration he was so much affected he turned round and withdrew a few steps to conceal his emotions.'[47] Nelson no longer complained of a gushing of blood but now felt 'Something rising in my breast' putting his hand on his left side. It is likely that by this time there was so much blood in his left chest the torn pulmonary artery bled into the collection of blood which Nelson could feel rising up against the pleura all round the lung, at the air/fluid interface associated with the left haemothorax (see p. 191). He now began to say 'God be praised, I've done my duty.' and complained of such severe pain he wished he was dead. [48] Beatty never indicated he gave Nelson opiates for his pain at any stage of his death agony. This may have been at Nelson's express request so as not to dull his intellect, but is more likely to be due to Beatty fearing they might cause Nelson further distress by making him nauseous or actually vomit – a potential side effect. Having said he wished he was dead his thoughts turned to Lady Hamilton and Nelson was heard to say 'One would like to live a little longer, too.' Hardy attended again after another interval of some 50 minutes:

> Lord Nelson and Captain Hardy shook hands again; and while the Captain retained his Lordship's hand, he congratulated him even in the arms of death on his brilliant victory: 'Which' he said, 'was complete; though he did not know how many of the enemy were captured, as it was impossible to perceive every ship distinctly. He was certain however of fourteen or fifteen having surrendered.' His Lordship answered, 'That is well, but I bargained for twenty.'[49]

There seems little doubt that all along Nelson had 'bargained for twenty' but the *Gibraltar Chronicle* said:

> About 5 o'clock, however, when he [Hardy] saw that the victory was completely decided, and the battle nearly ended, he was enabled to attend to the last wishes of the dying Hero, who eagerly inquired how many ships were captured? On being told by Captain Hardy, that he was certain of twelve having struck, which he could see, but that probably more had surrendered, his Lordship said 'What, only twelve! There should at least have been fifteen, or sixteen, by my calculation': however after a short pause, he added 'Twelve are pretty well!' [50]

Beatty then recorded the following exchange between Nelson and Hardy:

> Nelson then emphatically exclaimed, 'Anchor, Hardy, Anchor!' To this the Captain replied: 'I suppose, my Lord, Admiral Collingwood will now take upon himself the direction of affairs.' – 'Not while I live, I hope, Hardy!' cried the dying Chief; and at that moment endeavoured ineffectually to raise himself from the bed. 'No' added he 'Do you anchor, Hardy.' Captain Hardy then said: 'Shall we make the signal, Sir?' 'Yes' answered his Lordship 'For if I live, I'll anchor.'[51]

Nelson's anxiety with regard to the need to anchor after the battle was caused by his belief that the Atlantic swell experienced by the contending fleets presaged a severe storm and he was concerned for the safety of all the ships. His anxiety produced what was the most extraordinary and pathetic part of the whole death-bed account. The wound had in effect rendered Nelson quadriplegic. He had no right arm anyway; he had paralysis below his mid chest extending to both legs; he could move his left arm but his left shoulder was fractured; and in addition, his breathing was difficult due to two fractured ribs, a fractured thoracic spine, and blood leaking from 'a large branch' of the pulmonary artery. He now had extremely low blood pressure, yet with all the above, he still felt the need to anchor after the battle. After the effort to raise himself Nelson deteriorated rapidly.

The *Naval Chronicle* gave a slightly different account which nevertheless also rings true. The phrase, 'I am a dead man all over,' was all too apposite. The full account is given on pages 194-6 but here is the moment of death:

> Burke returned to the cockpit with Captain Hardy. Lord Nelson told the latter to come near him. 'Kiss me, Hardy!' he exclaimed – Captain Hardy kissed his cheek – 'I hope your Lordship,' he said 'will still live to enjoy your triumph.' – 'Never, Hardy' he exclaimed 'I am dying – I am a dead man all over – Beatty will tell you so – bring the fleet to an anchor – you have done your duty – God Bless you!' Captain Hardy now said 'I suppose Collingwood, my dear Lord, is to command the fleet?' – 'Never' exclaimed he, 'whilst I live' – meaning, doubtless, that, so long as his gallant spirit survived, he would never desert his duty … What passed after this was merely casual: his Lordship's last words were to Mr. Beatty, whilst he was expiring in his arms. 'I could have wished to have lived to enjoy this, but God's will be done!' 'My Lord' exclaimed Hardy, You die in the midst of triumph!' – 'Do I, Hardy!' – he smiled faintly – 'God be praised!' These were his last words before he expired.[52]

Beatty says when Hardy arrived the second time Nelson told him that 'He felt in a few minutes he should be no more.'

There is no doubt in all the accounts that Nelson asked Hardy to kiss him. There was a short interval between Hardy kissing him on the cheek and on the forehead but it was time enough for Nelson, after the effort of the 'Anchor, do you anchor' order, to deteriorate so far that when he was kissed the second time he had to ask who had kissed him.

Hardy now left (although the *Naval Chronicle* account suggested he was present when Nelson died) and Nelson asked to be turned on to his right side. This was done. Some years ago it was alleged Beatty ordered Nelson to be turned on to his right side and that this hastened his death. This was not the case. Nelson asked his steward Chevalier to turn him on to his right side. It was, of course, the only way he could get a little alleviation from his pain. Turned on to his left side would have caused pressure on his fractured left shoulder and first two left ribs. Lying on his back was causing severe pain in the area of the transected spine and lodgment of the ball. It was suggested blood from his left chest tipped over into his right and worsened his breathing but Beatty was emphatic that it was from the left chest that a quantity of blood extruded when he probed the track of the fatal ball the day after Nelson died.

The awful truth is that Beatty's account of Nelson's death did not describe the full horror of the wounds he sustained. Recently, it has been suggested that Beatty's book is simply a reconstructed account of the death of Nelson;[53] certainly it must no longer be accepted as gospel truth. It is known Beatty was economical with the truth at least once in his book when he said that Nelson's 'features were somewhat tumid, from absorption of the spirit; but on using friction from a napkin they resumed in a great degree their natural character.'[54] This was not true as Beatty had been forced to write to Alexander Scott on 25th December 1805, 'the features being lost,'[55] to prevent the coffin being left open at Nelson's Lying-in-State at the Painted Hall in Greenwich from 5th to 7th January 1806.

It is also known that the *Morning Chronicle* of 9th December 1805 reported that Nelson died with blood in his throat having 'convulsed' and this leads the author to wonder if one of the causes of Dr Scott's post traumatic stress disorder was that his hand, rubbing Nelson's chest, became covered in Nelson's blood as he died. It is Scott's account which shows just how much pain Nelson was enduring. Enough to stop him from talking, '…compelled to speak in broken sentences which pain and suffering prevented him always from connecting … There were frequent pauses in his conversation.'[56] Scott would be a reliable witness, replaying and replaying in his mind the nightmare that was the death of his patron and friend. The full account in *The Morning Chronicle* seems to have been provided by Lieutenant John Pascoe who had, as Signal Lieutenant, helped Nelson to send the pre-battle signal 'England expects that every man will do his duty.' Pascoe's name heads the list of wounded from *Victory*.[57] He had been wounded with grapeshot and was placed on the orlop deck near to Nelson as the latter lay dying.

The medical fact was that Nelson suffered that most terrible of deaths: with low blood pressure and in 'shock', he slowly suffocated in his own blood. The part of the left lung that was penetrated by the musket ball would have collapsed with blood in it – a haemopneumothorax. The ball in passing through the lung would destroy lung tissue and Beatty found at post mortem that a large branch of the pulmonary artery was also 'divided'.[58] Blood from the torn lung and artery would find its way into the trachea (windpipe) and be expelled as Nelson talked. It is significant that while none of the eye witnesses of Nelson's demise recorded it, Devis, who was the only artist to have direct access to his body, painted the dying hero with blood trickling out of his mouth.

In addition, if one lung collapsed there would have been a 'shift' of organs – the heart and the other lung – within the thoracic cavity causing more discomfort for Nelson. In a wounded man with compromised chest expansion externally due to pain at the sites of the bony fractures and with gross alteration of the function of the lungs, proper lung expansion is impossible and this produced what Beatty observed, 'His breathing was oppressed and his voice faint' (due to overall poor lung volume.)[59] Every single breath Nelson took after he was wounded would have been extremely painful. Reverend Dr Scott noticed this, and mentioned it in his letter to George Rose: 'He was ... compelled to speak in broken sentences which pain and suffering prevented him always from connecting.'[60]

This is where the suffocation comment earlier is so sadly fascinating. Nelson was bleeding to death internally within his chest cavity. He was suffocating. And he knew it. 'I feel something rising in my chest that tells me I shall soon be gone.' Given the torn pulmonary artery, his symptoms and the effect of the low blood pressure, as well as the other so very severe and painful injuries, it was, in the author's opinion, a measure of the physical toughness of Nelson that he lived for so long after being wounded. Many would have died of the pain and shock much more quickly. Moribund, he nevertheless seems to have retained his mental faculties until the very moment of death.

Victory's orlop deck had no natural light and no proper ventilation. It was below the water line of the ship and must have been extremely hot and practically airless, with guns continually firing on the decks directly above.

This primary early account of the behaviour of wounded men after a battle comes from a young war correspondent for the *New York Herald*, George Alfred Townsend, writing during the American Civil War. Yet there can have been very little difference between the scenes in the orlop decks of men-o'-war during and after naval battles in Nelson's day, and after land battles some 60 years later. Perhaps the air and light was better in the 'old barn', and there might have been chloroform for the most serious cases (although it was often unavailable, especially to the Confederate side in the later part of the war) but the reactions of the wounded would have been exactly the same and it is telling that Townsend invoked West's 'keen eye.'

> I went unrestrained, into all the largest hospitals. In the first of these an amputation was being performed, and at the door lay a little heap of human fingers, feet, legs, and arms. I shall not soon forget the bare-armed surgeons, with bloody instruments, that leaned over the rigid and insensible figure, while the comrades of the subject looked horrifiedly at the scene.

In many wounds, the balls still remained, and the discolored flesh was swollen unnaturally. There were some who had been shot in the bowels, and now and then they were frightfully convulsed, breaking into shrieks and shouts. Some of them reiterated a single work, as 'doctor,' or 'help,' or 'God,' or 'oh!' commencing with a loud spasmodic cry, and continuing the same word till it died away in cadence. The act of calling seemed to lull the pain. Many were unconscious and lethargic, moving their fingers and lips mechanically, but never more to open their eyes upon the light; they were already going through the valley and the shadow.

I think, still, with a shudder, of the faces of those who were told mercifully that they could not live. The unutterable agony, the plea for somebody on whom to call, the longing eyes that poured out prayers; the looking on mortal as if its resources were infinite; the fearful looking to the immortal as if it were so far off, so implacable, that the dying appeal would be in vain; the open lips, through which one could almost look at the quaking heart below; the ghastliness of brow and tangled hair; the closing pangs; the awful quietus ... I looked at these things:

'Gods!
Could I but paint a dying groan –'

How the keen eye of West would have turned from the reeking cockpit of the *Victory* ... to this old barn, peopled with horrors.[61]

The contrast between the medical quarters in the orlop deck of *Victory* and the medical efficiency of a modern hospital are enormous. So is the contrast between the treatments. A brief outline of the modern treatment of a major wound such as Nelson sustained on 21st October 1805:

Immediate treatment: (Not in order but all procedures must be done by the members of the medical team as soon as possible):
(a) Put in place intravenous drips
(b) Administer oxygen
(c) Insert a tube into the trachea so that artificial ventilation can be administered
(d) Insert a chest drain into the left chest
(e) Immobilise the whole spine and left shoulder
(f) Maintain body temperature
(g) Get to Thoracic Unit at hospital as soon as possible
(h) 'continuous early monitoring is fundamental to the severely injured patient'[62]

At Thoracic Unit at Hospital:
(a) Continue artificial ventilation
(b) X-ray to show:
  1. Sites of bony fractures
  2. Site of bullet
  3. Correct position of chest drain
  4. Correct position of tubes
(c) Open chest to:
  1. Find and suture torn pulmonary artery
  2. Suture and debride (clean up and remove) traumatised lung tissue
(d) Remove musket ball from lower right back muscles
(e) Provide adequate analgesia
(f) Blood transfusions
(g) Antibiotics
(h) Anti-tetanus
(i) Surgically stabilize spine/left shoulder
(j) Transfer to Spinal Unit once chest stabilized.

If successfully stabilised the long term effect would have been that Nelson would have had a permanently transected spinal cord, resulting in loss of control over bowels and bladder, impotence, and paralysis in both legs.

To sum up, Nelson died from a combination of severe injuries:

1. Traumatic blood loss occurred from:
    (a)   the five fractured bones and their attendant arterial supply
    (b)   the torn pulmonary artery
    (c)   the destroyed lung tissue in two segments of the left lung
    (d)   the destroyed spinal cord.
2. The destruction of the Autonomic Nervous System at the spinal level of thoracic ventebrae 6 and 7, resulted in severe pooling of blood and marked reduction in blood pressure in Nelson's body from the mid chest level downwards. This was due to loss of about two-thirds of his body's vascular tone.
3. The extremely severe pain experienced at several locations, most especially at the transected (cut) spinal cord, and in the fractured rib cage.
4. The reduced lung function associated with intra-thoracic blood loss, collapsed and destroyed lung tissue. and the rib cage pain.

Here is the full text of the *Naval Chronicle's* 'Addenda to the Biographical Memoir of Nelson', and Beatty's first account of Nelson's death which uses the words 'every instant' to describe Nelson's internal blood loss:

We are indebted to the following interesting statement, which has been authenticated by Mr. Beatty and Mr. Burke, the Surgeon and Purser of the *Victory*:

A few minutes before Lord Nelson was wounded, Mr. Burke was near him. He looked steadfastly at him and said, 'Burke, I expect every man to be upon his station!' Mr. Burke took the hint, and went to his proper situation in the cockpit.

At this time his Lordship's Secretary, Mr. Scott, who was not, as has been represented, either receiving directions from him, or standing by him, but was communicating some orders to an officer at a distant part of the quarter-deck, was cut almost in two by a cannonshot. He expired on the instant, and was thrown overboard. Lord Nelson observed the act of throwing his Secretary overboard and said, as if doubtful, to a Midshipman who was near him, 'Was that Scott?' The Midshipman replied, he believed it was. He exclaimed, 'Poor fellow!'

He was now walking the quarter-deck, and about three yards from the stern, the space he generally walked before he turned back. His Lordship was in the act of turning on the quarter-deck, with his face towards the enemy, when he was mortally wounded in the left breast by a musket-ball, supposed to have been fired from the mizzen top of the *Redoutable* a French ship of the line, which the *Victory* had attacked early in the battle.

He instantly fell. He was not, as has been related, picked up by Captain Hardy. In the hurry of the battle, which was then raging in its greatest violence, even the fall of their beloved Commander did not interrupt the business of the quarter-deck. Two sailors, however, who were near his Lordship, raised him in their arms, and carried him to the cockpit. He was immediately laid upon a bed, and the following is the substance of the conversation which really took place in the cockpit, between his Lordship, Captain Hardy, Mr. Burke and Mr. Beatty:

Upon seeing him brought down, Mr. Burke immediately ran to him 'I fear' he said, 'Your Lordship is wounded!' – 'Mortally! Mortally' – 'I hope not, my dear Lord; let Mr. Beatty examine your wound,' – 'It is of no use,' exclaimed the dying Nelson; 'he had better attend to others.'

Mr. Beatty now approached to examine the wound. His Lordship was raised up; and Beatty, whose attention was anxiously fixed upon the eyes of his patient, as an indication the most certain when a wound is mortal, after a few moments glanced his eye on Burke, and expressed his opinion in his countenance. Lord Nelson now turned to Burke, and said, 'Tell Hardy to come to me.' Burke left the cockpit. Beatty now said, 'Suffer me, my Lord, to probe the wound with my finger; I will give you no pain.' Lord Nelson permitted him, and, passing his left hand round his waist, he probed it with the forefinger of his right.

When Burke returned into the cockpit with Captain Hardy, Lord Nelson told the latter to come near him. 'Kiss me, Hardy!' he exclaimed – Captain Hardy kissed his cheek – 'I hope your Lordship,' he said, 'will still live to enjoy your triumph.' – Never, Hardy!' he exclaimed; 'I am dying – I am a dead man all over – Beatty will tell you so – bring the fleet to anchor – you have all done your duty – God bless you!' Captain Hardy now said, 'I suppose Collingwood, my dear Lord, is to command the fleet?' – 'Never,' exclaimed he, 'whilst I live;' – meaning doubtless, that, so long as his gallant spirit survived, he would never desert his duty.

What passed after this was merely casual: his Lordship's last words were to Mr. Beatty, whilst he was expiring in his arms, 'I could have wished to have lived to enjoy this; but God's will be done!' – 'My Lord,' exclaimed Hardy, 'you die in the midst of triumph!' – 'Do I, Hardy?' – He smiled faintly – 'God be praised!' These were his last words before he expired.

The above account is fully confirmed by the following official statement, with which we have been favoured by Mr. Beatty himself.[63]

His Majesty's Ship *Victory*, 15th Dec. 1805

About the middle of the action with the combined fleets, on the 21st October last, the late illustrious Commander in Chief, Lord Nelson, was mortally wounded in the left breast by a musket ball, supposed to be fired from the mizen-top of the *Redoutable*, French ship of the line, which the *Victory* fell on board of early in the battle. His Lordship was in the act of turning on the quarter-deck, with his face towards the enemy, when he received his wound; he instantly fell, and was carried to the cockpit, where he lay about two hours. On his being brought below, he complained of acute pain about the sixth or seventh dorsal vertebra; of privation of sense, and motion of the body, and inferior extremities; his respiration short and difficult; pulse weak, small, and irregular. He frequently declared his back was shot through; that he felt every instant a gush of blood within his breast; and that he had sensations which indicated to him the approach of death. In the course of an hour, his pulse became indistinct, and was gradually lost in the arm; his extremities and forehead became soon afterwards cold; he retained his wonted energy of mind, and exercise of his faculties, until the latest moment of his existence; and when victory, as signal as decisive, was announced to him, he expressed his pious acknowledgments thereof, and heartfelt satisfaction at the glorious event, in the most emphatic language. He then delivered his last orders with his usual precision; and in a few minutes afterwards expired without a struggle.[64]

Notes

1. Beatty p.74
2. ibid p.28
3. Nicolas vol VII p.224
4. Beatty p.60
5. Log of *Victory* ADM 101/125/1
6. Beatty p.42
7. ibid p.42–4
8. *Navy Magazine* October 1944
9. Naish p.374
10. *Nelson's Letters to Lady Hamilton* vol I p.34
11. Beatty p.49–50
12. ibid p.17
13. ibid
14. ibid p.15–17
15. *Dictionary of National Biography* 2004
16. Beatty p.iv
17. Minutes of the University of St. Andrews 14th October 1817 452/13 p.102
18. Catalogue of the Royal Society A00471
19. Gatty p.77
20. ibid p.195
21. ibid p.198
22. Morrison vol 2 letter 849 p.270
23. Gatty p.184-188
24. *Gibraltar Chronicle* Supplement 2nd November 1805
25. Crosland, Mrs. N. *Landmarks of a Literary Life* published privately mid 1870s
    Her parents knew Burke personally: 'A little fair man in a scratch wig'
26. Rev. E. Walker Personal communication to the Author
27. Beatty p.28
28. ibid p.34
29. ibid p.35
30. *Naval Chronicle* vol XIV p.40
31. Beatty p.36
32. ibid p.37
33. Mr. A. E. Rees, personal communication to the author
34. Beatty p.71
35. ibid p.69
36. ibid p.70
37. M. Crumplin personal communication to the Author
38. *Naval Chronicle* vol XIV 1805 p.38–40
39. Beatty p.38
40. ibid p.69
41. ibid

42. ibid p.40
43. ibid p.41
44. *Gibraltar Chronicle* Supplement 2nd November 1805
45. Beatty p.42–3
46. ibid p.43–4
47. ibid p.44–5
48. ibid p.45
49. ibid p.47
50. *Gibraltar Chronicle* Supplement 2nd November 1805
51. Beatty p.47
52. *Naval Chronicle* vol XIV p.38–40
53. Brockliss, L. et al *Nelson's Surgeon* 2005 p.154
54. Beatty p.73
55. British Library Add Mss 3492 Fo 49
56. Nicolas vol VII p.246
57. ibid p.223
58. Beatty p.70
59. ibid p.49
60. Gatty p.188
61. Townsend, G.A. 'Campaigns of a Non-combatant' Quoted in Commager, H.S. (ed) *The Blue and the Gray* 1950 vol II p.771–2
62. Colvin, M.P. et al. 'Early Management of the severely injured patient' *Journal of R.S.M.* vol 91 1998 p.26-9
63. *Naval Chronicle* vol XIV 1805 p.38–40
64. Beatty

CHAPTER XI

The Aftermath

Immediately after the battle three events occurred. Firstly, Collingwood, the new Fleet Commander, was forced to transfer to Blackwood's frigate *Euryalus* as his own ship, *Royal Sovereign*, was so badly damaged. He began to compose the elegant and accomplished Trafalgar Dispatch. In the middle of this very important public document is a paragraph of extraordinary private grief (see p.200-1) and this grief was mirrored by other correspondents in the Fleet.

Next, it was decided that Nelson's body should go back to England on board a fast frigate, but the crew of *Victory* seem, politely, almost to have mutinied. The decision was quickly revoked.

Thirdly, the decision to take Nelson's body back home slowly, in his battered flagship, via Gibraltar, meant that William Beatty, Chief Surgeon on board *Victory*, became responsible for the preservation of Nelson's body.

Victory arrived back in England on 4th December 1805 and a complex series of events occurred between then and 9th January, the date of Nelson's state funeral. The most important event was Nelson's post mortem.

Reactions to Nelson's death by writers on board ships in the British Fleet reflected the universal pall of grief which settled over the victorious crews once the news reached them (see p. xviii-xix). Captain Blackwood's letter (see pp. 215-7) was clearly penned by a man 'penetrated with the deepest anguish' as was Collingwood's dispatch. The whole of Collingwood's Dispatch was printed in *The Times*. It began with the words 'The ever-to-be-lamented death of Vice-Admiral Lord Viscount Nelson, who, in the late conflict with the enemy, fell in the hour of victory, leaves to me the duty of informing my Lords Commissioners of the Admiralty ...'[1]

The Times Editorial – all twelve paragraphs of it – caught exactly the mood of London, and then of the country as a whole, as the news of the victory and Nelson's death spread. Lieutenant John Lapenotiere of the *Pickle* schooner had arrived at the Admiralty at 1 a.m. on 5th November 1805 with Collingwood's Dispatches. William Marsden, First Secretary of the Admiralty, and the recipient of so many of Nelson's letters in the previous three years, was on his way to bed. Lapenotiere said to him 'Sir, we have gained a great victory; but we have lost Lord Nelson!'[2] and these double sentiments of elation and grief were universal. Furthermore, it was *The Times* which mirrored the recorded reaction of people to the events, not the other way round. Three paragraphs from this issue of *The Times* are given here, and it is interesting to note the alleged remark by Nelson that he would probably lose a leg:

The official account of the late Naval Action, which terminated in the most decisive victory that has ever been achieved by British skill and gallantry, will be found in our Paper of this day. That the triumph, great and glorious as it is, has been dearly bought, and that such was the general opinion, was powerfully evinced in the deep and universal affliction with which the news of Lord Nelson's death was received. The victory created none of those enthusiastic emotions in the public mind, which the success of our naval arms have in every former instance produced. There was not a man who did not think that the life of the Hero of the Nile was too great a price for the capture and destruction of twenty sail of French and Spanish men of war.

To the official details, we are enabled to add the following particulars respecting the death of as great an Admiral as ever wielded the naval thunder of Britain. When Lord Nelson found that by his skilful manoeuvres he had placed the enemy in such a position that they could not avoid an engagement, he displayed the utmost animation, and his usual confidence of victory. He said to Capt. Hardy, and the other Officers who surrounded him on the quarter-deck, 'Now they cannot escape us; I think we shall at least make sure of twenty of them. I shall probably lose a leg, but that will be purchasing a victory cheaply.'

If ever there was a man who deserved to be 'praised, wept, and honoured' by his country, it is Lord Nelson. ... If ever there were a hero who merited the honours of a public funeral, and a public mourning, it is the pious, the modest, and the gallant Nelson; the darling of the British navy, whose death has plunged a whole nation into the deepest grief; and to whose talents and bravery, even the enemy he has conquered will bear testimony.[3]

Hardy had sent a Lieutenant Hills to tell the British Second in Command that Nelson was dying. The command of the British Fleet thus devolved upon Nelson's friend, 'dear Coll,' Rear Admiral Cuthbert Collingwood. The death of his friend, which had reduced him to tears, provoked in Collingwood an extraordinary outpouring in the middle of his official Dispatch (paragraph nine) to the Admiralty:

Such a battle could not be fought without sustaining a great loss of men. I have not only to lament, in common with the British Navy and the British Nation, in the fall of the Commander-in-Chief, the loss of a hero whose name will be immortal, and his memory ever dear to his Country, but my heart is rent with the most poignant grief for the death of a friend, to whom, by many year's intimacy, and a perfect knowledge of the virtues of his mind, which inspired ideas superior to the common race of men, I was bound by the strongest ties of affection; a grief to which even the glorious occasion in which he fell does not bring the consolation which perhaps it ought: His Lordship received a musket ball in his left breast about the middle of the Action, and sent an Officer to me immediately with his last farewell, and soon after expired.[4]

Nelson in his writing immediately before Trafalgar, had hoped for 'humanity after victory' and what he prayed for came to pass. Six days after the battle, Collingwood wrote to His Excellency The Marquis de Solana, Captain-General of Andalusia, Governor of Cadiz:

Euryalus, off Cadiz, October 27th 1805

My Lord Marquis,

A great number of Spanish Subjects having been wounded in the late Action between the British and the Combined Fleets of Spain and France, on the 21st instant, humanity, and my desire to alleviate the sufferings of these wounded men, dictate to me to offer to your Excellency their enlargement, that they may be taken proper care of in the Hospitals on shore, provided your Excellency will send Boats to convey them, with a proper Officer to give receipts for the number, and acknowledge them in your Excellency's answer to this letter, to be Prisoners of War, to be exchanged before they serve again.

I beg to assure your Excellency of my high consideration, and that I am, &c., COLLINGWOOD[5]

The next day the Marquis replied:

Cadiz, October 28th 1805

Most Excellent Sir,

Your Excellency's letter of yesterday's date, which was brought to me today under a flag of truce, convinces me that you are not less distinguished for your humanity than for your valour in battle. The mode which your Excellency proposes for alleviating the lot of the unhappy persons who are wounded on board the captured Ships, is so honourable to your generous feelings, that I have resolved, on my part, with the assent of General [sic] Gravina, that tomorrow (if the weather permit) when the Frigates of the Combined Fleet go out to receive them, they shall convey to your Excellency, at the same time, the English Officers and other persons who have been made prisoners in those Ships which were recovered after the Action, and have re-entered this Port. In sending them, I entreat your Excellency to deign to fulfill the agreement for an exchange of prisoners, which I had adjusted with Vice-Admiral Orde and Lord Nelson, whose death has overwhelmed me with sorrow.[6]

The next important primary source is from the second part of Major Rotely's account which is concerned with what happened after Nelson's death:

On the morning after his death, I went below to view the body, and to procure a lock of his hair as a memento, but Captain Hardy had been before me and had cut off the whole with the exception of a small lock at the back of the neck which I secured. The hair, with the coat and waistcoat Nelson fell in, was preserved and sent to Lady Hamilton, the breeches and stockings came into my possession, and I have preserved them as valuable relics for upwards of forty years. To preserve the body, a large cask was procured and lashed on its end on the middle deck.

The body was brought up by two men from the cockpit. I received it and placed it head foremost in the cask. The head of the cask was then replaced and filled with brandy, and a Marine sentinel placed over it by night or day, so that it was impossible for anyone to approach it unseen.[7]

On 22nd October 1805, despite the fact that Beatty and his medical assistants had 105 wounded to care for, 'as soon as circumstances permitted the Surgeon to devote a portion of his attention to the care of Lord Nelson's honoured remains, measures were adopted to preserve them as effectively as the means then on board the *Victory* allowed.'[8]

Initially, Beatty only examined the body superficially but he then attempted to probe the course of the ball. This seems to have provoked 'a quantity of blood (which) was evacuated from the left side of the breast: none had escaped before. The ball was traced by a probe to the spine, but its lodgment could not at that time be discovered.'[9] Someone, probably Hardy, then cut off almost all the hair, (see above) as Nelson had wished (as was common practice in those days), and the body, stripped of all the ordinary clothes except the shirt, was put into the largest cask on board

Victory, a leaguer, head first, as described by Major Rotely, and placed on end on the middle deck with a marine sentry. The cask had an upper and lower opening so that brandy could be drawn off from below and replaced from above, and this was done once more, with brandy, before *Victory* reached Gibraltar on 28th October, where the brandy was replaced with spirits of wine. There had between no spirits of wine on board *Victory* although Beatty had felt it was 'certainly by far the best when it can be procured.'[10]

While still heading for Gibraltar there was a 'disengagement of air from the body to such a degree that the Sentinel became alarmed on seeing the head of the cask raised.'[11] (It would be interesting to know what the sentinel's heart rate was, when this happened!) At this stage Beatty observed that the body had absorbed a considerable quantity of brandy.

Victory left Gibraltar on 3rd November. The voyage back to England was prolonged by adverse winds and Beatty had to change the fluid in the cask twice more using a mixture of two-thirds brandy to one-third spirits of wine obtained at Gibraltar. Finally she arrived at Spithead on 4th December and was then sent round to the Nore. On 11th November, the day she sailed, Beatty performed Nelson's post mortem assisted by Arthur Devis, the artist who had come on board at Spithead. Throughout his book Beatty was at pains to record how well Nelson's remains were preserved apart from the bowels (intestines) which were 'found to be much decayed and likely to communicate the process of putrefaction to the rest of the Body: the parts already injured were therefore removed.'[12] The latter part of this sentence is ambivalent. Beatty clearly removed the intestines – he also removed the lungs in order to observe what he considered to be 'The immediate cause of His Lordship's death ... a wound of the left pulmonary artery, which poured out its blood into the cavity of the chest'[13] and also the other chest and abdominal organs in order to report on them.The heart was put back in the body (see p. 219). Beatty's letter to Scott of 15th December 1805)

Beatty's account of 'course and site of the Ball, as ascertained since death' is succinct and completely clear (and identical to the report sent under his name and that of Walter Burke to *The Times*, published on 30th December 1805).

The ball struck the fore part of His Lordship's epaulette; and entered the left shoulder immediately before the processes acromion scapulae, which it slightly fractured. It then descended obliquely into the thorax, fracturing the second and third ribs: and after penetrating the left lobe of the lungs, and dividing in its passage a large branch of the pulmonary artery, it entered the left side of the spine between the sixth and seventh dorsal vertebrae, fractured the left transverse process of the sixth dorsal vertebra, wounded the medulla spinalis, and fracturing the right transverse process of the seventh vertebra, made its way from the right side of the spine, directing its course through the muscles of the back; and lodged therein, about two inches below the inferior angle of the right scapula. On removing the ball, a portion of the gold-lace and pad of the epaulette, together with a small piece of His Lordship's coat, was found firmly attached to it.

W. BEATTY.[14]

After the post mortem the body was wrapped in cotton vestments and then rolled in cotton bandages. It was then temporarily laid in a lead coffin brought specially on board *Victory* and this coffin filled with 'brandy holding in solution camphor and myrrh.'[15] On 21st December the body was removed and put into Hallowell's L'Orient coffin, which had been obtained out of storage in London and sent down to *Victory*. Beatty said the facial features were 'somewhat tumid from absorption of the spirit but on using friction from a napkin they resumed in great degree their natural character,' and noted 'its [Nelson's body] undecayed state after a lapse of two months since death'.[16] This was *not* what he wrote to the Admiralty warning them privately that the face of the dead hero was in a poor state and could not be exposed to public gaze at the Lying-in-State which they now knew was to be at Greenwich. On the same day therefore, having been exposed for the last time to the view of *Victory's* Officers and some of Nelson's friends, the body, dressed in shirt, stockings, uniform small clothes, neck cloth and nightcap, was then placed in the *L'Orient* coffin which was in turn placed in a lead coffin. This was sealed and this in turn was placed in a wooden coffin. By this time the whole weighed some 400 lbs. The triple coffin 'was sent out of *Victory* into Commissioner Gray's Yacht *Chatham*'[17] and passed upriver to the Painted Hall, Greenwich, where it lay in (sealed) state for three days. More than 30,000 people came down from London to pay homage.

Meanwhile, Beatty had been writing. His 'Professional Report on His Lordship's wound and death' is dated 11th December 1805 from HMS *Victory* at Sea. Beatty sent it with a covering letter dated 15th December 1805 to the *Medical and Physical Journal* where it was published in January 1806. Even before that date Beatty had written to *The Times*. An article, which is almost identical to Beatty's two other reports, said to have been written jointly by Beatty and Walter Burke, the purser of the *Victory*, was published on 30th December. These extremely personal medical details so publicly available must have caused great distress to Nelson's family and friends but undoubtedly they brought Beatty's name to prominent public notice.

The *Medical and Physical Journal* article is illustrated with a hand-coloured reproduction in yellow, brown and pink of a drawing of the bullet which killed Nelson, almost certainly drawn by A.W. Devis, although there is no acknowledgment of this. Richard Walker wrote that Devis had gone on board *Victory* at Spithead and stayed on board as she sailed round to the Nore, making drawings of Nelson and the other officers (Beatty, Burke, Hardy and Dr Scott among others) for his painting 'The Death of Nelson.'[18] So he would be the obvious choice to draw and then engrave the drawing of the fatal ball. The private letter from Beatty to The Admiralty dated the same day as the covering letter to the *Medical and Physical Journal* was concerned with the poor state of Nelson's face; he also wrote to Dr. Scott on 20th December a letter which began: 'The Features being lost.'[19]

Beatty went on to higher things (see p. 179-80). His *Authentic Narrative of the Death of Lord Nelson* is a minor masterpiece and contains one of the first ever recorded accounts of traumatic paraplegia. Nelson would have found it amusing that even in death he was a 'first', medically speaking. Beatty's book contains the following notice:

> The Surgeon of the late illustrious Lord Nelson feels himself called upon, from the responsible situation which he held on the eventful day of the 21st of October 1805, to lay before the British Nation the following Narrative. It contains an account of the most interesting incidents which occurred on board the *Victory* (Lord Nelson's flag-ship) from the time of her sailing from England, in the month of September, till the day of battle inclusively; with a detail of the particulars of His Lordship's Death, the mode adopted for preserving his revered Remains during the subsequent long passage of the *Victory* to England, and the condition of the Body when it was deposited in Greenwich Hospital. This short statement of facts is deemed a small but necessary tribute of respect to the memory of the departed Hero, as well as a professional document which the Public had a right to expect from the man who had the melancholy honour of being his principal medical attendant on that occasion: and is presumed to be not inappropriately concluded by observations on the state of His Lordship's health for some time previous to his fall; with his habits of life, and other circumstances, strongly proving that few men had a greater prospect of attaining longevity, on which account his premature death is the more to be deplored by his Country.[20]

There is no acknowledgement in the book to Walter Burke or Alexander Scott; although since Beatty was not always with Nelson as he lay dying, and they were, it follows Beatty was quoting their recollections as well as his own.

Regarding Nelson's post mortem, why did Beatty go so quickly into print with his findings? The author believes the answer was two-fold. By publishing his findings as soon as he possibly could, firstly, in *The*

Times, the most important and widely read newspaper in London, next, in the *Medical and Physical Journal,* the most important medical journal in London (and probably in Britain) and finally in his own book on the subject, *Authentic Narrative,* Beatty established two things with all readers of any influence in the country. On the one hand, all now knew that no effort of his had been spared to look after and try to save the life of the Nation's hero; and on the other hand that no contemporary medical or surgical treatment could have prevented Nelson's death.

Beatty's account of his post mortem findings on Nelson's body, and the medical conclusions he made as a result of his findings, are provided in complete detail in his book:

> There were no morbid indications to be seen; other than those attending the human body six weeks after death, even under circumstances more favourable to its preservation. The heart was small, and dense in its substance; its valves, pericardium, and the large vessels, were sound, and firm in their structure. The lungs were sound, and free from adhesions. The liver was very small, in its colour natural, firm in its texture, and every way free from the smallest appearance of disorganization. The stomach, as well as the spleen and other abdominal contents, was alike free from the traces of disease. Indeed all the vital parts were so perfectly healthy in their appearance, and so small, that they resembled more those of a youth, than of a man who had attained his forty-seventh year; which state of the body, associated with habits of life favourable to health, gives every reason to believe that His Lordship might have lived to a great age.
>
> The immediate cause of His Lordship's death was a wound of the left pulmonary artery, which poured out its blood into the cavity of the chest. The quantity of blood thus effused did not appear to be very great: but as the hemorrhage was from a vessel so near the heart, and the blood was consequently lost in a very short time, it produced death sooner than would have been effected by a larger quantity of blood lost from an artery in a more remote part of the body. The injury done to the spine must of itself have proved mortal, but His Lordship might perhaps have survived this alone for two or three days; though his existence protracted even for that short period would have been miserable to himself, and highly distressing to the feelings of all around him.'[21]

The post mortem also enabled Beatty to trace 'Course and site of the Ball, as ascertained since death'.[22] This he did very correctly and very thoroughly.

Brandy was used in the leaguer to start the preservation of Nelson's body the day after he was killed. Beatty said he favoured spirits of wine for preserving bodies 'Spirit (sic) of wine, however, is certainly by far the best, when it can be procured' – but there was no spirits of wine on board. The brandy was drawn off and replaced once on the journey to Gibraltar – probably on 24th October. According to Beatty when the leaguer was examined, on *Victory* arriving at that port, on October 28th, 'the cask, showing a deficit produced by the Body's absorbing a considerable quantity of the brandy, was then filled up with it'[23] that is, with spirits of wine. Beatty records later that he used a mixture of spirits of wine and brandy in the ratio 2:1, and that a complete change of fluid in the cask was made twice on the voyage home, using the same mixture.[24]

Spirits of wine appears to have been a diluted form of brandy and water occasionally issued to sailors on board a ship if rum was in short supply. It had an alcohol concentration of approximately 20% proof.[25] This resulted in poor preservation of Nelson's body with unfortunate effects, and Beatty was wrong to believe in its efficacy.

So to the early medical reports. On 15th December 1805 Beatty sent a letter to the Editors of the *Medical and Physical Journal*, written from on board *Victory*. He sent the drawing of 'the fatal ball' and what Beatty called 'a statement of the site and nature of the wound' and what the Editors called 'Mr. Beatty's Account of the Death of Lord Nelson.'[26]

The *Medical and Physical Journal* had started life in 1781 as the *London Medical Journal*. In 1791 it changed its name to *Medical Facts and Observations* and it officially became *The Medical and Physical Journal* in 1799. It was published on a monthly basis and had two volumes per year. It was by no means the first medical journal in Britain. (That particular honour goes to *Medical Essays and Observations* published by the Society of Physicians of Edinburgh in 1731.)

It seems to have had several editors at the same time (hence Beatty's letters to 'The Editors'). It published papers and editorials on medical science as well as items on medical politics, reviews of books, notices of lectures and of societies, letters, obituaries and interesting cases. The article Beatty sent to the *Medical and Physical Journal* would have been of enormous interest and it was published in the very next issue of the Journal, Volume XV in January 1806, almost, one imagines, to coincide with Nelson's State Funeral. All the details, the editors were given to understand, were Beatty's alone. Beatty wrote:

TO THE EDITORS OF *THE MEDICAL AND PHYSICAL JOURNAL*
H.M.S. *Victory*, Dec. 15, 1805

Gentlemen,

I beg leave to transmit you a statement of the site and nature of the wound which produced the death of the exceedingly lamented and late illustrious hero, Lord Nelson; and request you will please to insert it in the next number of the *Medical and Physical Journal*; enclosed is likewise a drawing of the fatal ball, with its appendages, which were carried before it through the whole course it described.

I am, &c,

BEATTY, Surgeon.[27]

By an extraordinary coincidence in issues of the *Medical and Physical Journal* in the same volume as Beatty's account were two articles by medical men Nelson had known personally. Thomas Trotter, M.D., wrote a very long article from Newcastle on his intended publication, 'On the increasing prevalence, prevention and treatment of those diseases commonly called nervous biliary indigestion' giving the Journal's readers 'a kind of syllabus of my work.'[28] This was the same Thomas Trotter who had treated Nelson's left eye with cold spring water in 1801 and wrote about his treatment of the eye in 1803 (see p. 65). In 1782, J. B. Ruspini had treated Nelson's painful fleshy excrescence of the gum, and assured him he did not have a form of venereal disease. By early 1806 he was 'Surgeon Dentist to His Royal Highness the Prince of Wales' and had invented an instrument 'for the extraction of Balls from Gun-Shot wounds.'[29] (The engraving of said instrument showed it bore more than a passing likeness to the instrument with which the present author was inserting intrauterine devices in the 1960s.) The articles in the *Journal* would have intrigued a highly intelligent layman such as Nelson. For example, 'Dr Girdlestones's address to the inhabitants of Yarmouth on the pros and cons of Vaccination' would have fascinated him[30] as would an account by a doctor from Fulneck, near Leeds, Mr. J. Waiblinger, of 'two cases of eye disease cured by the Galvanic process'[31] and 'observations on the Nature and Cure of Fevers and Diseases of the West and East Indies, and of America...' by Thomas Clark, Surgeon.[32]

The *Journal*, however, did not have an exclusive. A letter with the title 'The following relation of the last moments of Lord Nelson given by Mr. Beatty, Surgeon, and Mr. Burke, Purser, of the *Victory*', was published in *The Times* of 30th December 1805; apart from two very minor differences it was identical to Beatty's account for the *Medical and Physical Journal* and published before it. This letter comes at the bottom of column three, and on the same quite extraordinary page there is a first account in English of the Battle of Austerlitz, a very long letter from one 'T.S.' on the already prepared monument to Nelson in St. Paul's Cathedral, and the justification, in English, by the French Captain Lucas and his surviving Officers from the *Redoutable*, as to why their ship was lost. Their justification of their actions, as captured enemy officers soon after a lost battle, is a rare thing in military history.

REPORT ON THE REASONS FOR SURRENDERING THE FRENCH SHIP *LE REDOUTABLE*

This day, October 23rd, we, the undersigned, Captain and Officer of the Legion of Honour, having the command of His Majesty's ship *Le Redoutable*, together with the Officers of the Staff, under Officers, & finding ourselves united on board the English ship *Swiftsure*, and having survived the loss of our own vessel, have drawn up the following report, containing the reasons and circumstances which occasioned the loss of *Le Redoutable*:

On the 21st of October, at half past ten, p.m., the Combined Squadron found itself to windward of the enemy, forming in line of battle, when *Le Redoutable*, according to the order of seniority, being the third ship to the rear of the Admiral's ship, the *Bucentaure*, the two head most ships, in consequence of a breeze springing up, after having begun to manoeuvre, left the Admiral's ship exposed, just at the moment when the enemy had made his disposition for attacking our centre. The Victory, of 110 guns, under Admiral Nelson, and the *Temeraire*, of the same rate, were at the head of the division which bore down upon the Admiral's ship, to surround it. Captain Lucas very soon perceiving the enemy's design, immediately manoeuvred, for the purpose of falling into the rear of the *Bucentaure*, in which he happily succeeded; and though the Admiral called to us several times to make sail, we had all unanimously determined rather to lose our own ship, than witness the capture of our Admiral. At a quarter before twelve the firing commenced on both sides between the shipping that were within gun shot. The enemy's two three-deckers directed all their efforts to the forcing of our line in the rear of the Bucentaure, and to force *Le Redoutable* on board her, in order to make the Admiral's ship cease her firing; but not being able to move us, we were ordered to lay ourselves along-side the Admiral, and in that situation gave and received a number of broadsides, but which, however, did not prevent us from lashing ourselves to the *Victory*. Our Commandant then giving orders to board; our brave crew, with their Officers at their head, instantly put themselves in motion. The conflict was immediately begun with small arms, *and upwards of two hundred grenades were thrown on board the* Victory. [Author's italics.] Admiral Nelson fought at the head of his crew; but still, as our fire was much more vigorous than that of the English, we silenced them in about a quarter of an hour. The deck of the *Victory* was covered with the dead, and Admiral Nelson killed. Still it was difficult to board the *Victory*, its upper deck being so much higher than that of *Le Redoutable*; however, the Ensign Yon, and four seamen, climbing up by the anchors, succeeded and would have been followed by the rest of their comrades on the larboard side. But the English ship, the *Temeraire*, perceiving that the fire of the Admiral's ship had ceased, immediately fell upon our starboard side, and after raking us with a heavy fire, the slaughter that ensued, was not to be described; more than two hundred of our men being killed, the Captain ordered the remainder to board the *Temeraire*, which was only prevented by the arrival of another of the enemy's ships within pistol shot of us, in which station it remained till we had struck our colours, and which took place about half past three p.m. for the following reasons:

Because out of the crew, consisting of six hundred and forty-three men, five hundred and twenty-two were no longer in a situation to continue the conflict: three hundred being killed, and two hundred and twenty-two badly wounded. Among the latter were the whole of the Staff, and ten inferior Officers.

Because the main and mizzen-masts were gone by the board; the first fell on board the *Temeraire*, and some of the yards of that ship fell on board *Le Redoutable*.

Because the bowsprit, and a part of the rudder, were shot away, and several of the guns dismounted; and in consequence of the bursting of an eighteen pounder on the second deck, and a carronnade of thirty-six pounds in the stern.

Because almost all the ports were knocked in, and the decks entirely bored through by the upper deck guns of the *Victory* and *Temeraire*.

Because both sides of the ship were shot thro' in such a manner, that numbers of the wounded were killed by the enemy after they had been removed from their quarters.

Because part of the ship was on fire, and had a number of leaks, so that, notwithstanding all the pumps were set a going, she must have sunk.

Throughout the whole of the fight, the *Victory* and the *Temeraire* never ceased their attacks upon *Le Redoutable*; nor did we separate from each other for some time after the battle had ceased in the rest of the fleets. The *Victory* lost its mizzen-mast; its rigging was nearly cut to pieces, and a great part of its crew was disabled. Admiral Nelson was killed by a musket-shot during the attempt to board. At seven in the evening the *Swiftsure* took us in tow, and in the morning sent a party on board to take charge of Captain Lucas, Lieutenant Duposel, and M. Duchees. About noon, the leaks had increased too much, that the Prize-master sending for assistance, the *Swiftsure* sent its boats to save the remainder of our crew, but had scarcely time to remove about one hundred and nineteen French. About seven in the evening, the whole of the stern being under water, the vessel sank, with all the wounded men on board. On the 23rd, the Captain of the

Swiftsure seeing some people at a distance upon a wreck, caused them to be brought in, to the number of fifty; but, including seventy of the wounded, that were taken up, not more than one hundred and sixty-nine were saved out of four hundred and sixty-three.

On board the *Swiftsure,* Signed by the Officers of the quarter-deck, and confirmed by

CAPTAIN LUCAS[33]

This account of the battle, from the French point of view, not unnaturally contains errors. For example, neither the *Victory* nor the *Temeraire* was a 110-gun ship. The British account of the battle says *Redoutable* only fired one broadside. *Victory's* crew were not disabled, although (not surprisingly, considering the fact that she was, with *Royal Sovereign,* foremost in the attack) she did sustain 105 casualties, killed or wounded.

This account by Lucas is not often quoted, so that Lucas' reported use of 200 grenades thrown on board *Victory* to facilitate the attempt at boarding, has usually been ignored.

After the joint article for *The Times,* Beatty and Burke seem to have gone their separate ways.

THE TIMES – 30th December 1805
The following relation of the last moments of Lord Nelson is given by Mr. Beatty, Surgeon, and Mr. Burke, Purser, of the *Victory:*
On his Lordship being brought below, he complained of acute pain in about the sixth or seventh dorsal vertebra, of privation of sense and motion of the body and inferior extremities; his respiration was short and difficult; his pulse was weak, small and irregular; he frequently declared his back was shot through; that he felt every instant a gush of blood within his breast; and that he had sensations which indicated to him the approach of death. In the course of an hour his pulse became indistinct, and was gradually lost in the arm; his extremities and forehead became soon afterwards cold; he retained his wonted energy of mind and exercise of his faculties until the latest moments of his existence; and when victory, as signal as decisive, was announced to him, he expressed his pious acknowledgements thereof, and heartfelt satisfaction of the glorious event, in the most emphatic language. He then delivered his last orders with his usual precision, and in a few minutes after expired without a struggle.

It has been ascertained since his death, that the ball struck the forepart of his Lordship's epaulette, and entered the left shoulder immediately before the processus acromium scapulae, which it slightly fractured; it then descended obliquely into the thorax, fracturing the second and third ribs, and after penetrating the left lobe of the lungs and dividing, in its passage, a large branch of the pulmonary artery, it entered the left side of the spine between the sixth and seventh dorsal vertebrae, fractured the left transverse process of the sixth vertebra, wounded the medulla spinalis, and fracturing the right transverse process of the seventh vertebra, it made its way from the right side of the spine, directing its course through the muscles of the back, and lodged therein, about two inches below the inferior angle of the right scapula. On removing the ball, a portion of the gold lace and part of the epaulette, together with a small piece of his Lordship's coat, were found firmly attached to it.[34]

In chronological order the early medical reports were:

1. That written by Beatty *and* Burke, published in *The Times* on 30th December 1805 and undated
2. The one written by Beatty alone dated 15th December 1805 from H.M.S. *Victory* and sent to the Editors of the *Medical & Physical Journal*
3. The one by Beatty alone printed in the addenda to the Biographical Memoir
4. The 1807 Book: *The Authentic Narrative.*

This last contained two descriptions of Nelson's symptoms, one which said he felt a pulse of blood every *instant*, and the one most often copied by other biographers, which said the blood pulsed every *minute*. This clearly could not be so, given the post mortem findings, but it did help to explain how all subsequent authors writing about Nelson's death were able to make it lingering but unhorrific.

What must be examined next are the accounts of Nelson's death from other sources. The Right Hon. George Rose, a lifelong friend of Nelson, and twice Treasurer of the Navy – dined on board *Victory* with Nelson just before she sailed for Trafalgar. Alexander Scott's letter to Rose gave Scott's account of Nelson's last hours. It is the one which shows most clearly what agony Nelson must have been experiencing as he lay dying.

To Right Honorable George Rose
H.M. Ship *Victory*, December 22. 1805

My Dear Sir,

In answer to your note of the 10th inst. ... which I received this morning, it is my intention to relate everything Lord Nelson said in which your name was in any way connected. He lived about three hours after receiving his wound, was perfectly sensible the whole time, but was compelled to speak in broken sentences, which pain and suffering prevented him always from connecting. When I first saw him he was apprehensive he should not live many minutes, and told me so; adding in a hurried agitated manner, though with pauses, 'Remember me to Lady Hamilton – remember me to Horatia – remember me to all my friends – Doctor, remember me to Mr. Rose; tell him I have made a will, and left Lady Hamilton and Horatia to my country.' He repeated his remembrance to Lady Hamilton and Horatia, and told me to mind what he said several times. Gradually he became less agitated, and at last calm enough to ask questions about what was going on. This led his mind to Captain Hardy, for whom he sent and inquired with anxiety, exclaiming aloud he would not believe the captain was alive unless he saw him. He grew agitated at the captain's not coming, lamenting his being unable to go on deck and do what was to be done, and doubted every assurance given him of the captain being safe on the quarter-deck. At last the captain came, and he instantly became more composed, listened to his report about the state of the fleet, directed him to anchor ... 'I shall die, Hardy', said the Admiral. 'Is your pain great sir?' 'Yes, but I shall live half-an-hour yet. Kiss me Hardy.' The captain knelt down by his side and kissed him. Upon the captain leaving him to return to the deck, Lord Nelson exclaimed very earnestly more than once. 'Hardy, if I live I'll bring the fleet to an anchor – if I live I'll anchor' – and this was earnestly repeated even when the captain was out of hearing. I do not mean to tell you everything he said. After this interview the Admiral was perfectly tranquil, looking at me in his accustomed manner when alluding to any prior discourse: 'I have not been a great sinner, Doctor', said he. 'Doctor, I was right. I told you so, George Rose has not yet got my letter – tell him' – he was interrupted here by pain. After an interval he said, 'Mr. Rose will remember – don't forget. Doctor – mind what I say.' There were frequent pauses in his conversation. Our dearly beloved Admiral otherwise mentioned your name indeed very kindly, and I will tell you his words when I see you; but it was only in the two above instances he desired you should be told.

I have the honour to be, etc.
A. J. SCOTT[35]

Next, in the *Gibraltar Supplement* of 2nd November 1805, there was an anonymous account which must have come from an eye-witness:

We have endeavoured, since the arrival of the *Victory*, the Ship on board of which Lord Nelson's flag was flying during the whole of the late action, to obtain every information in our power on the subject. It was his Lordship's intention to have broken through the enemy's line, between the tenth and eleventh of the enemy's Ships in the van; at the same time that Admiral Collingwood penetrated their line about the twelfth Ship from the rear: but finding the enemy's line in that part so close, that there was not room to pass, he ordered the *Victory* to be run on board of the Ship that opposed him; and the *Temeraire*, by which the *Victory* was seconded, also ran on board of the next Ship in the enemy's line, so that these four Ships were for a considerable time engaged together in one mass as it were, and so close, that the flash of almost every gun fired from the *Victory* set fire to the *Redoutable*, to which Ship she was at that time opposed: whilst our seamen, with the greatest coolness were at intervals employed, to the midst of the hottest fire, in throwing buckets of water to extinguish the flames on board of the enemy's ship, lest, by their spreading, they might involve both Ships in destruction. We question if ancient, or modern history, can produce a more striking instance of cool and deliberate valour; and it certainly reflects the highest honour upon the discipline and intrepidity of that Ship's crew.

Lord Nelson, on receiving his wound, was immediately sensible it was mortal; and said with a smile to Captain Hardy, with whom he had been talking at that moment, '*they have done for me at last.*' He was soon obliged to be carried off the deck; and as they were conducting him below, he remarked the tiller-rope being too slack, which he desired them to acquaint Captain Hardy with, and have it tightened. His anxiety for the event of the day was such as totally to surmount the pains of death, and every other consideration; he repeatedly sent to inquire how the battle went, and expressed the most lively satisfaction to find it favourable. Whilst bearing down on the enemy's line he had repeatedly said, 'that it was the happiest day of his life, and that from the plan of attack he had laid down, he expected that he should have possession of twenty of their Ships before night.' His lower extremities soon became cold and insensible, *and the effusion of blood from his lungs often threatened suffocation*: [author's italics] but still his eyes seemed to brighten, and his spirits to revive, at hearing the cheers given by the crew of the *Victory*, as the different Ships of the enemy surrendered. About four o'clock he became exceedingly anxious to see his friend Captain Hardy; and he sent for him several times, before that gallant Officer thought it prudent to quit the deck at so interesting a moment. About five o'clock, however, when he saw that the victory was completely decided, and the battle nearly ended, he was enabled to attend to the last wishes of the dying Hero, who eagerly inquired how many Ships were captured? On being told by Captain Hardy, that he was certain of twelve having struck, which he could see, but that probably more had surrendered, his Lordship said, 'What, only twelve! There should at least have been fifteen, or sixteen, by my calculation: (however, after a short pause, he added,) twelve are pretty well!' He now said 'that he felt death fast approaching, and that he had but a few minutes to live; He could have wished to survive a little longer, to have seen the fleet in safety; but, as that was impossible, thanked God that he had outlived the action, and had been enabled to do his duty to his country.' About this time, he was roused by another cheer from the crew of the *Victory*, at their seeing some more of the enemy's Ships strike their colours; at which he expressed the highest satisfaction on learning the cause, and shortly after expired without a groan.[36]

The Hon. Henry Blackwood was Nelson's chief frigate captain at Trafalgar. Nelson thought highly of Blackwood, regarding him as such a close friend that Blackwood was, with Hardy, witness to Nelson's signature to the famous codicil to his will. Blackwood was the man who tracked the combined French and Spanish fleet back to Cadiz in July 1805 and after he sailed back to England to report their whereabouts he called on Nelson (on his 25 day leave at Merton) to tell him that news *before* he informed the Admiralty. Most of Blackwood's letter to his wife is included because, as in Rotely's account, it gives a superb impression of the thoughts and feelings about the battle of an intelligent participant and his reaction to Nelson's death.

Tuesday, 22nd, 1 o'clock at night. – The first hour since yesterday morning that I could call my own is now before me, to be devoted to my dearest wife, who, thank God, is not a husband out of pocket. My heart, however, is sad, and penetrated with the deepest anguish. A Victory, such a one as has never been achieved, yesterday took place in the course of five hours; but at such an expense, in the loss of the most gallant of men, and best of friends, as renders it to me a Victory I never wished to have witnessed – at least, on such terms. After performing wonders by his example and coolness, Lord Nelson was wounded by a French Sharpshooter, and died in three hours after, beloved and regretted in a way not to find example … In my life, I never was so shocked or so completely upset as upon my flying to the *Victory*, even before the Action was over, to find Lord Nelson was then at the gasp of death. His unfortunate decorations of innumerable stars, and his uncommon gallantry, was the cause of his death; and such an Admiral has the Country lost, and every officer and man so kind, so good, so obliging a friend as never was. Thank God, he lived to know that such a Victory, and under circumstances so disadvantageous to the attempt, never was before gained. Almost all seemed as if inspired by the one common sentiment of conquer or die. The Enemy, to do them justice, were not less so. They waited the attack of the British with a coolness I was sorry to witness, and they fought in a way that must do them honour. As a spectator, who saw the faults, or rather mistakes, on both sides, I shall ever do them the justice to say so. They are however, beat, and I hope and trust it may be the means of hastening a Peace. Buonaparte, I firmly believe, forced them to sea to try his luck, and what it might procure him [in] a pitched battle. They had the flower of the Combined Fleet, and I hope it will convince Europe at large that he has not yet learnt enough to cope with the English at sea. No history can record such a brilliant victory. At 12 o'clock yesterday it commenced, and ended about 5, leaving in our hands nineteen Sail of the Line … They were attacked in a way no other Admiral ever before thought of, and equally surprised them. Lord Nelson (though it was not his station) would lead, supported by Captain Hardy, and Freemantle in *Temeraire*, and *Neptune*. He went into the thickest of it, was successful in his first object, and has left cause for every man who had a heart never to forget him. I closed my last sheet in a great hurry to obey my signal on board the *Victory*, and really I thought that I was sent for to take the command of one of the Ships vacant. It was, however, only to talk to me – explain what he expected from the Frigates in, and after, the action – to thank me (which he did, but too lavishly) for my intelligence, and the look-out we kept; and to tell me that if he lived, he should send me home with the despatches … I stayed with him till the Enemy commenced their fire on the *Victory*, when he sent me off. He told me, at parting, we should meet no more; he made me witness his Will, and away I came, with a heart very sad. The loss in the *Victory*, and indeed, I believe, in almost all the other Ships, has been sufficient to convince us the Enemy have learnt how to fight better than they ever did; and I hope it is not injustice to the Second in Command, who is now on board the *Euryalus*, and who fought like a hero, to say that the Fleet under any other, never would have performed what they did under Lord N. But under Lord N it seemed like inspiration to most of them. To give you an idea of the man, and the sort of heart he had, the last signal he made was such a one as would immortalize any man. He saw the Enemy were determined to see it out, and as if he had not already inspired every one with ardour and determination like himself, he made the following general signal by Sir Home Popham's telegraph, vis, 'England expects every officer and man will do their utmost duty.' This, of course, was conveyed by general signals from his Ship; and the alacrity with which the individual Ships answered it, showed how entirely they entered into his feelings and ideals. Would to God he had lived to see his prizes, and the Admirals he has taken! three in all: amongst them, the French Commander-in-Chief … but so entirely am I depressed with the private loss I have had, that really the Victory, and all the prize money I hope to get, (if our prizes arrive safe) appear quite lost by the chasm made by

Lord Nelson's death. … I can scarcely credit he is no more, and that we have in sight, of the Spanish shore obtained so complete, so unheard – of a Victory. Our prizes, I trust, we shall save. Ever since last evening we have had a most dreadful gale of wind, and it is with difficulty the Ships who tow them keep off the shore. Three, I think, must be lost, and with them, above 800 souls each. What a horrid scourge is war! Would to God that this may pave the way to a general peace.[37]

In a later letter Blackwood wrote:

I wish to God he had yielded to my entreaties to come on board my Ship. We all should have preserved a friend, and the Country the greatest Admiral ever was; but he would not listen to it, and I did not take my leave of him till the shot was flying over and over the *Victory*. Villeneuve says he never saw anything like the irresistible line of our Ships; but that of the *Victory*, supported by the *Neptune* and *Temeraire*, was what he could not have formed any judgment of.[38]

The Times recorded carefully and chronologically the progress of *Victory*, with Nelson's body on board, once she reached home waters:

DEAL Thursday, Dec. 19.

The *Victory* sailed this morning for the Nore. The gallant Hero of the Ocean was taken from the vessel of spirits, into which he had been immersed for preservation, on Sunday last. His remains were then deposited in a plain elm coffin, which was placed in the after cabin of the main-deck under a canopy of colours. In this state, the last tribute of respect to his memory has been paid by a number of visitors, who daily went off in boats, during the ship's stay in the Downs, for that purpose.[39]

25th December 1805

The *Victory*, with the remains of the ever to-be-lamented Lord Nelson, arrived off Sheerness on Sunday. On the following morning the body was removed from that ship, and placed on board the *Chatham* yacht at Sheerness, which proceeded immediately on her way to Greenwich.

All the English vessels, while the yacht was passing, hoisted their colours half mast high; and the fort on both sides the river at Tilbury and Gravesend, fired minute guns. Many foreign vessels also paid the same honourable tribute of respect to the corpse of our Naval Chieftain. About half past eleven, the yacht, with her honourable and glorious freight, passed by Gravesend. The coffin, covered with an ensign, was placed on the deck. As soon as the yacht was descried, the colours of the ships and forts were hoisted half-mast high. The bells were tolled, and afterwards rung a muffled peal. The wind being scanty and unfavourable it was found that the yacht could not reach Greenwich until the following tide.

Yesterday, about one o'clock, she arrived off Greenwich Hospital. The body is placed in the coffin made of the work of the Orient, which is put into one made of elm, then into a leaden one and soldered up, and the whole placed in another large coffin of elm, for the purpose of having the ornaments affixed thereon. ... The coffin weighs nearly four hundred weight, and; in consequence of the water not being sufficiently high, could not be removed till the evening.

The body was not landed until dusk. An immense crowd had been collected upon the terrace at Greenwich Hospital from the early part of the day. Towards two o'clock, a report was circulated that the remains of his Lordship would not be removed until the next day, and as the Hospital water-gate had been shut, and the Pensioners had retired, the rumour obtained full, though reluctant credit. About five o'clock, it was lowered from the Commissioner's yacht into a boat, and immediately conveyed to the lower Hospital stairs. The coffin was enveloped in the colours of the Victory, which were bound round it by a piece of rope about the thickness of one of the sheets of a first rate. As soon as it was landed, it was carried by sailors, part of the valiant crew of the *Victory*, to the Painted Hall, from whence, we understand, it was to have been removed, in the course of the evening, to the Record Chamber, in the Hospital, and where it is to continue until the preparations for its lying in state shall be completed ...

Lord Hood, immediately that the corpse arrived, left Greenwich for the Secretary of State's Office, and the Admiralty, to received further directions. It was then, we understand, finally determined, that the procession by water shall take place on the 7th of next month, from Greenwich to Whitehall; the body will be deposited in the Admiralty that night, and in the morning, the procession to St. Paul's to take place.[40]

The removal of the very heavy coffin from Commissioner Gray's yacht into a boat, and then from the boat to the lower Hospital stairs, must have been a very tricky procedure, especially in the cold and dark of a late December evening. If the coffin was carried thence to the painted hall and then to the record office, one wonders just how many sailors were needed to move it. Much more likely it would have been put on a wheeled hearse and dragged to its temporary resting places.

Beatty now had to inform Nelson's brother, William (the new Earl Nelson created in the post-Trafalgar Honours List), via a letter to Dr. Scott, that the body was *not* in a good state of preservation:

Private   H M Ship *Victory* 15th December 1805

When you have the honor of seeing the Earl Nelson, I beg you will have the goodness to inform him, that to check the progress of decay which was taking place, in the remains of his exceedingly lamented, and late illustrious brother, it was found necessary on the llth instant, to remove from the body, the greatest part of the contents of the Chest, and Abdomen; the body was afterwards surrounded with Cotton and Linnen [sic] Wrappers as were likewise the extremities, and rolled throughout with bandages of the same after the Ancient mode of Embalming; it was than placed in a Leaden Coffin, filled with strong spirits holding in solution Camphor and Myrrh, where it now remains in as perfect a State of Preservation as could be affected from modern Embalment; but it will be right to apprize his Lordship, that the features of his departed brother cannot at this distant period from his demise, be easily traced; from a knowledge of this circumstance, he will decide on the propriety of exposing the face during the time which the Body may lay in State. …

I enclose you for the information of my Lord Nelson, a concise history of the Nature of that fatal Wound …

W. M. BEATTY [41]

Five days later Beatty wrote again confirming the loss of facial features, and giving more medical details:

Memorandum for the Rev. Mr. Scott

The remains of the late Lord Nelson, are perfectly Plastic, and in such a state of preservation from being completely saturated with the Strong Spirit in which they have been so long immersed; That Embalmment is rendered not only unnecessary, but the process if undertaken may be attended with the unpleasant circumstances of the Skin coming off the body, when the Wrappers and Bandages with which it is surrounded are removed; the features being lost, the Face cannot with propriety be exposed during the time which the body may lay in State …

W. BEATTY

H.M. Ship *Victory* 20th December[42]

The next post-mortem pieces of evidence to be considered are the two most famous paintings of the death of Nelson by Benjamin West and Arthur Devis. On 22nd November 1805 newspapers in London announced a competition for a picture 'The Death of Nelson', for which the prize was to be 500 guineas. Both men entered the competition.

Neither is medically or historically accurate, but Devis must bear the greater guilt since he painted Nelson 'from the death', assisted at Nelson's post-mortem and must have been very aware of all the medical details of his injury. Moreover Devis was actually on board *Victory* for almost three weeks and had the unique opportunity of exploring, discussing and recording the awful event with all the major surviving participants – Hardy , Beatty, Alexander Scott, amd Walter Burke. Midshipman Westphal, Sergeant Secker and Lieutenant Rotely of the Marines would also have been eager to give Devis their first-hand knowledge of what happened on board *Victory*, on and after October 21st 1805.

Yet Devis and West (and Surgeon Beatty to the greatest extent) so glamorised Nelson's death that they created a new reincarnation of a very old legend, that of the hero who sacrifices his life to save his people. Devis and West produced pictures which were almost depositions, with Nelson shown in a Christ-like pose that verged upon the blasphemous. Beatty changed his original medical observations when he came to write the *Authentic Narrative* so that important symptoms experienced by Nelson were suppressed by the one medical witness who ought to have recorded them accurately; Beatty altered the details when he came to publish his book in 1807. Up until now, every Nelson biographer, (even those prepared to write less than eulogistically about Nelson) have nevertheless accepted Beatty's account and found no medical inaccuracies in the paintings of Devis and West.

Devis' painting of the Death of Nelson is a more correct version. The non-medical inaccuracies have frequently been commented upon: the two major ones being that the height of the orlop deck is portrayed incorrectly, and that Captain Hardy was not present at the exact moment of Nelson'sdeath. Medically, Devis' clinical inaccuracies are more serious, as they prettified what was in reality a most awful death, and enabled Beatty by *suggestio falsi* and *surpressio veri* to portray a written account of the hero gently drifting toward his demise, which actually diminishes the extraordinary bravery exhibited by Nelson at the end.

Devis depicts no blood at or around the entry site at Nelson's left shoulder. Indeed there is no blood anywhere at all, except the faintest suggestion of a trickle at the right side of Nelson's mouth. There is no blood on the body at all and Nelson's uniform coat instead of having been taken away, rolled up and used as a pillow for wounded midshipman Westphal, (as really happened) is lying in the front of Devis' picture, reinforcing the grandeur of the dying man, and perhaps reproving, just a little, the alleged vanity that lead to the wearing of so conspicuous a garment.

The American painter, Benjamin West, was born in 1738 in Pennsylvania. Having trained in Philadelphia he arrived in London via Italy in 1763. He became a close friend of Sir Joshua Reynolds, the first President of the Royal Academy, and achieved great fame with his painting 'The Death of Wolfe' popularizing modern costume in history painting. It was widely sold as a print. West was a charter (founding) member of the Royal Academy in 1768 and was elected its second President when Reynolds died in 1792. History painter to King George III from 1772 to 1801, West probably met Nelson through William Beckford – they were both guests at Beckford's house party in Christmas 1800.

Nelson is said to have attended a Royal Academy Dinner prior to his death and to have been seated next to West. He told West the one painting he really admired was West's 'Death of Wolfe' and said he always stopped to look at it if it was displayed in a print shop. Nelson then asked why West had not painted any other similar works. West replied that there had been no similar deaths amongst the leaders of Britain's armed forces, but added that he feared Nelson might provide such a death. 'My Lord, I fear your intrepidity may yet furnish me with another such scene, and if it should, I shall certainly avail myself of it.' Nelson is reported to have filled a glass with champagne and toasted West, exclaiming 'Well then, I hope I die in the next battle.'[43] This proved to be prophetic and West painted his Death of Nelson, now in the Walker Gallery, Liverpool.

Arthur Devis specialised in portraits and historical subjects but in 1804 had been imprisoned for debt, in the King's Bench prison. When the competition was announced Devis persuaded the King's Bench Authorities to let him out with leave to visit *Victory*, at Portsmouth after Trafalgar, and try to win the prize.

Devis went to Portsmouth, got on board *Victory* (which was at anchor at Spithead waiting for the orders that were to take her round to the Nore) and so ingratiated himself with the crew that he was allowed to stay – and was presumably given a berth and fed on board as well. He seems to have been on board for about three weeks. He made drawings of the members of the crew who had been present at Nelson's death, and also the cockpit itself. As soon as *Victory* sailed Beatty did the post mortem and Devis is believed to have assisted him. Beatty commissioned Devis to do a posthumous portrait of Nelson, a 'good likeness' with hints and by allowing him to see the body.[44] Beatty used an engraving of the portrait as the frontispiece for his *Authentic Narrative*. It is medically important because it is the only portrait which shows Nelson wearing a hat into which has been sewn one of the eye shades Lady Hamilton made for Nelson upon the recommendation of Thomas Trotter. As previously mentioned, Devis also drew the fatal musket ball and its attached cloth and gold bullion after it was removed by Beatty at post mortem. Although there are three different likenesses of the ball in existence each with slightly different annotations, the reproduction in the Medical & Physical Journal is the most like Devis' original drawing. The engraving from the *Authentic Narrative* is a direct engraving of his drawing and probably the reproduction in Addenda to the Biographical Memoir a second (inferior) engraving by an unknown hand from Devis's original drawing.

Devis' 'Death of Nelson' is his masterpiece. Although inaccurate in several ways it nevertheless gives a very powerful idea of what the scene must have been like, including as it does the portraits of the individuals closest to Nelson as he died – Alexander Scott, Burke, Chevalier and Beatty.

For a naval battle, the numbers of casualties in the battle are appalling. British casualties were given as 1,690 killed and wounded. Those in the Combined Fleet were said to be 5,860, but probably this was an understatement. The Combined Fleet was made up of eighteen French and fifteen Spanish ships. Collingwood's list of 'Ships of France and Spain showing how they are disposed of' (and what a typically ambiguous English phrase that is, both official and bloodlessly hard) gives part of the picture – 'sent to Gibraltar, wrecked, wrecked, wrecked all crew perished, burnt, sunk, wrecked, returned to Cadiz in a sinking state, burnt during the action, wrecked.'[45]

One of the casualties was the Spanish Second-in-Command, Admiral Gravina. He was in command of twelve Spanish ships at Trafalgar. At one stage in the battle his flagship, *Principe de Astorias* was opposed to three British ships at the same time and very severely damaged. At about 3.30 pm Gravina's left arm was shattered by grapeshot. Nevertheless he continued to fight, but towards the end of the battle, and with his own ship in tow, he collected ten of the Combined Fleet ships, and headed back to Cadiz. There, surprisingly, the doctors did not amputate his arm. The wound failed to heal and he died of that most terrible illness of the pre-antibiotic age, gas gangrene. On his death bed Gravina is reputed to have been visited by an Englishman to whom he said 'I am dying, but I die happy. I am going, I hope and trust, to join Nelson, the greatest Hero that the world has perhaps produced.'[46] One cannot think of any other pair of opposing leaders in any battle who might have felt the same. One cannot for example imagine the dying Montgomery saying 'I am going, I hope and trust, to join Rommel,' or Wellington feeling the same way about Napoleon. The *Gibraltar Chronicle* wrote 'Spain loses in Gravina the most distinguished Officer in her Navy.'[47]

THE AFTERMATH

POSTHUMOUS CHRONOLOGY

21st October 1805: Nelson killed

22nd October: Beatty probes Nelson's wound, and cuts off most of his hair. Rotely cuts off rest of his hair. Body, dressed in shirt, put head first into a leaguer filled with brandy. Leaguer put on end, on middle deck, guarded by a sentry. Gale, foretold by Nelson, comes on, Redoutable sinks.

24th October: Disengagement of air from body. Barrel spiled.

24th – 28th Oct: Brandy drawn off, cask refilled with more brandy. Body noted to be absorbing brandy.

28th October: Victory arrives in Gibraltar. Further absorption of brandy by the body noted. Spirit of wine procured and substituted for the brandy.

29th October: Wounded from Victory sent to hospital.

29th Oct – 2nd Nov: Temporary damage repair to Victory.

2nd November: Victory leaves Gibraltar for Tetuan Bay. Supplement to Gibraltar Chronicle published.

3rd November: Victory back at Gibraltar, embarks all but five most seriously injured crew. Victory sails for home.

4th November: Victory passes through Straits of Gibraltar.

5th November: Victory joins squadron outside Cadiz now commanded by Collingwood.

6th November: News of Trafalgar arrives in England.

10th November: Lord Hawkesbury writes to King George III stating Nelson will be buried in St Paul's Cathedral.

30th November: Design of funeral car by J Powell of Islington, Undertaker, published.

3rd Nov – 4th Dec: Leaguer drained twice, refilled with 2/3 spirit of wine and 1/3 brandy.

4th December: Victory anchors at St Helens

6th December: The Times announces 'The remains of the late Lord Nelson have at length reached this country.'

10th December: Victory sails for the Nore. A W Devis comes on board.

11th December: Nelson's body removed from leaguer. Beatty does post mortem. Devis assists. Beatty writes professional report. Body wrapped in cotton vestments, rolled in bandages, and put in lead coffin, with camphor, myrrh and brandy.

11th – 15th Dec: Devis draws Nelson posthumous portrait. Devis draws the bullet.

12th December: Victory arrives at Dover.

15th December: Beatty writes to The Medical Journal. Beatty and Burke write to TheTimes. Beatty writes to Reverend Scott regarding removing contents of chest and abdomen.

16th December: Victory weighs anchor.

17th December: Victory reaches the Downs.

19th December: Victory sails for the Nore.

20th December: Beatty writes to Scott, 'The Features Being Lost'.

21st December: Body removed from lead coffin and dressed in clothes. Hardy and friends view body for last time. Body put in L'Orient coffin, then into a lead coffin and then into a wooden shell. Coffin disembarked into Commodore Gray's Yacht. Coffin disembarked at Greenwich.

30th December: Beatty and Walter Burke's account of Nelson's death published in The Times.

Early January 1806: Three-day Lying-in-State commences in Painted Hall.

8th January: Body transported from Greenwich to Whitehall Stairs in three coffins, lies in ground floor room at Admiralty.

9th January: State funeral at St Paul's Cathedral.

January 1806: Medical Journal with Beatty's account of the death of Nelson and his post-mortem, published together with hand-coloured engraving of the musket ball.

References:

1. *The Times* 7th November 1805 p.1
2. Quoted in Pope, D. *England Expects* 1998 p.36
3. *The Times* 7th November 1805 p.3
4. ibid p.1
5. Nicolas vol VII p.227
6. ibid
7. *The Navy* October 1944
8. Beatty p.61
9. ibid p.62
10. ibid
11. ibid p.63
12. ibid p.67
13. ibid p.84
14. ibid p.70-72
15. ibid p.72
16. ibid p.73
17. ibid p/73–74
18. Walker p.160
19. N.M.M. MMS 51/040/2
20. Beatty p.iii-iv
21. ibid p.83–85
22. ibid p.70–71
23. ibid p.64
24. ibid p.66
25. Professor M. A. Green: personal communication to the author
26. *Medical and Physical Journal* vol XV January 1806
27. ibid
28. *Medical and Physical Journal v*ol XV p. 213–6
29. ibid p.455–7
30. ibid p.92
31. ibid p.150–3
32. ibid p.83–90
33. *The Times* 30th December 1805
34. ibid.
35. Quoted in *The Nelson Dispatch* vol 7 part 12 October 2002 p.847–8

36. *Gibraltar Chronicle* Supplement 2nd November 1805
37. Nicolas vol VII p.224–7
38. ibid p.226–7
39. *The Times* 21st December 1805
40. *The Times* 25th December 1805
41. N.M.M. MS 51/040/2
42. ibid
43. Hibbert p.384
44. Walker p.160
45. Nicolas vol VII p.220
46. Quoted in *The Nelson Dispatch* vol 5 part 12 October 1996 p.447
47. ibid

CHAPTER XII

Nelson's Genius

Persons of genius do not always possess that indefinable attribute 'common sense.' They can be – and frequently are – totally single-minded, anti-social, uncaring of the feelings of others, and possessed of 'one-track minds.' Nelson was not like this. He had abundant common sense, was extremely caring of others, not in the least antisocial; and he was also, if the word has any meaning, a genius.

In 1994 Buzan and Keene attempted to define genius in terms of ten qualities or categories which they described as a 'final measuring instrument' for assessing the top one hundred geniuses of all time. They included Nelson, using this group of qualities, in that top one hundred.[1] Rankings of this kind prove nothing; but Nelson featured, and consideration of the methods used can widen our knowledge of Nelson, not only as a genius of naval warfare but also of 'man management' and of the written word: two areas where he has not hitherto perhaps been considered to have excelled. The attributes of genius as delineated by Buzan and Keene were:

Superior intelligence (High I.Q.)
Dominance in the Field
Active longevity
Strength and Energy
Polymathy and versatility
Service Originality
Vision
Achievement of Prime Goal
On-going influence
Prolificness: bringing about results.

1. Intelligence

How can we tell that Nelson was possessed of superior intelligence? Early indications were present. As a young boy at Sir William Paston's School, Nelson stole pears from a tree belonging to the headmaster. 'I only took them because every other boy was afraid.'[2] That was one part of the episode, exhibiting perhaps no more than childish derring do; but then the boy thief refused to eat any of the spoil and shared it out amongst the other fearful scholars. That is an unusual act for a young boy, a calculated assay on the moral high ground. 'I never saw fear, what is it?'[3] is a remark a young Nelson is said to have made to his grandmother when he had become lost in the Norfolk countryside, and she managed to find him. It is the kind of comment intelligent children do make: early thoughts on abstract concepts are not common in the young.

Nelson appears never to have forgotten what he heard or read, and he remembered people from years past, and their names. He could recall, in detail, places he had visited many years after he had been to them.

Despite his brief formal education Nelson was also a master of English. His vocabulary was extensive. He quoted widely and constantly. His letters, especially those to his wife, have quotation after quotation (see page 166). He was a brilliant letter writer. His comment some four weeks after the Nile head injury 'My head is so wrong that I cannot write what I wish in a manner to please myself,'[4] is revealing. The post-Nile letters themselves show no loss of intellect. What seems to have been altered temporarily was Nelson's appreciation of his own efforts; or that what usually came easily to him was temporarily more of a struggle.

Nicolas's collection, Naish's superb book on Nelson's letters to his wife, *Nelson's Letters to Lady Hamilton* (thank goodness, she failed to obey his instructions to destroy them) and Colin White's collection of hitherto undiscovered letters reveal wide-ranging emotion and frame of reference. In his letters Nelson could be stern, unkind and (especially to his wife and the stepson who had saved his life) ruthless. He could make wrong decisions (the execution of Caracciolo), and be overwhelmed by suspicion and criticism. The letters reveal all these passions, but they also reveal compassion, generosity, humour, friendship, kindness, eroticism and love; they contain global assessments, strategic analysis, and consistent forward planning for the benefit of the fleets.

2. Dominance in the Field

This was best expressed by the novelist Joseph Conrad:

> In a few short years he [Nelson] revolutionised not only the strategy of tactics of sea warfare but the very conception of Victory itself. And this is genius. In that fact alone, through the fidelity of his fortune and the power of his inspiration, he stands unique amongst the leaders of fleets and sailors.[5]

There was a uniqueness about Nelson that his contemporaries recognised. 'There is but one Nelson.' wrote Earl St. Vincent.[6] Collingwood, his life-long friend, wrote 'Lord Nelson is an incomparable man ... he has the faculty of discovering advantages as they arise, and the good judgment to turn them to his use. An enemy that commits a false step is in his view ruined, and [he] comes at him with an impetuosity that allows no time to recover.'[7]

3. Active longevity

With the exception of the five years unemployed 'on the Beach' Nelson's whole life from the age of 12 to 47 was one of almost constant activity. Considering that many of Nelson's close relatives lived to a great age, that Surgeon Beatty, having performed Nelson's post mortem, stated his organs were those of a youth, not a man of 47, and that Nelson himself said 'I am not getting very fat. My make will not allow it,'[8] and that he was abstemious and ate a largely salt free diet, it is highly likely that had Nelson survived Trafalgar he could easily have lived another forty years. As did Wellington, Nelson would then have influenced three subsequent British Sovereigns: George IV, William IV and the young Queen Victoria. To say he died with his life's work achieved is nonsense.

4. Strength and energy

Linking these with activity, by 2nd August 1798 Nelson had already suffered from all the illnesses and the four serious wounds recorded in this book. He had a severe painful recurrent abdominal hernia and was very prone to coughs, colds, fevers of uncertain cause, and recurrent malaria. Yet his energy was unbounded and seemed the greater when difficulties were the greatest, or there was the most work to be done. The days of unremitting activity around the battle of Copenhagen or the months of constant toil on behalf of the British Fleet in the Mediterranean from 1803 to 1805 are two examples. Nelson was capable of unremitting 'grind' to the point of exhaustion, an attribute spotted by Lady Spencer who wrote about it in a letter to her husband, Lord Spencer (see p. 113).

5. Polymathy and versatility

At Copenhagen immediately after the battle, Nelson became a successful peace negotiator. His comment 'though I have only one eye, I see all this will burn very well,'[9] (referring to the building in which negotiations were taking place) to urge the negotiations along when they showed signs of stalling, is memorable. Immediately after the Battle of the Nile, despite a very serious head wound, Nelson's behaviour was exemplary. He fully realised the political and international effect of his victory, especially with regard to British rule in India, sending letters and dispatches to all relevant countries and most importantly and especially sending a Lieutenant Duval with dispatches to the Governor of Bombay. In a covering letter he gave to Duval for 'his Britannic Majesty's Consuls,' Nelson wrote:

> Having to forward with the utmost haste to India Lt. Duval of the Navy who will deliver you this, he being charged with dispatches of the greatest consequence to our possessions in that country – forward him as fast as possible.[10]

Yet one day earlier, he had written to Sir William Hamilton 'my head is so indifferent I can scarcely scrawl this letter.'[11] At various times in his life Nelson was an in-depth social observer, farmer, forestry reporter, negotiator, religious commentator, orator in the House of Lords and public speaker. All these occupations were in addition to his main roles of sailor, senior officer and manager.

In a letter to his old friend Dr. Moseley from *Victory* at sea in March 1804, Nelson wrote 'You will agree with me that it is easier for an Officer to keep men healthy, than for a Physician to cure them.'[12] He went on to tell Moseley about getting provisions for his crews 'plenty of fresh water,' and 'good mutton for the sick.'

An example of how he did it was shown in a letter written three days before to Captain Moubray, of *Active*. Nelson sent *Active* to the Bay of Rosas or Barcelona, where they were 'to remain for the space of seven days … to cause your people to be supplied with fresh beef every day with as many onions … to remove any taint of the scurvy …' Nelson went on to order Moubray to purchase 50 sheep plus fodder for them, '30,000 good oranges for the Fleet, with onions or any other vegetables … as many live bullocks as you can conveniently stow, with fodder … and return and join the Fleet … with the utmost expedition.'[13]

It had not always been so. Nelson contracted scurvy in 1782 (see p. 31) but after that one episode, he and his crews seem never to have suffered from scurvy again, since he clearly knew that fresh food prevented it. Thanks to Nelson's later efforts to feed and water the fleets under his command, Dr. Gillespie ('Physician to the Fleet under your Lordship's command') was able to write to Nelson on 14th August 1805: '… that over the two years from 13th August 1803 in total crews numbering from 5,000 to 8,000, there had only been 110 deaths on board, only 141 sent to the hospitals, and only an average of just over 18 men per ship on the sick list' (see pages 245-6).

6. Service originality

This is exemplified in his behaviour at the Battle of Cape St. Vincent and the battle plan of Trafalgar. Combined in Nelson were all the best traits of the British Admirals. He cared for the men under his command. He understood that these men had to be fed properly, kept healthy and maintained in a state of high morale. He achieved this by unremitting hard work and by his extraordinary ability to encourage, cajole and inspire subordinates. He was a brilliant delegator, but always, if necessary capable of doing the work he delegated himself. Whilst never a lax disciplinarian, nothing of relevance escaped his notice and he always rewarded deserving subordinates with deserved praise.

Certain aspects of the battle plan for Trafalgar had been used by Admiral Rodney at the Battle of the Saints twenty-three years prior to Nelson's Memorandum, 'The Nelson Touch'. Nevertheless the whole tenor of the 'Memorandum', as it was simply called, was 'new, was singular and was simple.'[14] It clearly stated that Nelson was aiming to *destroy* the whole of the Combined Fleet's centre and rear ships and to do so before the enemy van could come to their aid. 'The whole impression of the British Fleet must be to overpower from two or three ships ahead of their Commander-in-Chief, supposed to be in the Centre, to the Rear of their Fleet.'[15] Never before had a British Fleet sailed into battle with a determination to destroy or capture twenty ships of the Enemy. Nelson's Trafalgar battle plan ensured that they almost did. That was service originality.

7. Vision

Nelson's overriding vision was peace. It was the last word in his last letter to Lady Hamilton written just before he was killed. He had left the letter open in his cabin hoping to finish it after the battle. 'May God Almighty give us success over these fellows and enable us to get a peace.'[16]

Nelson has been called 'a natural born predator,'[17] and there is no doubt at all that he was one of the most successful war leaders ever. But the wars he successfully fought on behalf of his country were precipitated for most of his life by one man – Napoleon. The British had no territorial designs in continental Europe or, after 1782, in the new nation of America. Napoleon always had territorial designs in continental Europe and his ambitions extended to the invasion and conquest of England. From the time he came to power until his final defeat in 1815, the Royal Navy was the ultimate defence, guarding Britain from conquest. Nelson's methods with regard to fleet management ensured success in his lifetime and adherence to these methods guaranteed continued success after his death.

Nelson's vision was that the Royal Navy should be the bulwark of the British nation. This vision was achieved and subsequently its vital importance is said to have been acknowledged by Napoleon himself when he remarked that the Royal Navy had consistently thwarted his ambitions.[18]

8. Achievement of prime goal

In terms of Enemy ships destroyed, Nelson achieved his prime goal at the Nile and at Trafalgar. Nelson had planned meticulously for the Battle of the Nile. He had *five* different possible plans of attack, covering every contingency and had discussed each one with at least two senior captains of the ships under his command. Other captains were then informed by means of his Public Order Book – a notebook of day-by-day orders for the organisation of the ships in his fleet. He had also asked his captains for their advice, but always with the understanding that the final decisions and responsibility were his. The result was that every captain knew his leader's mind and Nelson's fleet was able to attack immediately, the instant they sighted the French Fleet at anchor in Aboukir Bay, even though night was rapidly approaching, and achieve what he had written in the Public Order Book six weeks before: 'The Destruction of the Enemy's Armament is the sole object.'[19]

By August 1798 Nelson had failed to destroy the French ships before they landed their army in Egypt, but, by winning the Battle of the Nile, he ensured that the French army was marooned in Egypt and so could not actively pursue the conquest of the Middle East. No British ships were captured or sunk; out of the French ships, six were captured, seven were destroyed and only four escaped, of which two were captured or sunk within the next 18 months.

In 1805 Nelson's prime goal was to destroy forever Napoleon's plans to invade England. The loss of 19 ships from the Combined Fleet at Trafalgar meant that Napoleon would never have a fleet powerful enough to take control of the English Channel for the short time he required to get his army across from Boulogne to England. At Trafalgar, Nelson's Fleet of 27 ships was opposed by 33 ships of France and Spain. In the actual battle, no British ships were captured or destroyed, and even those severely damaged, like *Victory* and *Royal Sovereign*, were able, by superb seamanship, to weather the horrendous storm that followed the battle and to limp away for repairs in Gibraltar.

9. Ongoing influence

His influence has persisted from the day of his death into the 21st century. Morale-boosting posters of the Abbott portrait and Nelson's Last Prayer were on hoardings in the London Underground in World War II. There are innumerable biographies of Nelson, and major exhibitions in naval museums at Greenwich and at Portsmouth devoted solely to him. All are witness to what Tom Pocock so accurately described as 'the flash and sparkle of the many sides of his character'.[20] Americans find him as interesting as Britons do, and the American Admiral Mahan's magnificent biography manages to explore Nelson's mind superbly. Field Marshal Bernard Law Montgomery (like Nelson in some ways) wrote in his book *A History of Warfare*: 'He seemed to have a magnetic influence over all who served with him,' and 'He knew how to win the hearts of men.' Montgomery went on to say that 'My problem in command was to win the hearts of the soldiers,'[21] and it is clear from his book that he used Nelson as a role model when in command in World War II. 'The period to Nelson's fame can only be the end of time.'[22]

10. Prolificness

Nelson achieved results because of his infinite capacity for hard work, taking pains and learning by his mistakes. He thus ensured that once he became a commander of ships, every ship under his command, was 'worked up' to an extraordinary level of efficiency, good health and high morale. Because he enjoyed the company of his captains and the officers of his own ship, he frequently entertained such men, and made them privy to his thoughts on all aspects of the welfare of the ships' crews.

Nelson had a ready wit and a nice turn of phrase. Throughout his life he 'played' with words in his letters and in his speech. At a levee at St. James's Palace in September 1797, Nelson was presented to King George III. Accompanying Nelson was Captain Edward Berry, who had been Nelson's First Lieutenant on board *Captain* at the Battle of Cape St. Vincent. Nelson was home on sick leave after the disaster at Tenerife. 'You have lost your right arm,' exclaimed King George. 'But not my right hand, as I have the honour to present Captain Berry!'[23] was Nelson's immediate, graceful riposte. Another example of Nelson's playfulness:

> Lord Nelson, shortly after the memorable Battle of Copenhagen, had occasion to write to his wine merchant, to whom he apologised for not answering his letter as he had lately been much engaged.[24]

Suffering with peripheral neuropathy, and convalescing at Bath after the Nicaraguan Expedition the 22-year-old wrote several letters to his erstwhile mentor, William Locker. One letter of February 1781 concerned his portrait painted by John Rigaud and commissioned by Locker himself. Knowing that Locker had commissioned portraits of other naval officers, Nelson wrote 'when you get the pictures, I must be in the middle, for God knows, without good supporters, I shall fall to the ground!'[25] a pretty heraldic pun on 'supporters'.

Very occasionally Nelson, the most lucid of writers, was obscure and never more so than with the famous phrase 'the Nelson Touch'; but there was a knowing ambiguity behind it. Several explanations have been suggested, two of the latest being that either it is an echo from his favourite Shakespearean play *Henry V* – 'A little touch of Harry in the night' – or that the Nelson Touch was a sexual joke between Nelson and Lady Hamilton. It is in two letters to Emma that Nelson uses the phrase. However, the phrase has many points of reference and one is even connected with Nelson's health.

On 17th September Nelson wrote to the Hon. George Rose while on board *Victory* off Portsmouth, just before she set sail, 'Nothing shall be wanting on my part ... I will try to have a Motto, at least it shall be my watchword 'Touch and Take.' I will do my best.'[26] Nelson's meaning here is to 'touch' or come into contact with the French Fleet and 'take' or capture them. His motto still seems to have been in his mind when *Victory* arrived off Lisbon, but he now used the enigmatic phrase 'the Nelson Touch'. On 25th September he wrote to Lady Hamilton 'I am anxious to join the fleet, for it would add to my grief if any other man was to give them the Nelson Touch, which we say is warranted never to fail.'[27] Then to Lady Hamilton on 1st October:

> I joined the fleet late on the evening of the 28th September ... I believe my arrival was most welcome; not only to the commander of the fleet, but also to every individual in it; and, when I came to explain to them the Nelson touch, it was like an electric shock. Some shed tears, all approved – 'It was new, it was singular, it was simple!' and, from Admirals downwards it was repeated – 'It must succeed, if ever they will allow us to get at them! You are, my Lord, surrounded by friends whom you inspire with confidence.'... the majority are certainly much pleased with my commanding them.[28]

His old friend Captain Alexander Ball, wrote 'He ... sent to me his plan of Attack which he said was called the Nelson Touch and he hoped it would be touch and take.'[29] The word 'touch' has acquired a multitude of associations in Nelson's phrase: to influence; to touch off – to fire a cannon; a fencing hit; the medical term 'to touch for the King's (or Queen's) Evil', the 'treatment' of touching with an object blessed by the sovereign, areas of skin tuberculosis, or Scrofula[30]; and touch and go – a naval expression meaning that a ship's keel touched the seabed without causing the ship to lose speed. And there is one more association.

Judging from what he wrote to Lady Hamilton in the last 'Nelson Touch' letter, Nelson achieved the element of surprise he wanted. But why did he use the words 'it was like an electric shock'? This was a reference he knew Lady Hamilton would understand. She may not have told him about her time working with James Graham, who used static electricity in his 'temple.' But the static electricity experiments of the Abbe Nollet would have been well known to everyone in society (see p. 67) and Nelson had had static electricity treatment on his right eye, in Palermo. Once Nelson explains his battle plan 'new ... singular ... simple ...it must succeed.' he has 'touched' all his Admirals and Captains (in the two dinners he gave on *Victory* on 29th and 30th September) and metaphorically completed the static electricity circle. Of course they would not jump into the air, but they would all act together; they were 'joined together' by what Nelson had told them at the dinners, and his explanation of what he wanted from them, in the forthcoming battle.

In view of the current debasement of the word 'charismatic', consideration of its original usage and the original research on the subject of charismatics can helping to identify just why Nelson was different from his contemporaries. When Carola Oman, one of the greatest of Nelson's biographers, described his return to England after the loss of his arm and his eye, she wrote:

> The fixed dim right eye, the empty right sleeve, were painful novelties to his family, but that his old infective high spirits were untouched was at once equally obvious; and these spirits were so distracting a characteristic that witnesses called upon for a description of a great man often confirmed on a note of surprise that he was not above middle height, very slight, far from handsome, unaffectedly simple in address, and of no great dignity, 'indeed, in appearance nothing remarkable either way.' ... The outstanding impression of those who encountered Nelson ... was of a man so active in person, so animated in countenance and so apposite and vehement in conversation that little else was recollected.[31]

The term 'charismatic' was probably coined by Max Weber, German Professor of Law and social scientist, who wrote upon the subject in the 1920s. The word comes from the Greek 'karis' meaning favour or grace. Originally considered a gift from pagan gods the word was adopted by the early Christian Church as a gift from God. Weber himself applied the term to people who were outstanding leaders and had a 'something', an extraordinariness which set them apart from their contemporaries. He gave such people five characteristics. They were:

1. Extraordinarily gifted persons
2. In a social crisis or desperate situation
3. With a set of ideas providing a radical solution to a crisis
4. A set of followers were attracted to the leader possessed of exceptional powers – believing that he or she was linked to transcendent powers
5. The gifted leader was validated in their exceptional powers by repeated success.

Kozubska conducted a further study of the phenomenon. She wrote 'Charisma is a word used to describe the qualities, behaviour and attitudes of others, not ourselves.' She felt it was characterized by:

> The warm glow we get from listening to truly charismatic individuals. It is about excitement ... belief ... [It] describes a social relationship in which followers give them (the charismatic, understood) loyalty and fellowship in exchange for the benefits the followers want ... they may be looking for ... a vision, a course, deliverance, clear leadership, excitement or inspiration.'

Kozubska added to Weber's five components:

6. Extremely high levels of self-confidence
7. Strong convictions about the moral righteousness of their beliefs
8. A strong need to have influence over others.[32]

These eight components apply to Nelson. Kozubska looked at great military leaders when discussing managerial versus leadership roles and came to the conclusion that such leaders (and she mentioned Alexander, Napoleon, Wellington and Montgomery, as well as Nelson) needed to be good as both managers *and* leaders – unlike, say, business entrepreneurs who tend to be good at *either* management *or* leadership. Kozubska wrote 'The real secret is energy which stems from being in love with yourself and what you do ... and if you believe in an Ultimate Being then love of that Being ... It is very difficult to make things happen when we are not committed to what we are doing. The formula is simple: Goals Persistence Energy.' She might have been describing Nelson alone.[33] John Scott, Nelson's public secretary, wrote to Lady Hamilton:

> I have heard much of Lord Nelson's abilities as an officer and statesman, but the account of the latter is infinitely short. In my travels through the service I have met with no character in any degree equal to his Lordship; his penetration is quick, judgment clear, wisdom great, and his decisions correct and decided: nor does he in company appear to bear any weight on his mind, so cheerful and pleasant,

that it is a happiness to be about his hand; in fact, he is a great and wonderful character, and very glad and happy shall I be if, in the discharge of my duty, private and public, I have the good fortune to meet his Lordship's approbation.[34]

The letter was dated 8th July 1803. A former purser of *Royal Sovereign*, Scott had only just embarked upon his employment with Nelson (which was to end so tragically when he was one of the first fatalities on board *Victory* at Trafalgar), when he wrote the letter. Similarly, Countess Spencer, wife of the then First Lord of the Admiralty, wrote of 'a sort of surprise that riveted my whole attention.[35]

Years before another young man, the third son of King George III, had made similar comments. The narrator – then Prince William Henry, later King William IV – gave the following account shortly after Nelson's death, to Clarke and M'Arthur:

I was then a midshipman on board the *Barfleur*, [Lord Hood's flagship] lying in the Narrow off Staten Island, and had the watch on deck, when Captain Nelson, of the *Albemarle*, came in his barge alongside, who appeared to be the merest boy of a Captain I ever beheld … Lord Hood introduced me to him. There was something irresistibly pleasing in his address and conversation; and an enthusiasm, when speaking on professional subjects, that showed he was no common being.'[36]

When one reads about the effect of his penultimate signal, just before Trafalgar, upon the whole British Fleet, for a fleeting moment one experiences the charismatic that was Nelson. 'They started cheering, more for love of their Admiral.'[37]

Kozubska divided charismatics into two kinds. Type A charismatics – so called 'personalised' charismatics, – are dangerous people. Charismatics like Hitler, Rasputin, arguably Napoleon. This type always promotes his own personal dream and is only interested in his followers in so far as they assist him to achieve his own very personal goals. It was said of the late Robert Maxwell: 'He just made a difference, even if you did not like the difference he made. There was never an occasion that he didn't make a difference.'[38]

Type B charismatics, so-called socialised charismatics, are anxious to develop their followers as individuals. They share their goals and visions with their followers, and they appreciate and rely on intellectual stimulation from their followers as they develop and formulate their goals and ideas. Nelson is an archetypal charismatic type B. Type B charismatics, when they are military or political leaders, also always make a difference. Queen Elizabeth I – so far as we can judge from the record an archetypal

Type B charismatic – made a difference to her people throughout her reign. Churchill made a difference in 1940 and he, too, must be adjudged a Type B.

Buzan and Keene outlined vision as 'the degree to which the goal of succeeding in life's ambition is absolute, imaginatively seen, precisely formulated, clearly stated and comprehensively understood.'[39] At the time of his death Nelson had brought his vision to total and practical realisation.

'He is to be buried in St. Paul's Cathedral under the Cupola, which will be his monument and may at the same moment, remind thousands of spectators of his merits and his loss,' the wife of Edward Codrington, Captain of the *Orion* in the battle, wrote to her husband.[40] At Nelson's funeral the body, in its three inner coffins, was lowered through the floor of the Crossing into the crypt: the hidden epicentre of the Cathedral, and by extension, the British Empire. Three of his friends of many years – Alexander Davison, William Hazelwood and William Marsh – acting for that day as Treasurer, Comptroller and Steward of his Household, at the end of the service broke their white staves of office and handed them to Garter King of Arms to be put upon the coffin as it was lowered by machinery into the black and white sarcophagus. This was designed by a Florentine sculptor, Benedetto da Rovezzano, for Cardinal Wolsey. After Wolsey's fall from grace and power the man who was almost certainly Nelson's ancestor through nine generations, King Henry VIII, had confiscated it but it had never been used. The Italian connection, the Royal Tudor link, and the use of an outer coffin 300 years old would have amused Nelson as much as the *L'Orient* coffin did.

Garter King of Arms' main role was to proclaim over the coffin, at the end of a burial service which lasted four hours, the styles and titles of the interred. In full these were:

> The Most Noble Lord Horatio Nelson, Viscount and Baron Nelson of the Nile, and of Burnham Thorpe, in the County of Norfolk; Baron Nelson of the Nile, and of Hilborough, in the same County; Knight of the Most Honourable Order of the Bath; Vice-Admiral of the White Squadron of the Fleet, and Commander-in-Chief of His Majesty's Ships and Vessels in the Mediterranean; also Duke of Bronte in Sicily; Knight Grand Cross of the Sicilian Order of St. Ferdinand and of Merit; Member of the Ottoman Order of the Crescent; Knight Grand Commander of the Order of St. Joachim.[41]

The motherless boy from an obscure Norfolk village had come, through major wounds and severe illnesses, via Mosquito Coast, Quebec, the West Indies, the East Indies, Cape St. Vincent, Bastia, Calvi, Tenerife, Aboukir Bay and Cape Trafalgar, a long way.

Notes

1. Buzan and Keene p.167
2. Clarke and M'Arthur vol I p.8
3. Eyre-Matcham M. *The Nelsons of Burnham Thorpe* 1991 p.57
4. Nicolas vol III p.108
5. Quoted in Bradford, E. *Nelson The Essential Hero* 1979 p.286
6. Mahan p.742
7. Quoted in Duffy, M. *Touch & Take* 2005 p.7
8. Nicolas vol I p.193
9. Clarke and M'Arthur vol II p.276
10. Nicolas vol III p.98
11. ibid p.94
12. ibid vol V p.438
13. ibid p.437
14. *Nelson's Letter to Lady Hamilton* vol 2 p.101
15. Nicolas vol VII p.90
16. ibid p.132
17. Coleman, T. *Nelson: the Man and the Legend* 2001 p.1
18. Quoted in Lincoln, M. (ed) *Nelson and Napoleon* 2005 p.xvi
19. White C. *Nelson: The New Letters* p.213
20. Pocock T. *Nelson and his World* p.126
21. Montgomery, B. L. *A Concise History of Warfare* 1968 p.215
22. Richard Brinsley Sheridan – Epitaph on the base of the Nelson statue in the Mansion House
23. Nicolas vol II p.448
24. *Naval Chronicle* 1805 vol XIV p.17
25. Nicolas vol I p.38
26. ibid vol VII p.42
27. Pettigrew vol II p.501
28. *Nelson's Letters to Lady Hamilton* vol II p.101–2
29. Ball, A. Quoted in Knight *The Pursuit of Victory* p.501, 505
30. *Shorter Oxford English Dictionary* vol II p.610
31. Oman p.252–3
32. Kozubska p.31
33. ibid p.135
34. Quoted in Mahan p.605
35. Edgcumbe, R. (ed) *Diary of Lady F. Shelley* p77–8 Quoted in Oman p.272
36. Clarke and M'Arthur vol I p.53
37. Quoted in Hibbert p.367
38. Kozubska p.28
39. Buzan and Keene p.13
40. Quoted in Oman p.645 Codrington vol I p.186
41. Nicolas vol VII p.417

A relic of Nelson's life and death

The top of the main mast of the French ship *L'Orient*, totally destroyed at the Battle of the Nile. When the flagship was seen to be on fire most ships manoeuvred away from the doomed vessel, knowing that it must explode when the fire reached its magazine. But one ship, *Swiftsure,* moved closer to *L'Orient*; her captain, Benjamin Hallowel, reasoning that the debris would then fly over his ship. This proved correct. Hallowel, an old friend of Nelson who had served with him in Corsica, pulled *L'Orient* main mast out of Aboukir Bay. He gave the topmost piece to Nelson, who kept it at Merton. The copper lightning conductor was 'High Tech' as such conductors had only been introduced three years previously. With another part of the main mast Hallowel had made a coffin, which he also sent to Nelson with the annotation, "My Lord, Herewith I send you a coffin made of part of *L'Orient*'s main mast, that when you are tired of this life you may be buried in one of your own Trophies." (Nicholas vol. III, p.89). Eventually stored in Peddieson's, a London upholsterer, Nelson is said to have visited it during his last leave before Trafalgar, and to have commented, "I think it highly probable that I will want it on my return" (Pettigrew vol I, p.132). He is buried in it (the second of the four coffins) in St. Paul's Cathedral. (Picture courtesy of National Maritime Museum)

Appendices

Appendix I

GILLESPIE, NELSON AND PREVENTATIVE MEDICINE

Leonard Gillespie M.D., was born in the same year as Nelson. He was appointed to *Victory*, as Physician to the Fleet, at the beginning of January 1805 and was with *Victory* on blockade and in the chase to Egypt and back. He missed the Battle of Trafalgar because he was on sick leave in Gibraltar suffering from gout. His service in the Royal Navy was as follows:

1781	First His Majesty's Ship (age 23)
15.7.81	Joined *St. Vincent*, sloop
16.8.87	Joined *Racehorse*, sloop. Carried until 5.1.91
6.3.93	Joined *Majestic*. Carried until 29.1.96
18.8.1804	Promoted to Fleet Physician. Carried *Swiftsure* also
2.1.1805	Joined *Victory* as Physician to the Fleet. Was also Inspector of Naval Hospitals
	in Malta, Sicily, Gibraltar
1819	Retired after 38 years service.
13.1.1842	Died aged 84 in Paris and buried there.

Gillespie wrote long discursive letters to his sister from 7th January to 16th March 1805, which provide a great deal of fascinating detail about life on board Nelson's flagship. He also wrote a careful letter to Nelson himself, the date of which almost coincides with Nelson's last return to England since it was written when *Victory* was nearing England after returning from the pursuit of the French Fleet to the West Indies.

These letters are reproduced because of the immense amount of first-hand information they contain. The first are to his sister in the winter and spring of 1805:

On board His Majesty's Ship *Victory*,
At sea off the Coast of Sardinia,
7th Jan., 1805.

Dear Sister,

I did myself the pleasure of writing to you in great haste on the 29th ult., being at that time on board His Majesty's ship The *Swiftsure*, off the coast of Catalonia, on my way to join this ship, which I effected on the 2nd inst., and I am at present fully established in my office as physician to this fleet, which is, thank God, in the best possible order as to health, discipline, spirits and disposition towards our gallant and revered commander, Lord Nelson. As a proof of the state of health enjoyed by the seamen, I may instance the company of this ship, which, consisting of 840 men, contains only one man confined to his bed from sickness, and the other ships (twelve of the line), of from eighty-four to seventy-four guns, are in a similar situation as to health, although the most of them have been stationed off Toulon for upwards of twenty months, during which time very few of the men or officers (in which number is Lord Nelson) have had a foot on shore.

You will perceive from this account, my dear sister, that the duties of my office are not likely at present to prove very laborious and my duty as Inspector of the Naval Hospitals will occasion me to visit, as may be found necessary, Malta, Sicily, Gibraltar and perhaps Naples, so that from all appearances and my experience hitherto, I have no reason to be displeased with the comforts, duties, or emoluments of the office I at present fill, my salary being £465 per annum, and being situated so as to live in a princely style, free from any expense. This exemption from expense arises from my having the honour of forming one of the suite and family of Lord Nelson, whose noble frankness of manners, freedom from vain formality and pomp (so necessary to the decoration of empty little great men), can only be equalled by the unexampled glory of his naval career, and the watchful and persevering diligence with which he commands this fleet.

On my coming on board I found that the recommendation which my former services in the Navy had procured me from several friends had conciliated towards me the good opinion of his lordship and his officers, and I immediately became one of the family. It may amuse you my dear sister, to read the brief journal of a day such as we here pass it at sea in this fine climate and in these smooth seas, on board one of the largest ships in the Navy, as she mounts 110 guns, one of which carrying a twenty-four pound shot, occupies a very distinguished station in my apartment.

12th Jan. – Off the Straits of Bonifacio ... To resume, my dear sister, the journal of a day. At six o'clock my servant brings a light and informs me of the hour, wind, weather and course of the ship, when I immediately dress and generally repair to the deck, the dawn of day at this season and latitude being apparent at about half or three-quarters of an hour after six. Breakfast is announced in the admiral's cabin, where Lord Nelson, Rear Admiral Murray, the captain of the fleet, Captain Hardy, commander of the Victory, the chaplain, secretary, one or two officers of the ship, and your humble servant, assemble and breakfast on tea, hot rolls, toast, cold tongue etc. which when finished we repair upon deck to enjoy the majestic sight of the rising sun (scarcely ever obscured by clouds in this fine climate), surmounting the smooth and placid waves of the Mediterranean which supports the lofty and tremendous bulwarks of Britain, following in regular train their Admiral in the Victory. Between the hours of seven and two there is plenty of time for business, study, writing and exercise, which different occupations, together with that of occasionally visiting the hospital of the ship when required by the surgeon, I endeavour to vary in such a manner as to afford me sufficient employment. At two o'clock a band of music plays till within a quarter to three, when the drum beats the tune called 'The Roast Beef of Old England' to announce the admiral's dinner, which is served up exactly at three o'clock, and which generally consists of three courses and a dessert of the choicest fruit, together with three or four of the best wines, champagne and claret not excepted; and what exceeds the relish of the best viands and most exquisite wines, if a person does not feel himself perfectly at his ease it must be his own fault, such is the urbanity and hospitality which reign here, notwithstanding the numerous titles, the four orders of knighthood worn by Lord Nelson and the well-earned laurels which he has acquired. Coffee and liqueurs close the dinner about half-past four or five o'clock, after which the company generally walks the deck, where the band of music plays for nearly an hour. At six o'clock tea is announced, when the company again assembles in the admiral's cabin, where tea is served up before seven o'clock, and as we are inclined, the party continue to converse with his lordship, who at this time generally unbends himself, though he is at all times as free from stiffness and pomp as a regard to proper dignity will admit, and is very communicative. At eight o'clock a rummer of punch with cake or biscuit is served up, soon after which we wish the admiral (who is generally in bed before nine o'clock) good-night. For my own part, not having been accustomed to go to bed quite so early, I generally read an hour, or spend one with the officers of the ship, many of whom are old acquaintances or to whom I have been known by character. Such, my dear sister, is the journal of a day at sea in fine or at least moderate weather, in which this floating castle goes through the water with the greatest imaginable steadiness, and I have not yet been long enough on board to experience bad weather.

18th Jan. – Madeline Islands, off Sardinia. We have been at anchor in this harbour, excellent of the kind, for five days, where we are supplied with wood, water, wine, provisions and other necessaries, and where I have commenced the duties of my office, without any difficulties to encounter, the business being very familiar to me. It consists in receiving returns of the state of the sick on board from their respective surgeons, visiting the ships as occasion may require, recommending to the surgeons the modes of treatment which to me seem most judicious, causing the surgeons and the sick under their care to be supplied with the medicines, refreshments and necessaries which they may require, all of which offices are very agreeable to me …

22nd Jan. – At sea, off the south-east end of Sardinia. The sudden arrival of a frigate, which had been stationed off Toulon to watch the motions of the enemy's squadron, on the evening of the 19th, *immediately changed* the whole system of our operations. This frigate informed us that the enemy's squadron, consisting of eleven sail of the line, had put to sea on the night of the 17th, and had chased the frigate apparently steering towards Cagliari, the capital of Sardinia. Although in the midst of the operations of wooding, watering, and victualling the fleet, every ship was under weigh in two hours' time, and put to sea through a narrow, rocky channel never yet well explored by any navigator. Since the night of the 19th we have been contending with adverse winds in heavy gales towards the east side of Sardinia, in hourly expectation of descrying the enemy, and having everything prepared to attack him with the well-known promptitude and decision of our gallant admiral, the more of whose conduct in dangers and critical situations I am witness to, the more I am forced to admire and revere him. For my own part I behold with great coolness the enthusiasm of all around me in anticipating the laurels to be gained in the expected battle …

12th March – Off Toulon … On the 15th (February) we were off the Morea in Greece, where we were joined by a frigate with the intelligence that the French squadron, apparently bound up the Mediterranean, had been disabled in a gale of wind and put back to Toulon, without effecting any purpose but that of disabling their own ships – a gale which we only regarded as a common occurrence and one which did not prevent us from sitting down to dinner as usual – and of rendering their unfortunate half-drowned freshwater sailors and soldiers sick to death of the sea. On the 12th of February we were off the capital of Malta, where we only remained a few hours, continuing our course down the Mediterranean, coasting along the island of Sicily, and after a stormy and tedious passage we arrived on the 27th at Cagliari, where we watered the ships and got a supply of cattle, about seventy or eighty head of oxen being embarked on board the fleet, which was then found and continues to be in the best state, there not being more than five or six men confined to bed by sickness; indeed the weather is so fine and temperate in this climate, that it is much more salubrious than a more northern climate …

16th March 1805. – Off Barcelona. His Majesty's ship *Renown* is just upon the eve of departure for England, by which I send this …

LEONARD GILLESPIE

To Vice Admiral Lord Nelson:
On board His Majesty's Ship *Victory*
At sea
14th August 1805

My Lord,
From the shores of the Nile to the gulph [sic] of Finland, the fame of your victories has been proclaimed; a nation, grateful for the important services you have rendered her, regards them with admiration; and the page of history has recorded them with eclat.

To me, as physician to the fleet under your Lordship's command, at the approaching close of the campaign, belongs the more humble yet useful and health in grateful task, to lay before your Lordship a concise statement of the state of the fleet during the two years campaign in the Mediterranean and West Indies, taken from the weekly reports made to your Lordship by my predecessor, Doctor Snipe, and by myself: together with a few remarks, contained in the enclosed Statement on the causes of the healthy state in which the men under your Lordship's command have been preserved during that period ... and the preserver of the gallant seamen, who, under the command of yourself, have achieved such wonders, by an unremitting attention to the furnishing the men under your command with every necessary refreshment and comfort, and by a steady and humane system of active discipline, as is demonstrated by the enclosed statement.

I have the honour to be, etc.
LEONARD GILLESPIE,
Physician to the Fleet.

[Enclosed statement]

Abstract of the Weekly Returns made by the Physician to the Fleet under the Command of the Right Hon. Vice Admiral Lord Viscount Nelson, Duke of Bronte, Commander in Chief in the Mediterranean Station, etc, etc, between the 13th of August 1803 and the 4th of August 1805, during which Time the said Fleet generally consisted of Ten or Twelve Ships of the Line, and Two or Three Frigates, manned by from 6,000 to 8,000 Seamen and Marines.

1803 From August 13 to end of the year,
Number of men deceased on board	18
Number sent to the hospitals	19
Medium number of men on the sick lists	185

1804
Number of deceased on board	43
Number sent to the hospitals	46
Medium number of men on the sick list	190

1805 to August the 4th

Number of deceased on board	49
Number sent to the hospitals	76
Medium number of men on the sick list	200
Total number of deaths on board	110
Total number sent to the hospitals	141
Medium number of men on the sick lists	190

Or eighteen to each ship nearly.

The above statement exhibits the most convincing and satisfactory proofs of the advantages arising from the practice of the improvements adopted in this fleet for the purpose of preserving the crews in good health, and the ships wholesome; and if compared with the accounts of the state of health of fleets or squadrons on foreign stations in former wars, the result will be found to show the importance of the regulations now used in preserving the health and lives of British seamen.

Thus, we find Dr. Blane, physician to the fleet in the West Indies, in the year 1781, in a memorial presented to him, in October of that year, to the Lords of the Admiralty, on the health of seamen, deploring the rapid expenditure of seamen in the navy, and stating, that during one year, in a fleet of twenty sail of the line, manned by 12000 seamen, there died on board 715, and in hospitals 862 men, forming a total of 1577 men, of which number only fifty-nine died in consequence of wounds; during the same period 850 men were invalided; the above shows that one man in seven died in the course of one year in the said fleet.

The following causes may be assigned for the high state of health in which the fleet under the command of Lord Nelson has been preserved for upwards of two years, unexampled perhaps in any fleet or squadron heretofore employed on a foreign station. lst. To the attention paid by his Lordship to the victualling and purveying for the fleet, in causing good wholesome wine to be used in room of spirits; fresh beef as often as it could possibly be procured; vegetables and fruit were always provided in a sufficient quantity, when they could be purchased; and an abundant supply of excellent sweet water was always allowed to the ship's company.

2nd The ships were preserved, as far as possible, from the baneful effects of humidity, by avoiding the wetting the decks (at least between the decks), by the use of stoves and ventilators below.

3rdly The constant activity and motion in which the fleet was preserved, being always at sea, and never exposed to the consequences of the idleness and intemperance which too often take place on board of ships lying in harbour, may doubtless be assigned as a principal cause of the good state of health of this fleet.

4thly. Intemperance and skulking were never so little practised in any fleet as in this, as ships were rarely or never in port; the opportunity of procuring spirits, or going to an hospital, by imposing on the surgeon, were difficult or impossible, hence these causes of disease were subtracted.

5th Cheerfulness amongst the men was promoted by music and dancing, and theatrical amusements, the example of which was given by the commander in chief in the Victory, and may with reason be reckoned amongst the causes of the preservation of the health of the men.

6thly. The sick were in general very comfortably accommodated, lodged in airy sick births, in many ships placed on a regular sick diet, and supplied with livestock, vegetables, fruit, soft bread, macaroni, and other articles of diet and refreshments, whenever the circumstances of the service, and the situation of the fleet would admit of these supplied being furnished.

7thly. By a standing order of the Commander in Chief, served to the men employed in the wooding and watering service; a drachm of Peruvian bark to one gill of spirits or two of wine, was the proportion allowed for each man; to be administered in divided portions, on going on shore, and on returning on board.

The method followed was to give the bark in a small quantity of wine or spirits, and to wash it down with a glass of water; it was found that the spirits answered better as a vehicle for the bark than the wine, as was experienced on board of some of the ships, in which wine had been used, but afterwards left off, and spirits were used in lieu thereof.

By the returns made by the respective surgeons of the ships to the physician in the fleet, reporting on the efficacy of the mode of prevention of the fevers, which might have been occasioned in consequence of the fatigue the seamen in wooding and watering; it fully appears that the practice entirely obviated every ill effect which might have been occasioned with regard to the health of the wooding and watering parties, and that it effectually prevented the occurrence of fevers, whether intermittent or continued.

This is the more worthy of remark, as it is well known to experienced officers in the navy, that on foreign stations, sickness very often finds its entrance into ships of war, from the wooding and watering parties being first attacked by fevers, in consequence of fatigue and exposure, which fevers often spread amongst the ship's company, and become a formidable and epidemic disease.

LEONARD GILLESPIE
Physician of the Fleet

Nelson clearly believed in preventative medicine, as shown in Gillespie's second letter. Nelson even endeavoured to persuade Lady Hamilton that his attitude to illness was the best course, as shown in his letter to Dr. Moseley of March 1804, when he wrote 'You will agree with me that it is easier for an Officer to keep men healthy, than for a Physician to cure them.'[1] He sent to Lady Hamilton the following well-informed (for a layman) commentary on vaccination:

> Yesterday, the subject turned on the cow-pox. A gentleman declared, that his child was inoculated with the cow-pox; and afterwards remained in a house where a child had the small-pox the natural way, and did not catch it. Therefore, here was a full trial with the cow-pox. The child is only feverish for two days; and only a slight inflammation of the arm takes place, instead of being all over scabs.[2]

Nelson typically knew about, and *understood,* vaccination – the major medical discovery of his day, the exemplar of preventative medicine. He understood first, that inoculations prevented subsequent infections despite exposure and second, that the inoculation reaction was a very mild one. Unfortunately Nelson added the words 'But, do you what you please!' and Lady Hamilton never had their daughter vaccinated. At the age of three, Horatia became severely ill with smallpox and although she did recover it was from a preventable illness.

Notes

1. Nicolas vol V p.438
2. *Nelson's Letters to Lady Hamilton* vol. I p.41

Appendix II

NELSON AND THE ARTISTS: THE PHYSICAL SIGNS

ARTIST	DATE	NELSON: PHYSICAL ABNORMALITY SHOWN
Rignaud	1777 – 81	None
Collingwood	1784	Wearing ill fitting wig to cover shaving of head as part of treatment for a fever.
At Calvi	**1794**	**Nelson wounded in right eye, right side of face.**
Leghorn. Miniaturist	1795	1) Curved linear scar outer aspect, upper right eyelid 2) Small curved scar inner aspect right lower eyelid 3) Small linear scar below outer aspect left lower eyelid 4) Loss of hair outer half right eyebrow
At Tenerife	**1797**	**Nelson wounded: right arm amputated**
Edridge	1797	1) Scar below outer aspect right lower eyelid 2) Right eyebrow less well drawn than left 3) 'Ties' in right sleeve. Amputation high up
Abbott. Kilgraston sketch	1797	1) Right iris and pupil distorted 2) Part of right lower eyelid missing
Abbott. Locker	1797	1) Right iris and pupil distorted 2) Part of right lower eyelid missing
Abbott minus hat	1797	1) Right pupil larger than left 2) 'Ties' in right sleeve. Amputation high up. 3) Yellow corneal colouration nasal side of pupil of both eyes
Gahagan	1798	Outer aspect right eyebrow irregular in shape (the right eyebrow deep indentation is *not* as in life).
At Aboukir Bay	**1798**	**Nelson wounded right side of forehead.**

Guzzardi	1799	1) Hat tilted backwards to prevent pressure on scar 2) Nile scar with horizontal and vertical components 3) Haggard face 4) Outer half right eyebrow absent 5) Yellow coloration of cornea 6) High amputation of right arm 7) Slightly sunken right eye
Head	1798 – 99 NMM	1) High amputation of right arm 2) Right side upper lip swollen
Head	1789 – 99 NPG	1) Bruising and swelling right side forehead 2) Bruising right side of face 3) Slightly sunken right eye
Grignion	1799	Right pupil smaller than left
Füger 'civvies' uni- form	1800 NPG	Nothing abnormal shown
Life Mask	1800 RNM	1) Right eyebrow outer half: hairs missing 2) Right eye slightly smaller
Life Mask	1800 NMM	1) Right eyebrow outer half: hairs missing 2) Right eye slightly smaller
Schmidt	1800	1) Right eyebrow outer half: hairs missing 2) Right eye slightly divergent to right 3) Right eye blurred with no corneal highlight 4) Linear scar below right eye lower lid 5) Right eye slightly sunken
Beechey. Sketch	1800	1) Right pupil enlarged and irregular in outline 2) Right eyebrow outer half distorted 3) Nile scar obvious above right eye 4) Yellow discolouration of corneal nasal aspect OBS 5) Right eye slightly sunken

Beechey. Oil	1801	1) Nile scar above right eye 2) Abnormal outer half right eyebrow 3) Right eye slightly sunken
Hoppner. Sketch	1800	1) Right pupil enlarged and irregular 2) Left eye blurred with no corneal highlight 3) Outer half left eyebrow hairs missing 4) Left eye (!) slightly sunken
Hoppner. Portrait	1800	1) Left eye blurred no corneal highlight 2) Left eyebrow hairs missing outer half
Bowyer	1800 – 1805	1) Hairs missing outer aspect right eyebrow 2) Nile scar above right eyebrow – inverted V shape 3) Absent corneal highlight right eye 4) Right eye slightly sunken
Devis	1806	1) Right pupil smaller than left 2) Eyeshade worn under hat
Andras	1805 –1806	1) Left eye blind 2) Vertical raised scar rising from middle of right eyebrow to middle right forehead 3) Absent hair outer third right eyebrow

Note: NMM = National Maritime Museum, Greenwich
NPG = National Portrait Gallery, London
RNM = Royal Naval Museum, Portsmouth

1. Portraits showing Nelson with head turned to the right so that his right eyebrow cannot be properly seen.
(a) Daniel Orme
(b) Abbott
(c) Head
(d) Grignion
(e) Fuger
(f) Devis
(g) Craig

2. Portraits of Nelson drawn left profile.
(a) De Vaere (Wedgewood)
(b) De Koster
(c) Downman
(d) Andras
(e) Whichelo
(f) Caulfield
(g) a Palermo artist

3. Portraits of Nelson with lock of hair in vicinity of, or covering, right eyebrow.
(a) Keymer
(b) Hoppner
(c) De Koster
(d) Bowyer
(e) Whichelo
(f) Devis
(g) Andras
(h) Flaxman

Appendix III

MERTON: NELSON'S LAST LEAVE: AUGUST/SEPTEMBER 1805

Nelson's last leave at Merton was extraordinarily busy and important. Having arrived back in England, at Spithead, in *Victory* on 18th August 1805, the next 27 days passed as follows:

August 1805:

19th (Mon) Nelson set out from Portsmouth to travel to Merton overnight. Wrote reference for John Scott.[1]

20th (Tues) Arrived at Merton at 6 a.m. By chance a Danish historian, J. A. Andersen, visited Merton bringing a copy of his book on the Battle of Copenhagen: 'The Admiral wore a uniform emblazoned with the different Orders of Knighthood. He received me with the utmost condescension.'[2]

21st (Wed) Travelled up to London where he called at the Admiralty, at the Navy Office; on Prime Minister Pitt at Downing Street; met with his Agents, Marsh & Creed; ordered silver-gilt cup from Salters, Nelson's sword cutler in the Strand, to be engraved 'To my much loved Horatia';[3] called on Lord Castlereagh and on Mr Addington.

23rd (Fri) The West India Merchants expressed their thanks re Nelson's 'bold and unwearied pursuit of them, [Combined Squadron] which had … been very instrumental towards the Saving of those colonies.[4]

24th (Sat) Lord Minto welcomed at Merton. Minto later wrote to his wife that 'Nelson sat down to dinner with his brother William and wife, their children and the children of a sister, Lady Hamilton at head of table and her mother at the bottom.'[5]

25th (Sun) All Merton House Party attended Merton Church.[6]

26th (Mon) Lord Minto met Nelson in Piccadilly, got hold of his arm 'So that I was mobbed too.'[7]

28th (Wed) Nelson booked rooms at Gordons Hotel, Albermarle Street, London, where he met with Lord Hood, Lord Braybrooke and a deputation of Directors representing the West India Merchants and Planters who thanked him 'for his sagacity in ascertaining the course of, and bold and unwearied pursuit of, the combined squadron, to the West Indies and back again. Nelson gave them all a very large breakfast at the hotel.[8] Lord Minto to dinner with Nelson and Emma at Lady Hamilton's house in Clarges Street, also Nelson's brother and wife, and Charles Greville (Sir William Hamilton's nephew).[9]

29th (Thur) Nelson wrote to George Rose, secretary of The Cabinet, to ask him to ask Pitt for a place in the Customs and Excise for his brother-in-law, Thomas Bolton.

31st (Sat)   Nelson noted by George Matchan (Senior) 'To be deeply
                    preoccupied throughout dinner'[10]

September 1805:
1st (Sun)   Nelson went to London to visit Prime Minister Pitt. Pitt asked
Nelson 'Now, who is to take command?' Nelson suggested Collingwood. Pitt
disagreed. 'No, that won't do, you must take command.' He then asked Nelson
if he could be ready to sail in three days. Nelson's response was 'I am ready
now.'[11]

2nd (Mon) 5 a.m. Blackwood called at Merton on his way to the Admiralty with
dispatches from Collingwood. He told Nelson the Combined Fleet including
Villeneuve were all at Cadiz. Nelson followed Blackwood to the Admiralty and
then saw Minto and told him what Pitt had said the day before.[12]

4th (Wed)   George Matcham (Junior) arrived at Merton 'Large company at
dinner' Lady Hamilton writes to Lady Bolton.[13]

5th (Thur)   Nelson's servants Henry Chevalier and Gaetano Spedillo left Merton
with his luggage to go to *Victory* at Portsmouth

6th (Fri)   Nelson summoned to Admiralty to collect his orders and attended
a Council at Downing Street. Wrote to Davison.[14] Stands sponsor for child
of Colonel Suckling christened at Merton Church. Duke of Clarence dined at
Merton

7th (Sat)   Nelson paid bill to Barrett, Corney & Corney for five sets of his four
silver embroidered stars.[15] Visited Peddison's shop in Strand and viewed the
L'Orient coffin. Asked for his name on the lid.[16]

8th (Sun)   Sidney Smith visited Merton and talked about siege of Acre.[17]

9th (Mon)   Reverend Doctor and Mrs. Nelson left Merton.

10th (Tues) Nelson drove in the morning to Richmond Park where he visited
Henry Addington, Lord Sidmouth and drew a plan in wine with his finger on
a small table (which Sidmouth afterwards kept) detailing how he would attack
the Combined Fleet if he could bring them to action.[18] Went to London with
Lady Hamilton for dinner with James Crawford and his wife. Also present were
the Duke of Devonshire, Lady Bessborough and Lady Elizabeth Foster.[19] Nelson
now knew he would be leaving Merton on 13th September.[20]
11th (Wed) William Beckford visited to sing and play the harp.[21]

12th (Thur) Nelson by command visited Prince of Wales at Carlton House,
London.[22] Then visited Lord Castlereagh (Secretary at War) and met Duke of
Wellington for first and only time (see pp. 154-5). Visited Lord Mulgrave at
Downing Street and drove home to have dinner (two hours later) with James
Perry, Editor of the *Morning Chronicle* and Lord Minto.[23]

13th (Fri)   Drove to Admiralty in morning to get final orders. Spent rest of day at home with Emma, Horatia, nieces and nephews. Left Merton for the last time in the late evening and stopped at Anchor Inn, Liphook, to write penultimate prayer.

14th (Sat)   Arrived Portsmouth (The George) at 6 a.m. early morning. Wrote to Lady Hamilton.[24] Found ships *Royal Sovereign*, *Defiant* and *Agamemnon* not ready so instructed them to follow *Victory* as soon as possible. Collected Sir Howe Popham's new signal book to be given to each ship in his fleet. Pushed through cheering crowds to leave by boat from Sally Port. Rowed to *Victory*. Dined with George Canning, Treasurer of the Navy, and George Rose (both of them were Pitt's friends) on board *Victory*.

15th (Sun)   *Victory* sails towards Trafalgar.

During the 24 days, at dates not specified, Nelson visited Abraham Goldsmidt, a neighbour who lived near Merton at Morden Hall. He also visited Abraham's brother Benjamin, who lived at Roehampton. Admiral Sir Peter Parker visited him at Merton, as did his sister Susannah, and all his Bolton relatives.

From the above account of Nelson's last leave, it can be seen that he was required to be at the very heart of the governance of the country and the most senior ministers were looking to him for advice. In addition, Nelson settled his finances, especially monies owing for work done at Merton, although he never knew exactly how much more money Lady Hamilton owed for repairs and renovations that she had not told him about. He had his family about him, his last remaining brother plus wife and two children, his two sisters and their spouses with more children, Emma's mother (who seems to have supervised the running of a very complicated establishment) and even his late brother Maurice's common law wife, the blind Mrs Sarah Ford. One of the family was George Matcham Junior, the eldest son of Nelson's favourite sister Katty. George kept a diary of his visit to Merton which, together with his letter to *The Times* on 6th November 1861 gave a clear picture of Nelson less than two months before his death. Matcham wrote:

> I visited my Uncle …at his house at Merton in 1804…Lord Nelson in private life was remarkable for a demeanour quiet, sedate and unobtrusive, anxious to give pleasure to everyone about him, distinguishing each in turn by some act of kindness, and chiefly those who seemed to require it most. During his few intervals of leisure, in a little knot of relations and friends, he delighted in quiet conversation, through which ran an undercurrent of pleasantry not unmixed with caustic wit. At his table he was the least heard among the company, and so far from being the hero of his own tale, I never heard him voluntarily refer to any of the great actions of his life…he seemed to me to waive homage with as little attention as was consistent with civility…It would have formed an amusement in the circle at Merton if intemperance were set down to the master of the house, who always so prematurely cut short the sitting of the gentlemen after dinner. A man of more temperate habits could not … have been found … in his plain

suit of black, in which he alone recurs to my memory, he always looked what he was — a gentleman ... his disposition was truly noble ... it revolted against all wrong and oppression. His heart, indeed, was as tender as it was courageous. Many like myself could bear witness to his gentleness, kindness, good breeding and courtesy.[25]

At some time at the very end of his leave, Nelson arranged to take Communion with Emma in the local parish church at Merton after which service they exchanged rings, attempting to confirm what he had for some time been saying and writing: that Emma was now his wife in his own eyes and, he hoped, those of Heaven.

Notes:
1. Nicolas VII p.14
2. Pocock p.307
3. Gerin p.90
4. Clarke and M'Arthur Vol 2 p.420/421
5. Gerin p.93
6. ibid. p.91
7. Minto Vol iii p.363
8. Oman p.589
9. Gerin p.93
10. ibid. p.96
11. ibid. p.96/97
12. ibid. p.97
13. Nicolas VII p.28
14. ibid. p.30
15. Coleman p. 311
16. ibid p.310
17. Gerin p.95
18. Oman p.600
19. Clayton and Craig p.70
20. Gerin p.95
21. ibid p.95
22. Clayton and Craig p.70
23. Oman p.602
24. Gerin p.101
25. Edgecombe R (Ed) Diary of Frances, Lady Shelley (1912) quoted in Pocock T *Nelson's Women* p.218

Bibliography

Sources consulted in the preparation of this book.

MAJOR SOURCES: BIOGRAPHIES OF NELSON
Beatty, W. *The Authentic Narrative of the Death of Lord Nelson* 1807
Bennett, G. *Nelson, the Commander* 1972
Bradford, E. *Nelson: The Essential Hero* 1977
Clarke, J. S. and M'Arthur, J. *The Life of Admiral Lord Nelson, K.B.* 2 vols 1809
Knight, R. *The Pursuit of Victory* 2005
Mahan, A. T. *The ife of Nelson: the Embodiment of the Sea Power of Great Britain* 2 vol. 1897
Naish, G. P. B. (ed) *Nelson's letters to his Wife and Other Documents* 1958
Nicolas, Sir N. H. *The Dispatches and Letters of Vice-Admiral Lord Viscount Nelson* 7 vols 1844–1846
Oman, C. *Nelson* 1947
Pocock, T. *Horatio Nelson* 1987
Sugden, J. *Nelson: A Dream of Glory* 2004
Warner, O. *A Portrait of Lord Nelson* 1958
White, C. *Nelson: The New Letters* 2005
Logs relating to: *Hinchinbroke, Theseus, Victory*

OTHER BOOKS & SOURCES ABOUT NELSON
Anon. *Letters of Lord Nelson to Lady Hamilton* 1815
Beckford, W. *Memoirs* 1859
Beresford, Lord C. and Wilson, H. W. *Nelson and His Times* 1897
Blumel, T. *Nelson's Overland Journey* 2000
Britton, C. J. *New Chronicles of the Life of Lord Nelson* 1946
Brockliss, L. et al *Nelson's Surgeon* 2005
Charnock, J. *Biographical Memoirs of Lord Viscount Nelson* 1806
Coleman, T. *Nelson: the Man and the Legend* 2001
Dawson, W. (ed) *The Nelson Collection at Lloyds* 1932
Dixon, N. *On The Psychology of Military Incompetence* 1976
Duffy, M. *Touch and Take* 2005
Edgcumbe, R. (ed) *The Diary of Frances Lady Shelley 1787-1817* 2 vols 1912
Edinger, G. and Neep, E. J . C. *Horatio Nelson* 1930
Eyre-Matcham, M. *The Nelsons of Burnham Thorpe* 1911
Fraser, F. *Beloved Emma* 1986
Freemantle, A. (ed) *The Wynne Diaries* 3 vol. 1935–1940

French, G. R. *The Royal Descent of Nelson and Wellington* 1853
Gatty, A. and Gatty, M. *Recollections of the Life of the Reverend A. J. Scott D.D.* 1842
Gerin, W. *Horatia Nelson* 1970
Goodwin, P. *Nelson's Ships* 2002
Harris, D. *The Nelson Almanack* 1998
Harrison, J. *The life of the Right Honourable Horatio Lord Viscount Nelson* 2 vols 1806
Hibbert, C. *Nelson: A Personal history* 1994
Howarth, D. *Trafalgar: The Nelson Touch* 1969
Hudson, R. (ed) *The Grand Quarrel* 2000
James, Sir W. *The Durable Monument: Horatio Nelson* 1948
Jeaffreson, J. *Lady Hamilton and Lord Nelson* 2 vols 1888
Jennings, J. (ed) *Correspondence and Diaries of J. W. Croker* 2 vol. 1884
Kennedy, L. *Nelson's Band of Brothers* 1951
Laughton, J. K. *The Nelson Memorial: Nelson and His Companions in Arms* 1896
Lavery, B. *Nelson's Navy* 1989
Lavery, B. *Nelson and the Nile* 1998
Leigh, *Chronical Scrip Book Part IV* 1879
Lincoln, M. (ed) *Nelson and Napoleon* 2005
Lloyd, C. *The British Seaman* 1968
Lloyd, C. *Nelson and Sea Power* 1973
Lloyd, C. *The Nile Campaign: Nelson and Napoleon in Egypt* 1973
McCarthy, L. *Remembering Nelson* 1995
Minto, Countess of (ed) *Life and Letters of Sir Gilbert Elliot, First Earl of Minto* 3 vol. 1874
Moorhouse, E. *Letters of English Seamen* 1910
Morrison, A. (ed) *The Hamilton & Nelson papers* 1893–1894
Morriss, Roger et al *Nelson: An Illustrated History* 1995
Nash, M. (ed) *The Nelson masks, Proceedings of the Symposium on the Nelson Masks, Portsmouth,* 1993
'Nastyface, J.' *Nautical Economy* 1836
Pettigew, T. J. *Memoirs of the life of Vice-Admiral Lord Viscount Nelson, K.B.* 2 vol. 1849
Pocock, T. *Nelson and his World* 1968
Pocock, T. *The Young Nelson in the Americas* 1980
Pocock, T. *Nelson's Campaign in Corsica* The 1805 Club 1994
Pocock, T. *Nelson's Women* 1999
Pope, D. *England Expects* 1998
Pugh, P. D. G. *Nelson and his Surgeons* 1968
Russell, J. *Nelson and the Hamiltons* 1969
Tute, W. *The True Glory* 1983
Van Der Merwe, P. (ed) *Nelson: An Illustrated History* 1995
Vincent, E. *Nelson: Love and Fame* 2003
Walker, R. *The Nelson Portraits* 1998
Warner, O. *Nelson's Battles* 1965
Warner, O. *Nelson's Last Diary and the Prayer before Trafalgar* 1971
White, C. (ed) *The Nelson Companion* 1995
White, C. *The Nelson Encyclopaedia* 2002

BIBLIOGRAPHY

White, C. 1797: *Nelson's Year of Destiny* 1998
Wilkinson, C. *Life of Nelson* 1931

ARTICLES FROM:
The Gibraltar Chronicle supplement 1805
The Naval Chronicle 1805, 1806
The Nelson Dispatch (Journal of the Nelson Society)
The Times
The Trafalgar Chronicle (Year Book of the 1805 Club)

BOOKS CITED IN TEXT AND FURTHER READING
Asprey, R. *The Rise and Fall of Napoleon Bonaparte* 2000
Bernier, O. *The World in* 1800 2000
Commager, H. S. (ed) *The Blue and the Gray* 2 vol. 1950
Cooper, J. *Great Britons* 2002
Cragg, G. R. *The Church in the Age of Reason* 1995
Harvey, A. and Mortimer, R. *The Funeral Effigies of Westminster Abbey* 1994
Keevil, J. J. *Medicine and the Navy* 2 vol. 1959
L'Eaing, H. *The Pathology of Leadership* 1969
Longford, E. *Wellington: The Years of the Sword* 1969
Louda, J. and Maclagan, M. *Lines of Succession* 2002
MacNalty, Sir A. S. *Henry VIII – A Difficult Patient* Christopher Johnson 1952
MacNalty, Sir A. S. *Elizabeth I : The Lonely Queen* Christopher Johnson 1954
Montgomery, Field-Marshal B. L. *A Concise History of Warfare* 2000
Moran, Lord *Courage* 1945
Porter, R, *Enlightenment* 2000
Stuart, J. D. M. *Dearest Bess* 1955

BOOKS AND ARTICLES – MEDICAL AND PSYCHOLOGICAL
Appleby, L. et al (eds) *Postgraduate Psychology* 2nd edition 2001
Becket, J. B. *An Essay on Electricity* 1773
Bolby, John *Attachment and Loss: Vol.3, Loss* 1998
Buzan,T, & Keene, R, *Buzan's Book of Genius* 1994
Cameron, Peter et al (eds) *Textbook of Adult Emergency Medicine* 2000
Carter, R. *Mapping the Mind* 1998
Carvallo, T. *An Essay on the Theory and Practice of Medical Electricity* 1780
Cecil: *Textbook of Medicine* 2004
Chaloner et al 'Amputation at the London Hospital 1852' *Journal of R.S.M.* vol 94
August 2001 p.411
Cheyne, G. *An Essay of Health and Long Life* 1734
Cooper, J. *Great Britons* 2000
Coran, S, *Sleep Thieves* 1996
Crumplin, M. K. H. *Journal of R.S.M.* 1988 vol 81 p.40
Da Costa, J.M. 'On Irritible Heart, a Clinical Study of a Form of Functional
cardiac Disorder and its Consequences' *American Journal of Medical Sciences* 1871
vol 761 p.17
Dandy, D. J, and Edwards, D. J, *Essential Orthopaedics and Trauma* 3rd *Edition* 1998
Fisher, S. H. *Archives of Physical Medicine* 1960 vol 41 p.62

Haslett, C. et al (eds) *Davidson's Principles and Practice of Medicine* 19*th* edition 2004
Heller, R, *Effective Leadership* 1999
Hooper, R. *The Anatomists' Vade-Mecum* 9*th* edition 1820
Hutchinson and Hunter *Clinical Methods* 12*th* edition 1949
Katz, H. 'Phantom Limb Pain' *The Lancet* vol 350 1997
Kozubska, J. *The 7 Keys of Charisma* 1997
Kuvan and Clark *Clinical Medicine* 5*th* edition 2002
Mitchell, B. J. *Materia Medica & Therapeutics* 1890
Murray Parkes, C. and Napier, M. M. *British Journal of Hospital Medicine* November 1970
Porter, R. *The Greatest Benefit to Mankind* 1997
Ridley, M. *The Origins of Virtue* 1997
Rowbotton and Susskind *Electricity and Medicine: History of theirInteraction* 1984
Ruspini, J. B. 'A brief Description of a Newly Important Instrument, for the extraction of Balls from Gunshot Wounds' *Medical & Physical Journal* vol XV no. 85 p.456
Shaffer, D. R. *Developmental Psychology* 4*th* edition 1985
Stannard, C. F. 'Phantom Limb Pain' *The Lancet* vol 350 1997 p.13–38
White, P. 'Da Costa's Syndrome or Effort Syndrome' *B.M.J.*
Yanuf & Fine *Ocular Pathology* 4*th* edition 1966

JOURNALS
American Journal of Medical Sciences
British Journal of Hospital Medicine
British Journal of Surgery
British Medical Association News
British Medical Journal
Hospital Doctor
Journal of the Royal Society of Medicine
Journal of The Society of Genealogists
The Lancet
Magazine of the Friends of the National Maritime Museum
Medical and Physical Journal
The Morning Chronicle
Organorama
Stand To! (Journal of the Western Front Association)